Bumps in the Road

Maria McErlane

a memoir

GREAT NORTHERN

Great Northern Books
PO Box 1380, Bradford,
West Yorkshire, BD5 5FB

www.greatnorthernbooks.co.uk

ISBN: 978-1-914227-61-5

Design by David Burrill

CIP Data
A catalogue for this book is available from the British Library

FSC
www.fsc.org
MIX
Paper | Supporting
responsible forestry
FSC® C013604

To

Jeremy Langmead

"You must live in the present, launch yourself on every wave, find your eternity in each moment. Fools stand on their island of opportunities and look forward to another land. There is no other land; there is no other life but this."

Henry David Thoreau
July 12, 1817

CONTENTS

Introduction: 7
Converted Marin e-Bike

Chapter 1   **Once a Catholic:** 13
Dad's Green Raleigh Work bike

Chapter 2   **A Life Before God:** 23
Priest's Butcher's Bike

Chapter 3   **The End of Play:** 34
Peugeot PX8

Chapter 4   **An Alternative Education:** 49
Pinky the Foundling with Silver Wheels

Chapter 5   **Who Shall I Be?** 68
My Own Bike – Hercules, God of Strength

Chapter 6   **London Living:** 78
Dawes Lady Racer

Chapter 7   **A Dangerous Obsession:** 85
Peugeot 1976 Drop-Handlebar Tourer

Chapter 8   **An Actor's Life for Me:** 94
The Gunmetal Grey Falcon Tourer

Chapter 9   **Boom, Tish!** 113
The Falcon Tourer Lives On

Chapter 10   **Real Life Hits:** 123
The Falcon Tourer

Chapter 11   **Famous Folk:** 137
White Mountain Bike – Built to Own Specification

Chapter 12   **Daniel:** 144
Mountain Bike

Chapter 13   **Being 40:**.. 150
White Mountain Bike

Chapter 14   **Daniel Goes Mad:**.................................. 161
White Mountain Bike

Chapter 15   **Copy and Print!**..................................... 178
White Mountain Bike

Chapter 16   **A Difficult Age:**.................................... 185
White Mountain Bike

Chapter 17   **The Power of Dog:** 195
Death of the White Mountain Bike

Chapter 18   **Follow Your Dreams:** 202
Marin Mountain Bike

Chapter 19   **Agony Aunt:**.. 214
Day-Glo 90s Marin

Chapter 20   **Understanding Vulnerability:** 223
Day-Glo Marin

Chapter 21   **Flirting:** 238
Rolls Royce Gifted Marin

Chapter 22   **Advice to Self:**..................................... 245
Junk Shop Marin and Claud Butler Racer

Epilogue... 250

Introduction:

Converted Marin e-Bike

knew something bad was about to happen.

After all, this was not my first rodeo. I had been cycling for 50 years and falling off comes with the territory. As the back wheel of my bike buckled on the storm drain and flung me through the air, I knew this wasn't going to be pretty. My first reaction was, sensibly, to try and protect my head (the other bits of your body are less complicated and easier to mend). The other thought that flashed through my mind before I hit the rain-soaked cobblestones was why the feck was I wearing a Toyah Willcox wig instead of a safety helmet?

'Darling, will you come and judge the Halloween competition?' Coco Canal, a local drag queen had asked me a few weeks before. He was organising a grand bash at a swanky club in Hastings, the seaside town on the south coast of England that had been my home for some years. 'I will love you forever and smother you with unwanted gay kisses,' Coco added as an afterthought.

'You really need to get a celebrity,' I countered.

'Well, yes, I know, my sweet, but I've been let down and you will have to do.'

I had been up since 6am as I'd had to be in London that morning for my slot on Graham Norton's Virgin radio show. I'd then rushed back again to Hastings and was running late. I had promised Coco I'd dress up, and so a silver-sequinned bodycon dress, cinched-in jacket with sequinned sleeves, platform boots, false eyelashes and a pink and blonde ombre Toyah wig were pulled from wardrobes and the back of cupboards. I slung a raincoat over the whole ghastly ensemble and clambered aboard the e-bike.

The e-bike had recently been acquired. There was deep shame attached to this purchase. I was somehow betraying my people. As a true dyed-in-the-wool cyclist, I knew that this wasn't proper biking.

It was a sham, I was a sham.

There was also a creeping suspicion that having succumbed to the horrors of assisted pedalling, it would be a mere stepping stone to the end game of assisted walking and then assisted dying. But at least tonight it would enable me to get to the event more quickly and then I could make a smooth getaway and would be happily ensconced in bed by midnight.

I hadn't, however, factored in the possibility of rain. Five minutes from the club, the sky emptied its contents directly onto my head. Not the irritating pin pricks that sting your face and make you damp but ludicrous enveloping surges of water that cloud your vision and drench you in seconds.

The instinct to speed up and get there more quickly was tempered by long experience of such treacherous conditions and I slowed down before very gently squeezing both brakes as I came out of a corner. There was no way of knowing that I was directly over a metal storm drain that offered zero grip to my inadequate tyres.

A woman screamed as I crashed to the ground. 'Oh my God! That was a terrible fall,' exclaimed another onlooker as he loomed over my splayed body. I must have been out for a second or two as his words were too much for my bandwidth and I just stared at him blankly.

His wife kneeled down beside me in the rain. 'Are you OK?' she asked my unresponsive head.

'I don't know,' I eventually muttered, prodding all the areas on my body that were emitting pain. Ouch, my head. I had hit my head at the front and there was a worrying egg beginning to grow under the ridiculous Toyah wig. Only a small amount of blood though, which I wiped away with the back of my hand and, as I could still remember who our hopeless prime minister was, it was possible I had got away with it.

The wife helped me up and noticed my tights were ripped at the knee.

My right leg was bleeding, as was my arm, the sequinned sleeve of my jacket now stripped of its glittery content from wrist to elbow.

'I think we should take you to hospital,' she said, as I staggered theatrically.

'Noooo! All good. I'm FINE!' I said with as much authority as I could muster.

Embarrassed by my outfit and wig, I garbled out the reason why, plus the pressing need to carry out my promised judging duties and continue on my way.

'We will walk with you to the club,' said the husband emphatically. 'Just to make sure you are really OK.' Gathering up the contents of my bag, which had spread across the wet ground, the rain stopped as suddenly as it had started and we ambled off soggily with the kindly husband pushing my stricken bike and the wife clutching my elbow in case of imminent collapse.

Small talk with strangers is difficult at the best of times, but as they had been my saviours and were seeing me at my worst, both physically and sartorially, I chatted to them like old friends. Jeff and Catherine had been out for dinner, were from Pett Level, a village out of town, and were sheltering in a shop doorway when they witnessed my spectacular stunt.

I insisted on buying them a drink when we reached the venue, to thank them for their kindness. Then had the brilliant idea that they should come and watch the show. They looked doubtful, before Catherine suddenly said, 'Yes, why not! We were only going to go home.' Jeff locked up my bike and obediently trudged in behind us.

They were quite a 'straight' middle-aged couple (teacher, bank manager) and when we got inside, I saw the scene before me entirely through their eyes.

Outlandish costumes, drag queens with massive eyelashes and three-foot-high back-combed wigs, bare-chested biker boys in leather shorts and Sam Brown harnesses, plus a waitress behind the bar serving drinks in a bejewelled gold lame bikini. To the uninitiated, it must have looked like a scene from the film *Blade Runner* or a pre-war Berlin cabaret.

Wide-eyed they took their seats, I bought them drinks and then rushed off to check in and do my duty.

A few people noticed my déshabillé, torn tights, blood on my forehead, but I laughed it off as part of the costume. It was Halloween, the place was awash with ghouls, bloodied zombies and a very realistic Carrie from the film of the same name after she has materialised from her watery grave.

My head was beginning to throb, but I gleefully watched the parade of hopeful fancy dress competitors as they paraded through the club to cheers and catcalls. Coco Canal took control and affected my glittering introduction along the lines of 'you may know her from a list of TV shows from the early 90s, she's all we could get so show her some love!' and I bounded onto the stage in my capacity as 'celebrity judge'.

'I told a few self-deprecating jokes in an attempt to get the audience onside, noticed Coco pointing at her watch to indicate we were running late and announced to the expectant faces my top three prize winners. 'In third place, the vicar from *The Exorcist*!' I exclaimed. Hearty appreciative applause. He attempted to put on his winner's medal but the realistic ice spike protruding from his neck put an end to that. 'In second place, the exceptionally spooky twins from *The Shining*!' I boomed. 'You would have come first but for the mismatched trainers,' I told them. They shuffled off, mildly disgruntled.

'And in first place, with prizes galore, it's Norma Desmond from *Sunset Boulevard*!' Much whooping and cheering for a deserving winner. He was an old chap of around seventy-five and had made a spectacular effort with a beautiful purple and black gown, gorgeous headdress and impeccable make-up.

Norma may have been a little drunk. Although delighted to have won, when I thrust the microphone in front of her and said, 'We can't let you leave the stage without hearing the famous quote,' she looked panic-stricken and searched my face for a clue. Without wishing to humiliate the poor gal I tried to assist by whispering the line into her hearing aid.

She faltered slightly but announced with some gusto, 'I'm NOT small, it's just the pictures got too, um, what was it?'

'Well yes, something like that,' I laughed, before asking the audience to help out.

'I AM BIG, IT'S THE PICTURES THAT GOT SMALL!' they shouted in unison. Gotta love a gay crowd.

Foolishly I tried again with Norma: 'Now Ms Desmond, what is it you're ready for?' Her make-up was starting to run under the harsh lights on the stage and the dark magenta lipstick was settling into the heavy crevices around her lips. 'Ready for?' she repeated nervously. 'Er, bed?'

The audience guffawed and again came to the rescue: 'READY FOR MY CLOSE-UP MR DE MILLE!'

Relieved the ordeal was over, Norma was cheered from the stage and on came another drag queen in full Michael Myers *Halloween* mask who began singing, 'I am what I am.'

It was gone Midnight as I made my way out of the club. 'You're a trooper!' shouted Coco Canal from the stage. I spotted Catherine and Jeff chatting to a bear of a man who had come as the American Werewolf in London and a six-foot Carol Channing drag queen. They seemed to be having a ball and I thanked them once again for their exceptional kindness.

As I unlocked my bike, a very large gentleman, naked but for a nappy and a dummy which was sharing its place in his lipsticked mouth with a cigarette, spat the dummy from his mouth and said, 'Aren't you a bit too OLD to be riding a bike?'

Mentioning the 'O word makes me see red. The irony of a grown man wearing a nappy was clearly lost on him. As we live in a time where you can be who or what you want to be, it is progress that body-shaming has no place. Age-shaming though seems to be another matter. I smiled and said, 'If I can walk, I can pedal!' before scooting away.

Wounds washed and dressed, ice pack on giant impact egg, and the comfort of pyjamas, I caught sight of myself in the mirror.

Maybe it was delayed shock, but I wondered who that person was? She wasn't the twenty-four-year-old who lives in my head, happily oblivious to what others see, but a bashed and bruised older lady with sad eyes. Sad because maybe my cycling adventures 'should' be brought to an end? How many times could I get away with falling off? Norma Desmond's line swam into my head: 'I am big, it's the pictures that got small.' An image started to form of Liza Minnelli forgetting the words to her songs and falling from the stage in Lake Tahoe after a hip replacement and drug problems. I had been in the second row but couldn't save her. This vision was replaced by Bruce Forsyth and his massive cue cards when he could no longer read the autocue and a negligent agent who should surely have said, 'Enough now, Brucie, go and enjoy your golf.' I was, of course, momentarily elevating myself to their level, but perhaps I needed someone to tell me? 'Park the bike lady, you gotta get off!'

That my love of cycling and an open road defines me in the same way Cabaret defines Liza, is camp and grandiose I know, but the thought of not being able to continue pedalling would surely end me as quickly as any of the killer diseases encountered in Sniper Valley, the one-way boulevard we enter at a certain age.

Nodding off to sleep, ALL the bicycles I have ever had swam into view and I started to remember them like lost children. It wasn't about the make or model, about cost or how cool they were, it was about what was happening in life during the sometimes brief time we travelled together. Each machine came with its own quirks, each carrying me through chapters of my life, changing fashions, joyous discoveries, sadness, disappointment and more fun than should be legal.

You should probably write about them, I thought.

So I did.

As in life, with cycling, the wheel goes up and the wheel goes down. As long as we keep pedalling, we keep on moving forward.

Chapter 1

Once a Catholic:

Dad's Green Raleigh Work bike

I used to pray every night on the first star for God to bring me a bicycle, but it never happened. My faith in the big man was tenuous to begin with, that he continued to ignore my prayers caused quite a rift. Difficult given my early indoctrinations.

'So . . . MAR-EEE-AAAA . . . McErlaaaaane,' Sister Bernadette annunciated my name, to shame me in front of the other children. 'Do you think it is right to use the word toilet and God in the same sentence? . . . DO YOU?'

'Um . . . should I have said lavatory?'

'BE QUIET GIRL! I am here to tell you, Maria McErlane, that it is NOT right! It is blasphemy! Blasphemy to use the word toilet in Our Lord's house with our Lord's name and you will stay here until I decide how to punish you. God in his righteous glory will guide me.'

Rooted to my chair, it seemed only Mum or Dad could save me, if I could only get home. Could they though? Would they? My heart told me no. Collaborators both.

I spent the rest of the class in quiet petrification, unable to grasp why I deserved such punishment. I was frightened of the nuns in company, so to be alone with one and no witnesses was unthinkable.

I contemplated running away. If I could get through the heavy double doors of the church and run like the wind they would never catch me. Run! Run! Past my house and down under the bridge to the Grand Union canal. I was the Pied Piper of Hamelin, and like rats the nuns would follow, down to the banks where they would tumble one by one into the murky slime, their thick black habits absorbing putrid water and pulling them down to their rightful deaths.

Home was a mid-50s council house in Sycamore Avenue on a tree-lined estate, imaginatively titled 'The Trees Estate' in Bletchley, Bucks. A little-known new town fifty miles or so north of London. Fifteen years before I was born, Bletchley Park was where the Enigma code was cracked by Alan Turing and other secret service agents. A massive contribution towards the defeat of Hitler.

Hoorah. What else is Bletchley known for? Er, that's about it.

Ever since I could remember, I was told that my grandma had helped to build the Catholic church. An imposingly stark building at the top of our tree-lined street. Something of a literal child, I had images of my five-foot grandma in a yellow hard hat yelling orders to burly bulldozer operators and single-handedly erecting the welcoming twenty-foot crucifix that hung at the altar, with a ladder some pulleys and a few rusty nails.

It was only much later that I realised she had campaigned, raised money and joined forces with the growing swell of Irish Catholics in Bletchley, Buckinghamshire, to create the 'building of suffering' as I came to know it. My grandfather seemingly did very little, all I remember of him was a fug of cigarette smoke and a disapproving stare. As WB Yeats wrote, 'Being Irish, he had an abiding sense of tragedy, which sustained him through temporary periods of joy.'

St Thomas Aquinas church was a stone's throw from our house and sat at the top of Sycamore Avenue. At the bottom of the street, Pinewood Drive ran parallel to the Grand Union canal and large playing fields beyond. The Grand Union canal was totally out of bounds for us as children, on account of the barges carrying coal and the absolute certainty we would be abducted by the dirty barge men who would do unspeakable things, kill us and throw us in the canal.

The church was very much 'in bounds' and became my something of a second home. There was never any mention of men in dresses who may do unspeakable things.

Mum and Dad (Jack and Jean) married at twenty-one and twenty respectively, moved in with aforementioned Grandma in Larch Grove on the same Trees Estate before being given their own council house. The third of four children, I was a happy child, until the big house at the end of the road, where Jesus lived, became my nemesis. Jean had a fondness for Crimplene, fuchsia lipstick (no other make-up) and I never saw her naked but for the neck up and the knees down. Jack had a fondness for Brylcreem and a pint.

We seemed to be in church ALL the time. Jean had converted to Catholicism on marriage and seemed determined to prove her devotion to holiness by offering up her children as a sacrifice to the mind-boggling experimental teaching of the Catholic faith.

Good manners were very important to Mum and Dad, that they loved us was never in doubt, but there was an element of control that seemed to be born out of fear. Fear that something would happen to us and/or the opinions of others. It was very important to Mum especially, that we should never do anything to draw attention to ourselves either good or bad. To be invisible was to never cause concern. Modesty was a prized virtue as was best behaviour at all times.

The best schooling for well-behaved children was deemed to be the Catholic Church. Being packed off every Sunday to be taught the Penny Catechism was a kind of child-minding correction unit. We were taught by nuns using well-thumbed copies of a small booklet to recite in parrot fashion,

'Who made you?'

'God Made me.'

'Why did God make you?'

'God made me to know him, to love him and to serve him.'

'Where is God?'

'God is Everywhere.'

The Penny Catechism: 'A summary or exposition of doctrine, which serves as a learning introduction to the sacraments.' This was the Catholic faith as a compressed and systematised booklet for a child's understanding. It contained everything you needed to know to stay on the path towards Heaven, along with stark warning of your fate should you stumble and fall into the darkness (Hell). It also stated that 'the difference between Mortal and Venial sin was quite obvious to someone who had attained the use of reason.

At six years old, I had NOT yet attained the use of reason.

The book was filled with countless Q&As, all offering the same mystifying responses about some old bloke who lived 2,000 years ago but was also hovering in the ether, watching my every move and ready to come down on me like a ton of hot lava if I stepped out of line in ANY way.

There was NEVER any explanation or actual teaching, the thinking was that if you say the words often enough at some point they will begin to have some semblance of meaning.

The nuns were unpleasant, unsmiling penguins who never once wavered from the teachings of the magic booklet. They would brook no complaint and stymied all attempts at dialogue. As a precocious six-year-old trying to grasp the metaphysical concepts, I had innocently asked, 'If God is everywhere, can we pray to him without coming to church? On the toilet or cleaning our teeth?'

This was met with titters from the other children (toilet) and a steely stare from Sister Bernadette. The other nuns looked at me with pity. Class was finally over, everyone shuffled off. Leaving just me and Sister Bernadette who busied herself packing away the catechism booklets. I was very frightened and very alone, but for Jesus, of course, who is everywhere.

Finally, she came and loomed over me. 'Who exactly do you think you are?' she began. 'With your silly little girl questions and your need to be the centre of attention? Do you think our Lord's teachings are amusing?'

I remained silent and hung my head. I could feel tears behind my eyes and I blinked hard to make them go away.

'DO YOU?' she repeated.

'No,' I whispered.

'Speak up girl!'

'NO,' I said again, with greater conviction.

'Come with me,' she commanded, and I followed behind her to the front of the chancel.

Feeling sure I was about to be beaten, or worse, the temptation to run or to faint, or to scream for someone to hear me, whizzed around my brain, but before I could do any of the above, Sister Bernadette instructed me to lay face down on the chancel floor.

I did as I was told. Bare knees on cold flagstones, arms by my side, head down, resting my forehead on the ground.

'You will remain here and you will beg God for forgiveness,' she said. 'I will go and speak to Father Carey and he will dismiss you when he feels your soul has been cleansed. DO YOU UNDERSTAND ME?'

'Yes,' I mumbled into the floor.

With that, she was gone. And I heard the echo of the church doors banging behind her.

I started to cry. Not with shame or contrition, but fear of being in the church alone (apart from Jesus). I was cold, my knees and head hurt resting on the cold floor and I wasn't sure how long I would be there.

I tentatively lifted my head and looked at Jesus on the cross. Not really sure how to ask for forgiveness, I just said 'sorry' very softly.

When you're a child, a minute feels like an hour so I have no idea how long I was lying there. I got pins and needles in my legs and even though I felt I was probably being watched, I got up and sat on my haunches.

No one came. I waited. I sat on a chair. No one came.

I scanned the white-painted brick walls of the church for help or inspiration. Nothing, just misery from every Station of the Cross. Fourteen carved pictorial vignettes of the journey Christ made to Mount Calvary.

1.   *Jesus is condemned to death.*
2.   *Jesus carries his cross.*

3. *Jesus falls for the first time (very heavy cross).*

4. *Jesus meets his mother Mary (always found this one unbearably sad).*

5. *Simon of Cyrene helps Jesus carry the cross (guards tell him not to).*

6. *Veronica wipes the face of Jesus (crown of thorns causing much sweat and blood. Later the Shroud of Turin). Also, who was Veronica?*

7. *Jesus falls for the second time (someone tripped him over).*

8. *Jesus meets the women of Jerusalem (they are really sad and crying).*

9. *Jesus falls for the third time (so very exhausted).*

10. *Jesus is stripped of his clothes (but they let him keep his loin cloth).*

11. *Jesus is nailed to the cross.*

12. *Jesus dies on the cross. But to make sure, they stab him in the side.*

13. *Jesus is taken down from the cross.*

14. *Jesus is placed in the tomb.*

It was very clear that Jesus had endured an awful lot of suffering and I was sorry about that but saying 'toilet' in his presence, especially since he was dead anyway, felt pretty mild in comparison. Also, how was he here when he clearly wasn't here?

There was no way of knowing if I had been granted forgiveness or not, but I was cold and starting to get hungry so I genuflected to the altar, made the sign of the cross on my head, chest and each shoulder and scurried home.

I made no mention of this drama at home, but had a convenient tummy ache for the following week's class and convinced Mum that I should stay at home. A lie I told God about in my prayers. When I returned to catechism class, Sister Bernadette was nowhere to be seen. Had she been taken off the job? I secretly hoped that she had died but didn't feel any enquiry would be wise or welcome.

My question was never answered about the omnipresence of the Lord but I think I figured it out.

A year later I was deemed compliant and knowledgeable enough to make my Holy Communion.

For this, I was taught the seven gifts: Wisdom, Understanding, Counsel, Fortitude, Knowledge, Piety and the Fear of the Lord.

These were not gifts I had any interest in. I wanted a Tiny Tears doll or a fully working Dalek (the black and most evil one). By now though, like an early handmaid, I had come to realise it was just best to go along with whatever they told me and to treat the whole charade like a fairy story.

At communion, a disc of unleavened bread is placed on the tongue by the priest. Moments earlier, this disc has been turned into the 'body of Christ' (host). This was achieved by a process called transubstantiation. There is wine too. This becomes the blood of Christ.

I can't explain this to you now and I couldn't then, in a nutshell you either believe it or you don't believe it.

The nuns told us a precautionary tale to frighten us.

'There was a woman who DID NOT believe that the host would become the body of our Lord. She was a BAD woman. As she kneeled at the altar to receive the host (disc), she took a handkerchief from her pocket and when the host had been placed on her tongue by the priest, when no one was looking, she took the host from her tongue, wrapped it in the hankie and put it back in her pocket. When mass was finished she rushed to her home and took out the handkerchief containing the host.

'Then she went to the shed, found a block of wood, a hammer and some nails. She placed the host on the wood, took the nail and hammered the nail through the host, attaching it to the wood. AND OUT CAME BLOOD! THE BLOOD OF OUR LORD!'

Cue gasps and screams from the tiny, gullible students and an everlasting irrational fear that if the disc of unleavened bread should jag your teeth when it's placed on your tongue, your mouth will be filled with blood.

One of the most annoying events in the Catholic calendar was Lent, the six-week period that leads up to Easter. In the gospels, Jesus spent 40 days in the wilderness to fast and pray and over the years this has been passed down to normal mortals as a time to abstain from something that gives you pleasure.

Giving up chocolate or booze are the usual choices. As we lived moments away from the church, it was decreed by Mum and Dad that we girls aged 14, ten and eight (me) would give up an hour of sleep on school days and attend morning mass.

If memory serves correct, mass was from seven-thirty until eight-fifteen, whereupon we would dash home, grab our school bags and head off for the bus. There was one other person who attended that mass, Mrs Williams. An elderly lady who spent almost all her time in the church, putting in the hours for her ultimate salvation. Mrs Williams never spoke to us as she was constantly praying under her breath, lost in a reverie to the Lord.

In those days, masses were said entirely in Latin. Utterly incomprehensible to me, I was forced to while away the time with a selection of sleepy daydreams until the moment of holy communion which was something of a highlight. If there was to be a funeral that day, the undertakers usually brought the coffin in the evening before, where it would sit at the front of the altar awaiting its final journey. I never found out if this practice was for the body to absorb all the Godliness it could before being placed in the ground or if it was just expedient to allow the undertakers a morning lie-in. Either way, it was a new source of great fascination. Over the three or four years of attending 'Lent mass' I became something of an expert in the lives and fates of those hapless souls I imagined in their boxy abodes.

The cost of coffins varies enormously, but I could always tell if the inhabitant came from money. Handles are often where the cash is spent, brass curlicues of elaborate design would give way to cheaper plain metal handpieces designed merely to do the job.

The colour of the wood was another social indicator. Light blonde or veneered wood was much cheaper than the dark hard wood like mahogany which was always polished to such a shine you could see your reflection. The most expensive of all were the wide-brimmed caskets which were bigger and often had elaborate, intricate carvings. Sometimes I would spend the entire mass conjuring a back story for the now deceased souls that lay only feet away from me. Ruminating on how they died, what they looked like alive and, more thrillingly, how they looked after death.

I knew that by the law of averages most people were old when they died which was way less interesting. If there was a purple coffin sitting on its stand at the altar, this meant it was to be cremated. The family eschewing the costs of fancy final furniture for what looked like balsa wood and a quick coat of emulsion. I would imagine how long it took for a corpse to be burned and if any body parts remained amongst the ashes.

The most poignant of all the coffins were the children and babies. These receptacles would usually be white to indicate the purity and unsullied nature of the sad little creatures within, denied their go on the merry-go-round. The smaller the tiny casket, the greater my sorrow and I would always remember to say a prayer in the hope that the babies had been baptised in order to avoid floating around for all eternity in limbo. If, while walking to the altar for communion, I was able to brush past the coffins or touch them, it gave me a momentary thrill.

Given the amount of time I spent so close to the dead at such a young and impressionable age, it is unsurprising that death became something of an obsession. Stories I wrote at school were littered with tragedy and anguish. Such were the byproducts of leading a holier than holy life. It is not something I would want for any child and in retrospect was something of an error.

A story I wrote in 1970 aged 12 shows a love of the dramatic, an alarming obsession with death and an appalling grasp of the rudimentary principles of spelling:

I was six years old when Mum deserted us. I had an older sister of seven and a younger brother of six months. My Dad was in Borestal (sic) and the squalid flat we lived in on the outskirts of Cambridge had only one room. We waited for her to return, it got cold and dark, we were very hungry.

It got light and then dark so many times, our tummies rumbled and we were very frightened. One day baby Paul never moved or cried. He never woke up from his sleep/ Susan knew he was dead and we cried by his cot until I was sick with hurt and sadness.

There was an enonomous (sic) tip off to a welfare agency and a lady came to collect us. I was taken to a sichiatryst (sic) who said she would look at the stain on my mind and try to help me not hate Mum or the World.

When I showed this to the therapist Philippa Perry, she asked me if it were true.

Chapter 2

A Life Before God:

Priest's Butcher's Bike

As we grew older, all three McErlane girls joined the Legion of Mary, an organisation founded in 1921 to help Catholic layfolk fulfil their baptismal promises and live their dedication to the church.

Essentially, we were a do-gooding troupe who would help clean up the church vestry, polish altar candlesticks, raise money for good causes and babysit for vast Catholic families worthy of our free services.

This activity would also bring us into close contact with the resident priests. One who lived in the grace-and-favour house alongside the church and another who would pass through as a sidekick, until being appointed to his own parish if and when the bishop of the diocese deemed him suitable.

It was pretty much a revolving door for the latter category. One minute they were there and then, without explanation, they would be gone.

Any attempt to glean information from Jean, as to the reasons for a priest's departure, would be met by stony silence and the 'where do babies come from' brush-off.

All enquiries to do with sexual matters or conversations Jean deemed difficult (for her) would be closed down with a wave of the hand and a curt response.

'MUM! Why do men have willies?' we would giggle.

'I don't know!' she'd reply. 'Go and brush your teeth!'

As a result of my curious questions remaining unanswered, I was always on the lookout for illicit information and once overheard my Auntie Anne discussing Father Veyzey.

He was a ruddy-faced bear of a man with very little finesse and a fondness for the 20-minute sermon of bewildering blarney. It turned out this was no coincidence as he had also developed a fondness for Communion wine and for accompanying parishioners to the Dukes Head, the Swan at Fenny Stratford and the Dripping Spring. The announcement at Sunday mass of his sudden absence and hasty return to Ireland caused very little upset, other than to the tutting morality biddies who had all signed the pledge (never to drink) and, when not engrossed in prayer, would be pressing envelopes of money into a priest's hand for the next stained-glass window.

Whenever I visit churches as an adult, I marvel at the beauty of all the windows, paid for by bony-knuckled widows secure in the knowledge that their pitiful lives on earth would be rectified by a world of joy in the hereafter.

Father Veyzey's replacement was a softly spoken, floppy-haired, gentle soul with blue eyes and an Irish lilt akin to Val Doonican. He was called Father O'Leary.

I first met him at school. Catholic children were granted leave from C of E school assembly and would be ushered into a separate room where, more often than not, the priest would visit, to read prayers and to discuss the Bible.

At Water Eaton junior school, a ten-minute walk from home, the Chosen Ones (Catholics) were few and it would often be only two or three kids attempting to feel in some way superior for their faith while also suffering exclusion from the gang.

During the mini assembly, Father O'Leary dispensed with the prayer and Bible schtick and would prefer instead to just chat; engaging us in conversations about who we were and what our lives were like. There would invariably be some form of ecumenical conclusion to our discussions along with laughter and a few verses of 'Kum Ba Yah'.

I really liked Father O'Leary, liked the way he laughed; and even at nine years old, I could tell he liked me back.

There was no way of knowing how old Father O'Leary might have been. He was a grown-up and he was a priest. Both categories were never to be questioned.

He would often be pottering about in the vestry while I was carrying out my Legion of Mary duties and we would chat about this and that. I was playing 'The Wind' in a junior school play called *The Gas Lamp* and sometimes I would recite my lines to him and he would offer his own versions of what they might mean.

'I am not wanted here but I am needed to blow away the leaves, the dirt of the day and to whistle through the space in the branches!'

In the play an old gas man would come to light the street lamps and would implore the wind not to blow. 'The lamps are needed to keep the children safe, why wind do you need to blow them out?' The wind was lonely, everyone she met would be blown away, this made her sad and cross, why should she care that the children weren't safe? During the course of the play she is shown the error of her ways and works with the other elements, rain, snow and sun, to find joy in the happiness of others and the necessities of self-sacrifice. It was a good part 'with a very good emotional arc', said my teacher Mrs Cave.

For my costume, Mum had reluctantly given me some old net curtains long since turned grey with age and Mrs Cave had fashioned them into an ethereal costume that represented the fleeting, floating nature of blowy air.

We could never afford dance classes, but I would attend the local church hall every Saturday where my best friend Lynn Matthews took ballet and tap lessons.

It had a tiny stage and parquet flooring that echoed to the sound of a slightly off-key piano and tiny tap shoes attempting unison.

I would sit on the side lines with the mums and watch; concentrating hard to learn and remember the positions, angles and steps before rushing home at the end of the class to practise in the dressing-table mirror of our three-girl, shared bedroom.

It was the only mirror in the house, a triptych with hinged sides that reflected back three different images from the waist up.

Then I would race downstairs to show Mum my newly learned steps.

Mum had been a dancer in her youth and had once danced as a chorus girl in the Arthur Askey summer season spectacular on the North Pier in Blackpool.

She was terribly homesick though and would recount stories of walking back to her lonely digs while peering mournfully through people's windows.

The sight of happy families inside made her heart sick to be so far away from her own. It was not a life she wanted for her own children and encouragement for anything remotely theatrical was never forthcoming.

It was in the vestry that I showed Father O'Leary my movements as the wind. A jerky dance routine, which consisted of a few ballet spins, some pointy-toed leaps and a few inappropriate gyrations I had lifted from the Young Generation, a dance group that preceded Pan's People and appeared on the Rolf Harris television show.

Rolf Harris was an Australian genius who would paint massive pictures with cans of coloured paint slopped onto the canvas in copious amounts. It was impossible to tell exactly what he was painting until the very last minute. 'Can you tell what it is yet?' he would ask before launching into 'Tie Me Kangaroo Down Sport' with his didgeridoo, while the Young Generation would high-kick behind him in skimpy tops and flapping bell-bottom trousers. Rolf Harris now occupies the position of 'disgraced TV star' after being convicted of paedophilia in 2014.

The fact that Father O'Leary laughed at my contemporary masterpiece was a little disconcerting, but he made up for it by breaking into hearty applause as the wind crouched down to the floor, fluttering slightly, and silently dying (spoiler).

I once asked Father O'Leary why he had chosen to dedicate his life to God and was he ever lonely as God can't answer you? He laughed and told me that God doesn't always KNOW the answers and that his cousins and brothers were also priests.

He then told me that he had 'the calling from God'. I understood that phrase then about as much as I do now and spent many hours worrying that I too might get 'the calling'. I really did not want that and asked God in my prayers to send 'the calling' to my sister Clare instead.

Many of my Catholic friends wanted to be nuns or priests and I remember telling Father O'Leary that I would prefer to be a saint. He laughed and told me I would have to wait until I died.

'Why will you be canonised?' he asked.

I told him it would be for kindness, which made him laugh again.

I confided to Father O'Leary about my desperation for a bike and he asked me why? I told him that as long as I was strong, I could cycle to eternity. He corrected me with a gentle smile: 'For eternity,' he said. In my head, I had made eternity a place, a bit like Heaven where I would be able to cycle all the time and be happy but without being dead.

Evenings after school, would often see me atop my dad's green boneshaker bike after he'd ridden home from work. I couldn't reach the saddle but saw this as only a minor irritation. It was a ladies' bike he'd bought from a man in the pub and I would hurtle around the relatively car-free estate pedalling furiously and careering down hills. Legs stiff on the pedals, saddle out of reach, willing my fear and my fingers not to clutch the brakes as I reached what felt like the speed of light.

I so longed for my own bicycle, but money was tight. There was once talk of Father Christmas bringing a bike to share with sister Clare, but would it cause arguments?

'It won't,' I promised. 'Tell Father Christmas we won't argue, will we, Clare?'

Clare said, 'As I'm older, I get first choice when to use it!'

And then a fierce argument ensued, so that was that.

Once, when I was washing up cups after a Legion of Mary

meeting, Father O'Leary came into the vestry and suggested I could have a go on his own trusty steed, the one that he used to get around town and visit 'parishioners in need'. This phrase puzzled me. 'In need of what?' I would ask.

The answer would invariably be, 'They are struggling with their faith and NEED guidance'. This platitude covered a multitude of sins, from divorce through to prostitution, alcoholism, domestic violence and murder.

It was a revelation to find out all of these heinous sins could be instantly cleared by a quick visit to confession. 'Bless me, Father, for I have sinned', you told the priest, who sat behind a screen and listened to your failings.

Being cheeky to my mum, having impure thoughts and unkindness to those in need were my go-to sins. The priest may sometimes ask for further details (impure thoughts) before instructing you to recite a few Hail Marys and a couple of Hail Holy Queens. Whereupon your soul would be wiped clean like Fablon. A miracle!

Father O'Leary's bike was of the old, butchers' variety. Black with a large protruding basket on the front, along with a very heavy frame which was way bigger than I was used to.

No matter. I had accepted his offer and ride the bike I must.

He held it steady while I clambered on and then he attempted to run alongside me like a dad with a child on stabilisers.

'I can do it myself,' I shouted, and wobbled off into the road.

The brakes were very stiff and positioned too far away for my tiny hands to negotiate, but I was confident I could slow myself by turning 'up' into the hill by the church.

Alas, my plan could not be put in place. I was still going too fast as my right foot slipped forward from the pedal, forcing my toe to the floor, scraping my plimsoll and bending my ankle to near breaking point.

Painful as that was, it also forced my front bottom down onto the crossbar with full force, filling my eyes with tears and rendering me momentarily sightless.

The plimsoll scraping the floor had the effect of slowing me down slightly and the nimble priest in his dog collar had now caught up and was pulling at the back of the saddle in an attempt to save my trapped foot from further damage.

As every nine-year-old knows, physical pain is nothing compared to the mental anguish of looking foolish and losing face. I tried so hard not to cry and instead let out a strangled yelp and an embarrassed laugh. My front bottom was throbbing and becoming numb, my sock was ripped and the front of my ankle now oozing blood into my plimsoll. It is only as an adult that I can see how impossible it was to tell a priest that I had broken that bit between your legs that you can't even talk about to your mum.

We walked back to the vestry and Father O'Leary cleaned up my ankle with tissue and made me some hot chocolate usually reserved for the altar boys.

He told me he was very sorry, which was puzzling. Then he handed me the red ribbon that had come free from one of my plaits. I remembered how Mum had made me return to school to find a lost plait ribbon some weeks before, along with the instruction, 'Don't you dare come home without it!' His kindness at retrieving my ribbon filled me with gratitude. I loved Father O Leary.

Getting into my pyjamas before bed, I realised my front bottom injury had been bad, as I noticed the vivid blood stain on my white pants, the colour of my almost-lost plait ribbon. When I brushed my teeth, I ran the pants under the tap and scrubbed at the gusset with pink Camay before patting at them with a towel.

They remained a little damp in the morning, but I was relieved to see no evidence of further blood loss in my pyjama bottoms.

My sister Clare also liked Father O'Leary, as he would talk to her about nuns, a nonsensical notion she briefly toyed with – my prayers having been answered about her getting 'the calling' as opposed to me.

I used to tell her, 'Clare, you'll be a brilliant nun!'

Father O'Leary would often come to visit at Sycamore Avenue, an occasion that meant the television in the corner being switched off and the kettle being boiled for tea.

It also meant that there weren't enough chairs in the front room and that I would have to sit on the floor clutching my knees. He would tell my dad stories of Ireland and his time at the seminary. Mum would cluck about offering sandwiches, all the while knowing she had nothing to put in them.

You can't really give the priest a jam sandwich, can you? These offerings were mercifully always refused on account of his housekeeper making tea.

Shortly after my rather lacklustre performance as the wind where, despite much praise for my dancing, I had suffered terrible nerves and forgotten a large and integral chunk of my emotional arc, there were whispers in Catholic assembly that Father O'Leary was leaving the parish.

Sure enough, one Saturday afternoon during *Grandstand* there he was at the door to confirm his imminent departure. He asked if he could take me on a drive to say goodbye.

Mum seemed a bit flustered, saying, 'Yes, of course, I'll just get their coats.' I was buckling up my red Clarks sandals when I heard him say, 'No, no. Just the little one.' I was secretly pleased.

Clare didn't seem that bothered about going for a drive, so I pulled on my gabardine school mac over blue, bri-nylon slacks, complete with annoying stirrups that were always getting rucked up in my too-big shoes. 'You'll grow into them', being the mantra for most attire.

Father O'Leary had a navy blue Ford Anglia and I was delighted to be sitting in the passenger seat. A thrill previously unknown to me as we didn't have a car.

Whenever we borrowed my Auntie Anne's car to go on fraught holidays to Ramsgate, we were always bundled in the back, where one by one, in beautiful human synergy, we would be carsick throughout the journey.

Father O'Leary drove us in the Anglia to Brickhill woods three miles away and parked in a leafy layby.

I can remember us chatting, facing each other in the passenger seat, and his hand brushing back some hair on my face, and that's it. No further memory whatsoever of anything that took place in the woods.

I don't even remember how long we were gone.

All that is available in the memory banks is the car drawing back up to the house when it was dark. I saw my mum peering out from behind the curtains and she was not smiling.

Then I remember feeling very guilty.

Guilty because I had gone on a jaunt without my sister Clare? Guilty that we had been gone too long? Guilty that it was now dark and I had missed my turn in the weekly Saturday bath?

I don't know. I just remember the heavy weight in my stomach that I had done something very wrong.

Before I got out of the car, Father O'Leary gave me a ten-shilling note, said goodbye. Then, he was gone.

The atmosphere inside the house was chilly. 'Where did he take you?' was all that Mum could manage. 'Brickhill woods,' I told her, and handed over the ten-shilling note.

She stared at me for a long time before shouting, 'You will SHARE this with your sister Clare.' Why was she shouting at me for having ten shillings?

That Mum was paranoid about us being taken by strangers is an understatement. Whenever we were out shopping, we were either on leather reins or our hands were held in a vice-like grip for fear of us getting snatched or lost in the crowds. For Mum, her children were her life.

And yet she allowed her unaccompanied ten-year-old daughter into the car of a priest to be driven to deserted woods?

In the olden days (for that is surely what they are) the working classes were not encouraged to question figures of authority or anyone in a uniform.

Policemen, doctors, lawyers, priests, even teachers were beyond reproach. In 1964, I remember we went to see our local Buckingham MP Robert Maxwell who was opening a local fete. There is a photograph at home taken with him, a rather oleaginous fella, who Mum and Dad declared to be 'a marvellous addition to the Labour party'. The party of the working man.

Mum said nothing further about my outing. How could she? To ask me details would be to invite information that may blow her world apart. I was a wide-eyed innocent child; it was inconceivable to her that anything could have changed that.

As I went up to my bath, I noticed one of my white plait ribbons was missing. Preparing myself for Mum's fury, I pleaded, 'It must have fallen off in Father O'Leary's car! I can run up to the vestry and ask him to look?'

'Forget the ribbon!' she said. It looked like she was near to tears which made me scared. It was only a stupid ribbon.

I really couldn't understand why I felt so guilty. Looking back, it would have been impossible for me to vocalise any wrongdoing, I just wouldn't have had the words, so perhaps as has been suggested, it was a form of traumatic amnesia.

It was while working for the *Sunday Times* many years later, that I tried regression therapy. Would I be able to unlock this secret?

It is never a good idea to allow total indoctrination when a child is so young. That everything I was taught at such an impressionable age was never questioned or explained feels like an act of negligence. The total blind devotion asked of me, to a Catholic faith I didn't really understand or believe in, sat uneasily with the rest of life as I saw it.

On a rare occasion, I once plucked up the courage to ask the priest, 'If God loves us all equally, why does he let little children die?' The answer troubled me further: 'God lets little children die in order for us to demonstrate our faith, that in the face of our own suffering, we still believe in his wisdom.'

The priest also told me that 'God will only allow us the suffering we are capable of'.

Even then this sounded bogus. As I understood it, the greater the pain you are forced to endure the stronger you will have to be. If you cannot endure the agony then you will be deemed weak. A sort of competition on who has the greatest capacity for torment.

I gave up all ambitions to become a saint and turned my back on Catholicism as soon as I was able.

The devotion expected of me toward the superior beings that were nuns and priests left me with a sometimes debilitating relationship with figures of authority. A need to question why some humans have the right to superiority over others and a very firm belief in social democracy.

When my dad was dying and suffering from Parkinson's disease, and I once rather cruelly mentioned that 'at least he had his faith to comfort him', it transpired that sadly there was no comfort to be found in his predicament and he felt that his faith had deserted him.

My relationship with Father O'Leary is a difficult one to unpick. It can be a dangerous moment if a child receives special attention, especially from someone outside the immediate family, where it might be expected.

He was interested in me (as I saw it) and listened to what I had to say. As many children who have been groomed report, he made me feel special.

That Mum and Dad allowed to me travel alone, into the woods with a priest was a decision born of their unquestioning beliefs towards a man of the cloth. Any possibility of wrongdoing was incomprehensible.

Whenever I think back to that time, I am reminded of the quote by Robert Browning: 'Ignorance is not innocence, but sin'.

Chapter 3

The End of Play:

Peugeot PX8

'We do not remember days, we remember moments'
– Cesare Pavese

Accessed via a small alleyway from the Limes, a two-minute dash from home, was a patch of land half the size of a football pitch, surrounded on three sides by the gardens of houses in Pinewood Drive, Oakwood Drive and Laburnum Way; all part of the 1950s council-built Trees Estate.

This recreation ground contained an old sand pit filled with dog poo and a dirty brown crumbling substance that smelled of wee. The grass in the rec was mostly worn away to dry mud and the creaking see-saw was badly in need of oiling, along with repair to the bleached and broken wooden seats.

This was my favourite place in the world to play.

An after-school Mecca for the inhabitants of Manor Road Infants and Water Eaton Junior school.

At the end of the school day I would race home, rip off my good school jumper, pleated skirt, white shirt and tie, and pull on Blue bri-nylon slacks with stirrups under the foot and my faded Oxfam Walk '69 T-shirt. These were my designated play clothes.

Oxfam Walk '69 T-shirts filled our small shared bedroom; a result of my sister Clare helping to organise a 30-mile sponsored walk from Harpenden in Hertfordshire to Wembley Stadium, with all the funds raised going to Oxfam.

Aged 12, sister Clare wasn't strong on marketing know-how and many of the T-shirts remained unsold.

Despite the fact that I was ten years old, I completed the walk in six hours wearing a summer dress, my school shoes and knee-high socks. Possibly the first time I can recall something being really difficult. Aching legs, throbbing feet and exhaustion couldn't compete with the starving children Oxfam would be able to feed with my sponsor money, though, and I pushed on in the summer heat.

As we approached the outskirts of Wembley and the air started to smell dirty, I fell slightly behind the others as they picked up the pace, eager to get to the stadium where the Lovin' Spoonful were due on stage.

Out of the shadows of a small alleyway a man appeared, he was smiling and I was sure he was going to donate some money for the cause. Instead he held my arm and mumbled into my ear, 'If you wanna see a stiff cock, don't tell the others and follow me!'

Totally flummoxed by this, I hesitated for a moment. I DID want to see a stiff cock but the following him part caused me some concern. What WAS a stiff cock? Where was it and why couldn't the others come and see it too?

My eyes darted towards the walkers, twenty or thirty yards ahead, it seemed quite important that I catch them up despite this kind offer. The man was sporting a worn black leather glove on his free hand and I wondered what deformity it was covering. He looked at me hopefully, two white globules of congealed spit either side of his lips.

'Oh, no. You see I'm completing this walk for starving children,' I said as politely as I could. 'Thank you, though!' My arm fell free from his clutches.

There was no drama and he quickly slunk back from whence he came as I fast-skipped as nonchalantly as I could back to the safety of the group.

The encounter had both delighted and horrified me, his face, the smell of his breath on my cheek and the dirty black glove stayed with me for the rest of the day, but I never thought to mention it to anyone. A stiff cock was obviously rude and it was all probably my fault.

I can't recall much of the Lovin' Spoonful, other than I didn't know any of the words to the songs, it was really loud and I very much wanted to be home. The stiff cock conundrum was the only thing whirring around my head; that, and the fact that I had raised 19 shillings for the children of Biafra.

The Oxfam Walk T-shirts were now ragged and worn. Once my school uniform had been removed and folded, I would dash to the see-saw rec to meet my friends. It was the perfect place to shout and scream, let off steam and use up all the energy left over after class.

Running, singing, shouting and laughing. British Bulldog would see us careering the length of the rec singing 'Fox on the Run' by Manfred Mann.

The see-saw was an area of danger. Not for us the 'one on each end' gentle, rhythmic, up-and-down motion; no, we would pack as many as we could on each end causing the see-saw to groan under the great weights. If you could bounce people off the top with the ferocity of your downward bang, points were scored.

We seemed to really enjoy hurting ourselves and broken arms, noses and chin scabs were commonplace.

The rec was also a place we would sing pop songs. The boys said singing was for girls and we were only too glad they didn't join in. We all wanted to be Bobbie Gentry and knew by heart the words to 'I'll Never Fall in Love Again'. We would bellow into the wind,

What do you get when you fall in love?
A guy with a pin to burst your bubble
That's what you get for all your trouble
I'll never fall in love again
I'll never fall in love again

The next verse apparently was in code:

What do you get when you kiss a guy?
You get enough germs to catch pneumonia
After you do, he'll never phone ya
I'll never fall in love again
I'll never fall in love again

Kelvin Hansen told me that the 'germ' Bobbie sang about wasn't pneumonia at all but was actually VD (venereal disease) and you got it from kissing boys, which made you cheap and the boy who kissed you would be too ashamed to see you again or 'never phone ya'.

The thought of kissing a boy was abhorrent to me and we didn't have a phone so none of it applied. VD was also something of a mystery, but it didn't sound good and it really didn't surprise me that it came from boys.

Kelvin Hansen often hung out with the girls, he had ginger hair and pale, freckly skin. Gentle and softly spoken, he was very clever and played the clarinet beautifully. He also had a racing bike which was one of the reasons I liked him. It was a Peugeot PX8 that his dad had brought back from France on the ferry. It was a machine of great beauty. If Kelvin was in a generous mood, he would allow me to borrow this drop-handlebar, sleek, black, multiple-geared piece of engineering and leave the rec for half an hour. I'd speed away to the distant sounds of Kelvin yelling 'Don't be too long!', before navigating the empty roads of the Trees Estate and pretending I was on a mission for Illya Kuryakin in *The Man from U.N.C.L.E.*

I relished being on my own, lost in imagination and the knowledge that if I successfully completed my task, I would almost certainly marry Ilya Kuryakin, get promoted to the United Network Command for Law and Enforcement (U.N.C.L.E.) and replace Gaby the beautiful East German mechanic/British spy in the television programme.

I was very sad when Kelvin Hansen and his bicycle moved to Watford with his family. Kelvin was taunted a lot at school, called a nancy boy and often got in fights that he would invariably lose. We hung out together and he taught me strange facts about nature and how to change a tyre. It was many years later that I heard he had lost another fight, not one of his choosing, but he 'got another germ and caught pneumonia' – Kelvin died from AIDS at the age of 31.

Put kids together and they can be unspeakably cruel to those who are different, but in the see-saw rec there was very little bullying. Instead we would come up with all manner of games, old wives' tales, Chinese whispers, rules that made no sense, momentary hierarchies, and *Lord of the Flies*-type dares.

I loved the rec. Every night was different, and we would come home for tea ruddy-faced and scuffed of knee, smelling of night-time and ready for bed.

Puberty hits at different rates and many of the boys who used to play with us were older. I was always an enthusiastic tomboy and would wrestle and race with the boys without any thought. Until I hit 13, when something imperceptibly changed and I had no idea what it was or how to stop it.

The boys started to notice me, whereas previously I had just been part of a gang.

As far as I was concerned, their behaviour was mystifying, I wore the same old wellies, plaits and anorak, still sang and played the fool, but a definite uncomfortable shift had taken place in boy response.

There was a boy called Richard Palmer who lived in Laburnum Grove on the Trees Estate and went to Water Eaton school. I was friends with his sister Jackie who was a year younger than me and had pretty brunette hair and freckles. Jackie was a tip-top netball player.

Richard was tall and quite skinny, two years older, thin-lipped, but handsome in the manner of Peter Tork from the Monkees. Kind of a doofus.

He was funny and cheeky and would always be the one to push things a tiny bit too far, resulting in someone sulking or getting hurt, and which meant it would be time to go home. We would all lope off grumbling and blaming Richard for being an idiot who never knew when to stop.

Richard used to stare at me quite a lot and for reasons I couldn't fathom started to be unkind.

The boys used to hold 'flobbing' competitions, clearing the backs of their throat and spitting phlegm as far as they could, then using the length of the see-saw as a measuring tool. The girls found this singularly unappealing and we would remove ourselves to a different part of the rec for the duration of this disgusting peacock display.

On one such occasion, I was collecting my bag of old tennis balls while this macho spit fest was going on and although I was nowhere near the flob ball target area, a massive splat of phlegm landed on the sleeve of my anorak. Richard Palmer had deliberately changed his trajectory and spat directly at me.

It made me physically heave and the girls rushed in with tissues and hankies to remove the horror while everyone told him off and called him names.

He said nothing but looked on sullen and unrepentant.

As far as flirting goes, this was not a winning tactic.

The sleeve was washed under the tap when I got home, telling Mum it was a grass stain and that I had fallen over. Upsetting to be singled out in such an unpleasant way, it made me a bit anxious.

I determined to steer clear of Richard Palmer in the see-saw rec. As Kelvin Hansen told me, 'There are nicer people to play with.'

One rainy weekend journey, returning from a trip to see relatives in Nottingham in Auntie Anne's borrowed Morris Minor, we stopped for a family-sized wee at a service station. I discovered that finally, aged thirteen and a half, I had become a woman. My period had finally come. As I was one of the last girls in my class to experience this momentous rite of passage, I was greatly relieved. The horror of remaining forever a child had seemed a very real possibility that caused much anguish. While the rest of the family were busy getting orange squash and rich tea biscuits, I found a photo booth and popped myself in to record this joyous day of leaving girlhood behind. Greasy hair, spots and oily skin were captured forever in black and white with four poorly timed poses and impossible-to-gauge flashes.

Despite being a quiet child, the monstrous amount of ego required to believe that history needed this pictorial transition from girl to woman documented at Scratchwood Services is rather telling.

I kept my news and painful cramps to myself for the rest of the journey, waiting until I could get Mum alone at home before I let her into my wonderful secret.

Nothing of a sexual or reproductive nature had ever been discussed in the McErlane household. Any daring enquiries about where babies came from were quickly squashed with a curt reply of 'I'll tell you when you're older'. Even the Virgin birth of Mary was out of bounds for knowledge-hungry children.

In hindsight, it was quite an irresponsible and foolish course of action.

Whether it was embarrassment, not wishing to light a fire under our curiosity or just the sadness of little girls becoming women, I have never found out.

Unable to utter words to convey this natural phenomenon, I merely showed Mum what had happened in my pants.

Without a word, she scurried to the top kitchen cupboard, the contents of which had previously been a mystery, gave me what seemed like a small house brick and some sort of elasticated suspender attachment then hurried me into the loo.

Rather crestfallen and feeling a bit ashamed, I twisted and turned, contorting my body trying to secure this new part of grown-up fashion into position under my winceyette pyjama bottoms. The stomach pains were now quite ouchy and the novelty was wearing off. Later, Mum told me to wrap the discarded and used house bricks in newspaper and place them under the curtains which ran the length of the sink and draining board in the kitchen. 'What happens to them then?' I asked. 'They are BURNED, of course!' Mum seemed cross which made it all feel grubby and bad. No mention was made of how often I needed to change this cumbersome nappy or what to do about the pain. It was literally never spoken of again.

My coming-of-age moment was clearly a dirty secret that must not be discussed.

In bed that night, I looked at the hastily posed kiosk photos taken at Scratchwood Services. My gormless face and slightly smug smile made me sad. I cried some hormonal tears but couldn't understand why.

Our nightly trips to the rec continued but the songs we sang changed. Detroit Emeralds' 'Feel the Need in Me' was a favourite along with 'Crazy Horses' by the Osmonds. We choreographed dance routines in the style of the Young Generation and performed them for the boys.

Richard Palmer sidled over to me one day and said, 'If you got rid of your spots and that fringe, you might be quite pretty.'

I went very red and wracked my brains for a response. Nothing came.

'Oh, shut yer cakehole,' I shouted and ran off to girl safety.

The film *A Clockwork Orange* by Stanley Kubrick had just been released and some of the older girls were desperate to see it. Knowing that this would be out of the question for me, on account of it being corrupting and that I was only 14 and it was X-rated. I told Mum I was babysitting for a Catholic family with innumerable children and would be home late. A white lie I would reveal to the priest, when next I went to confession.

Along with babysitting, my other job was delivering Sunday papers at 6.30am before Mass. My collection point was five minutes away, IF I took the back route. The back route was a bit scary as it was past the unused garages and through a dark narrow alley which bordered the graveyard of St Martin's Anglican church.

I was given strict instruction by Mum never to use this route, on account of almost certain abduction and murder. This ruling was gleefully ignored, although I was always a tiny bit trepidatious on dark mornings and would run all the way, only stopping once I could see the light of the paper shop opposite the old church.

Mountains of newspapers would be stacked in piles, each pile marked for its hapless delivery urchin. Mr Parker, the smoke-raddled old owner who only ever wore worn-out carpet slippers, would then stuff the papers for my round into the canvas delivery bag with its heavy leather strap, before it was slung over my shoulder and off I would stagger.

At its heaviest before any drops had been made, the bag would almost reach the ground. Once outside the shop, I would rearrange the strap behind my head and under each arm like a backpack, then trundle off like a tiny pit pony overburdened by coal.

Britain was plagued by strikes in 1972, miners, dockers, building workers, with everyone complaining about food prices as a result. The front pages of the papers screamed out grim headlines. Mr Parker in his worn-out carpet slippers once told me I could take a paper home to read: 'It'll be up to you young uns to sort out this mess,' he laughed, and I noticed that he only had three or four teeth.

My round would take two hours and I was paid ten shillings, or 50 pence as it had just become after decimalisation. The first few years of decimalisation were spent with people in shops asking, 'How much is that in old money?' Laying down a selection of coins on counters for some helpful shop assistant to fathom. Having my own wages meant I was able to buy whatever I wanted, as long as it didn't cost more than ten shillings – and what I really wanted was to go and see *A Clockwork Orange*.

Although shuffling into the Bletchley picture house with the older girls meant less scrutiny as to my age, I had nevertheless edged my eyes in heavy black eyeliner and borrowed a pearlised Rimmel lipstick in sickly coral.

The ticket lady in her booth didn't even bother to look up which emboldened me to use this method again. Going on to see *Fritz the Cat* (a very rude cartoon) and *The Exorcist*. All before I was 15.

A Clockwork Orange was beyond me. I loved the music and was mesmerised by Malcolm McDowell with his eyeliner, fake eyelash and bowler hat, but I didn't really know what the Droogs were talking about in their strange Nadsat language, nor why everyone was getting beaten up and hurt.

The brutality of the gang paled into insignificance when we saw the even more bloody and violent attempts at rehabilitation which were barbaric and ultimately didn't work.

Someone said that 'THAT was the point!' although it made no sense to me. Without the necessary tools needed for full analysis, we cooed and clapped the film, then declared it 'genius'.

The see-saw rec gang decided to call ourselves the Children of the Revolution after Marc Bolan's hit song, despite us having little knowledge or interest in what a revolution actually was and no longer considering ourselves children.

We would blather about TV programmes, *Magpie* being a big favourite with all the girls fancying the bubble-haired Mick Robertson; *Kung Fu* meant we called everyone 'Grasshopper' and spoke in portentous tones when imparting homegrown wisdoms, and we all loved *The Waltons*, but were way too cool to admit such a fondness for the cheesy stories of family morality and survival.

Films on the big screen, especially those illegally seen, were the real talking point and gave you an extra unspoken amount of respect.

Discussing *A Clockwork Orange* endlessly in the rec, one of the girls bought the album that she home-recorded and played to us on a tiny, tinny, battery-operated tape recorder while we marched around the see-saw in unison.

There was often a large, black Labrador roaming about the rec which we named Droog. It never answered to that name but would instead bumble about its business leaving deposits in the sand pit and snuffling around for snacks. Dogs seemed to roam more freely in the olden days and would return home as and when they needed feeding, with nary a thought for getting lost or harmed. I'm not sure anyone stole dogs either as they had no currency.

Being afraid of dogs, Droog the Lab didn't much interest me. Whilst he seemed pretty harmless there was little need for us to interact in any way. An arrangement that suited us both.

Apart from, that is, one occasion he kept coming over to me

every time I turned my back, sniffing and snuffling around my coat as though I may have something tasty in my pockets.

Each time this happened I would remove myself, running to another part of the rec to escape him. Droog would be side-tracked for a while before once again picking up my scent and following me.

I didn't like this at all and started to get scared. Richard Palmer told me it was better to stand still, that the dog thought it was a game and I should just stay where I was and ignore it. Thinking he was helping me, I settled by the see-saw and dutifully turned my back on the dog.

Before I knew what was happening and without the benefit of sight, Droog lurched at me, launching its front legs over my shoulders, thrusting wildly at me with his lower body and a great deal of force.

Richard seemed pleased by this.

The dog knocked me front ways over the see-saw and was too heavy for me to wriggle away, all the boys gathered around with Richard Palmer laughing and shouting, 'YES! That's what you need!' Despite pleading for assistance and to 'get the dog off me!' Richard merely stroked the dog's shuddering back until it suddenly fell away and lumbered off panting.

I was upset, had grazed my leg on the broken wooden seat and had no idea what had just happened.

Richard then delighted in pointing out the large white streak of glutinous matter all over the back of my gabardine school mac and everyone started to laugh and call me the dog's girlfriend.

'She made the dog come,' he screamed. 'She must be on the blob!'

I started to cry. 'There is something WRONG with you!' I shouted before running home to get the vile stuff off my coat in case Mum found out that not only had a dog pushed me over, but it had left its nasty slime on my back.

I hated Richard Palmer, hated that he knew I was on my period and vowed never to play with him again.

Leaving church after Mass the following Sunday, we learned that a terrible thing had happened. A man had been beaten to death with a paving slab in the doorway of St Martin's Anglican church. Nothing like this ever happened in Bletchley and the entire community was in disbelief. The church and the scene of the murder was opposite the paper shop where I would collect the Sunday newspapers for delivery. For days the whole area was cordoned off with flapping police ticker tape. People gathered in huddles nearby, trying to divine information or seek reassurance that it must have all been a terrible accident. Everyone knew there was a bad person at large and that this wasn't an episode of *Columbo*. That Sunday on my paper round, I was too afraid to take the short cut. Instead, I chose the long way round, where street lights illuminated the roads and early morning dog walkers made their way to the canal tow-path.

Everyone was jittery and afraid. It had been a brutal and horrifying killing of a defenceless man. Some said he was a tramp (as they called homeless folk in the 70s) or someone befuddled by drink who had stumbled into the church graveyard to relieve himself. Speculation was rife with very few facts available as to how and why such a gruesome act had occurred.

My thoughts were filled with this man's last moments, what had he done wrong? Had he known his killer? How much blood was there? At what point did his spirit leave him, defeated and resigned to death? How had the police not managed to find the person who did this? It was their job to keep us safe, after all.

Running home from school one sunny afternoon that week, eager to get out to play, it was impossible to miss two police cars parked by the see-saw rec. Any evidence of the police always made me feel guilty. A good Catholic girl ready to shoulder blame for any inexplicable wrongdoing:

'Did you kill the Lord our God?'

'Yes, yes, I believe that was indeed me.'

The police were there to protect us but also to be feared and avoided. There would be no playing in the see-saw rec that day. Maybe someone had reported us for being too unruly? Or perhaps the dreaded black Lab Droog had gone missing?

Even though you wanted to know more than anything, you must never ask the police about their existence and only approach them if you were in danger. Everyone knew that.

Dad had decided that after the horrific murder opposite the paper shop, I was not allowed to continue with my newspaper round until the murderer had been identified and imprisoned. In my heart and the fearful part of my stomach, there was some relief at this diktat, but knowing I had put down a deposit on a Prince of Wales check dress for the school disco, I needed the money urgently to pay for it in the allotted time. A row quickly erupted before it was decided that Dad would undertake my delivery duties and the money would be loaned to me, until such time it was deemed safe to resume my Sunday deliveries.

There was never any question that he would gift me the money because 'that was not the way life worked and the sooner I understood that the better'.

I was to go into the paper shop the following day after school to explain to Mr Parker and his worn-out slippers that this would be the new, necessary and temporary arrangement regarding my employment. I had wanted Dad to tell him, man to man, but in our house 'taking responsibility' was held in high regard and some old meaningless guff like 'soonest done soonest mended' put an abrupt end to the conversation.

Rounding the corner to Laburnum Grove, practising what I would say to Mr Parker, I was stopped from walking, breathing or moving by the sight of police tape at the house opposite.

Outside this unprepossessing semi-detached council house with white lace curtains, glossy painted door and red polished step, there were hastily erected thin poles plunged at angles into the once pristine grass which divided the shared lawn. The tape extended to the side entrance of the house and covered the gate and nearby brick shed.

It was Richard Palmer's house. The police were at Richard Palmer's house. I must have remained there for some minutes, staring at the tape flickering in the wind, all thoughts of my difficult paper round conversation with Mr Parker evaporated.

Of course the police were there. It was Richard. Richard had killed someone. How was that even possible? Had he gone too far as usual? Not known when to stop? He had wanted to taunt a tramp? To humiliate, debase, abuse? He had battered him to death with a paving stone. A living breathing man was now dead because Richard Palmer had made him dead with his own spindly arms and white, hairless, kicking legs.

I ran to the paper shop, blurted out that Dad would do my paper round before Mr Parker interrupted me and said, 'But they've got him! They've arrested the killer. A young lad round your way, apparently. There's no need to worry anymore. What a terrible shock for his mum! See ya Sunday, love.'

That night it was on the national news. No names, no photograph, just that a local man had been arrested. 'Man'. He wasn't a man, he was a goofy, hopeless boy.

They called it the Clockwork Orange Murder because of its similarities to the senseless kicking to death by Alex DeLarge of an innocent tramp.

Had Richard seen the film? Was he with us that night? None of us could remember. We had certainly all talked about it in the see-saw rec.

The psychiatrist for the prosecution described in detail the similarities in the brutal attack, but the defence argued that Richard had not, COULD not, have seen the film as it had an X-rated certificate and he was only 16, not 18 as the ruling required.

His sister and the family disappeared from the house overnight, we speculated that they were probably in police protection. The ticker tape disappeared, the house loomed out at you empty, desolate and holding onto its many secrets.

We had been learning about the Norwegian painter Edvard Munch at school and every time I passed the abandoned house I would see in my mind the image of *The Scream*, Munch's iconic painting of emotional pain. Often, I would emit a small silent scream as I passed. A scream for lives ruined, for an impetuous moment with devastating consequence. For the memories of our time in the see-saw rec where no one ever played anymore; time was passing, we were growing up and our evenings were more likely to be spent playing Tamla Motown records in teenage bedrooms and talking of sexy boys. I thought of Richard Palmer often, of his sister and his mum and dad, of the manner of death inflicted on an old defenceless man, the speed at which lives can change and at Charles Dickens's opening line to *A Tale of Two Cities*:

It was the best of times, it was the worst of times, it was the age of wisdom, it was the age of foolishness, it was the epoch of belief, it was the epoch of incredulity, it was the season of Light, it was the season of Darkness, it was the Spring of hope, it was the Winter of despair, we had everything before us, we had nothing before us, we were all going direct to Heaven, we were all going direct the other way.

After Richard was convicted of murder and for many years after, I was always fearful that, somehow, I would murder someone, quite by accident and that I would be taken away.

The alternate scenario was that I would be wrongly convicted of a murder and no one would believe my innocence.

In later years I had a recurring dream that, along with my then partner, we had conspired to murder someone and hide him away behind concrete in a subsequently abandoned building. Freudians would of course claim this to be a part of oneself that needed to be locked away and perhaps that is true.

Bad things happen all the time but mainly to other people, until the bad thing happens to you. At no point did I ever feel or think that Richard Palmer was evil. It was as important then as it is now to maintain that belief.

Chapter 4

An Alternative Education:

Pinky the Foundling with Silver Wheels

'Make yourself one small republic of unconquered spirit'
– Rebecca Solnit

So, I messed up my exams.

I am still not entirely sure why. The fact that I spent at least three months skipping school, staying on the bus and riding around the streets and estates for most of the day, seemed preferable to the tedium that awaited me during lessons. I had been a model student for the first year or two at Leon County Secondary School, coming either first or second in class and competing with my best friend Lynn Matthews for those prized placings.

What went wrong? The whole debacle haunts me still and I wish there was some way of tapping into the 'what's the bloody point' reasoning that engulfed the teenage me. A sense of hopelessness, laziness and apathy took hold and I think I just gave up.

That I was able to conceal my educational absences for as long as I did felt at the time like a triumph but a Pyrrhic victory as it turned out. Even my English tutor Mr Shiner felt it was too late for me to catch up on coursework and that taking my exams would be a waste of everyone's time.

Mum and Dad were furious and disappointed and felt my only option was to leave school and get a job. In a different time and from another background I may have been sent to a crammer or been given extra tutoring, perhaps even some form of investigation into why a once bright teenager had thrown all the balls in the air and made no attempt to catch them as they fell.

I left school and got a job in the Tetley tea company as an office junior. This involved early morning coffee pots for the men with job titles like Brand Manager or Head of Marketing. They all had large, plush offices and their own secretaries; they were clearly very important. Filing, typing invoices and ordering stationery were my other high-end chores. I would also be sent on errands through the vast halls of production in the factory. Humid and dusty, the entire place stank of tea and was filled with endless conveyor belts tended to by stony-faced workers in overalls and J-cloth shower caps.

It was grim and relentless. Automatons collecting, packing and stacking. Eight-hour shifts doing the same thing over and over again. Thankful that I was to be in the offices, it was something of a wake-up call to know that this form of employment even existed. One Monday morning I was sent to London with an important package to be delivered to Bayswater Road. I was given £5 in petty cash and set off to the station with instructions to take taxis from Euston and back.

Instead, I fathomed the complex underground system and took the tube to Bayswater Road. Once my oh-so-important package of tea had been delivered to a duke or a princess (as I imagined) I walked back along Bayswater Road, passed Marble Arch and on to the wonder that was Oxford Street.

So many cool and groovy shops, Jane Norman's window display had a skinny mannequin in a baker-boy Donny Osmond hat, gingham miniskirt and two-tone platform boots. She was majestic and it was the most glamorous outfit I had ever seen. I wandered around C&A, British Home Stores and Selfridges, agog at the prices and possibilities, my only previous trips to London having been to Petticoat Lane Market to get cheap schmutter (as the stall holder once called it) and poorly made knock-offs of Prince of Wales check dresses.

I was in retail heaven with nothing in my wallet but pretend pounds to purchase whatever I wanted.

This was a wonderful game and I kept a tally of everything I 'pretend' bought.

Chelsea Girl saw me try on a brown midi coat in thick corduroy for nine pounds, almost an entire week's wages. Then a floral maxi dress with an extra large white collar. The skirts dragged on the floor as I swept over to the full-length mirror to admire my newly invented self. 'It's too long,' I told the bored assistant. 'What a shame,' she drawled, without looking up.

In Dolcis I tried on two pairs of Chelsea boots and pretend bought a pair in pink suede.

Lilley and Skinner offered platform clogs with leather uppers and a wooden base. They were impossible to walk in but I fell in love and pretend bought them for £7.50 – an absolute fortune.

In Bourne and Hollingsworth I decided it would be a brilliant job to work behind the make-up counter. All the girls had heavily pasted foundation, pale frosty lips and blue eye shadow with the sexiest flicked-out eyeliner. What fabulous lives they must all be having!

With aching legs and having spent 28 pretend pounds on shoes, a shiny plastic coat, two mini dresses (in the sale), a bedside lamp and a Mary Quant eyeliner, I trudged back to Euston invigorated by what I had seen. Bletchley had little mystery and I knew that my time at the Tetley tea company held no further excitements. There was a big world out there and it was time for me to change things up.

At Euston station, I asked a taxi driver to give me two return receipts to and from Bayswater Road, claiming I had foolishly forgotten to ask my drivers. He dutifully complied and I pocketed the two pounds I had saved. My first act of fraud felt like I now fully understood the wicked ways of the world. No one was going to give me a leg-up, so I had better get used to using whatever methods necessary.

A few weeks later, a friend mentioned she was thinking of taking a summer season job as a chambermaid in a hotel in Newquay,

Cornwall, and did I want to go? Of course I did! A passport out of Bletchley was what I had been praying for. We were to live in staff quarters, would have our meals provided, work from 7am till 2pm daily, plus an hour for bed turndown at 6pm. The rest of the time would be ours to frolic in the sea and enjoy the hostelries and delights of the town.

My plan was met with resistance from Mum and Dad: I had miraculously acquired a good, reliable job with prospects at Tetley tea company, why would I want to throw it all away on a frivolous summer season?

I had no credible answer other than that I had already thrown away my education and there seemed to be a pattern emerging.

Bredon Court Hotel was a large, imposing building set back from the road, flanked by tennis courts and rather splendid gardens and grounds. I was to share a room with my friend in a converted Victorian house 300 yards from the main entrance. It was the attic room with two single beds under the eaves, a brown wardrobe with a broken door, a scuffed chest of drawers and a small sink by the window which looked out over the tennis courts. It made me very happy.

All the other rooms in the house were taken by staff and we collectively shared a bathroom and loo. The chambermaids each had ten hotel rooms on one of the four floors to clean every day. The housekeeper Margaret instructed us how to make beds, change sheets, clean skirting boards and hoover the rooms. Then, the correct way to clean and polish the bathroom and wash the floors, and mirrors must be cleaned last to avoid splashing.

The first job of the day at 7am was to prepare and deliver tea trays to the guests' rooms from our service stations on each floor. This was a tiny cupboard containing a water boiler, sink, fresh cotton bedding in a fetching magnolia stacked neatly on high shelves, plus cleaning paraphernalia and our own personal hoovers which were to be emptied daily, checking amongst the dust for small objects of jewellery that may have been mistakenly sucked into the bag.

Each tea tray had to contain a small silver tea pot, a silver hot water jug, silver milk jug, spoons, silver sugar bowl with sufficient cubes and two china cups and saucers. All silver jugs and tea pots were to be taken weekly to the burnishing unit in the large hotel kitchen in order to maintain their sparkling sheen and pretence of grandeur.

I was given the three corner rooms on each of the three floors, plus a ground-floor 'suite' which was exactly the same as the other rooms but slightly bigger, with the addition of a pink velour sofa and French windows which opened onto the garden.

My tea trays had to be carried up many flights of stairs and were dropped on countless occasions, spewing hot tea, milk and sugar cubes over the carpets and walls. The consequent refilling and frantic cleaning would often make me late for staff breakfast taken in a large refectory an hour before guest breakfast began.

This was such a happy time. Despite the menial and repetitive tasks, there was a sense of pride in managing each room, and noticing small improvements on how long it took and how quickly I could turn a dishevelled pit into a spick-and-span room of dreams.

People behave quite differently in a hotel room to the way they would in a room of their own.

The knowledge that a small cleaning fairy in a white collar and cuffed tunic will magic away the detritus, return the bed to tight-sheeted order and eliminate nasty bathroom secrets, turns some folk into slobs of the highest order – or should that be lowest?

One couple who stayed for two weeks in the ground-floor 'suite' would toss the entire contents of their wardrobes onto the floor every day. They would bring pastries into the room from the restaurant and stub out multiple cigarettes using the cake as an extinguisher. They left used condoms on the bedside tables and vomit around the loo most mornings. Whether it was pregnancy or bulimia I will never know, but the room took as long to order as the other nine in total. I blame them entirely for my folding obsession. Every 24 hours, I would pick up multiple items from the floor and fold them carefully.

It felt too personal to return them to the wardrobe and it wasn't my place to open it.

The lady's clothes would be laid in an ever-higher pile over the chair and the man's clothes would be placed atop the velour sofa.

Shoes would be paired by the door, socks, panties, bras underpants and stockings all placed in a laundry bag and hung on the door. Condoms would be picked up with rubber gloves and binned. Then the large dildo, which I found in the middle of the bed, was placed upright on the bedside table as an acknowledgement of its discovery by an innocent who didn't really understand what it was.

Their bath was always full of scummy water, the toilet remained unflushed of its ugly contents, shower plug blocked by bleached and broken hair and the bathroom floor cluttered with dirty towels, dropped and fallen powder pots and make-up.

Every morning for two weeks I would hesitate before using my key, afeared of the horror I would find on the other side of the door.

The other chambermaids told me I was a shoo-in for a very large tip. Instead, on the morning they left, I was told as they hastily rushed for departure that there were two cakes from the restaurant I could have along with instructions on a pile of dirty clothes they were leaving: 'Please take anything you like as I don't want them anymore'.

It was all binned.

In contrast there were beautiful souls who made their own beds, left bathrooms looking as though they were never used, tidied their personal effects daily and left massive tips and thank-you cards. Classy folk.

Ever since my chambermaid days, I have always been mindful to leave hotel rooms as tidy and pleasant as I can, for the simple reason that I DID that job once and I care about those who are doing it now.

Quite the best life lesson for anyone to learn.

The first week of my summer season was marred by the arrival of mum, eldest sister and younger brother who had booked a bed and breakfast to come and visit. A source of great irritation as I could only view it as checking up on me. It was such a source of joy to have sought independence and I couldn't contain my fury to be undermined in this way. Of course there was also guilt, as the surprise visit had been spun into a nice and kindly thing to do, in case I was homesick. I wasn't fooled and only agreed to meet them on a few occasions. Forming new friendships and reinventing myself, their presence only succeeded in making me feel babyish and mollycoddled. I had severed the apron strings only for the bloody apron to turn up on my doorstep. Not what you need when you have made a monumental break for freedom.

That Mum had always feared my accidental entry into prostitution and the sordid underbelly of life said more about the shame she would feel rather than my safety, wellbeing or questionable character. An oft quoted catchphrase being, 'What will the neighbours think?'

It was a glorious summer and afternoons would be spent on Fistral beach, sunbathing, swimming and making new friends. *Jaws* was the blockbuster of the summer and we nicknamed the beach 'Amity'. We would hold parties in our rooms listening to the Eagles singing 'One of These Nights' and 'The Best of My Love' on my tiny record player, then go dancing at discos to 'Kung Fu Fighting' and the Average White Band's 'Pick Up the Pieces'. It was a carefree existence.

There was extra money to be made at the hotel by joining the babysitting roster. One night a week meant patrolling the rooms where small children slept while their parents got drunk in the bar or went out into town.

One evening on babysitting duty I was sent to the kitchen during dinner service in order to warm a baby's bottle. Uniforms were not needed for babysitting and I was wearing a baby pink Angora polo neck which accentuated my teenage bosoms, blue high-waisted oxford bags and white platform clogs which were very much the footwear du jour.

I had seen Martin the silver-service waiter at staff mealtimes, but he had never seen me out of chambermaid tunics.

Rushing through the busy kitchen complete with the obligatory raging and half crazed head chef, it was clear I had made an impression on Martin and I felt his eyes on my bottom as I hurried away to feed the abandoned baby.

To quote Julius Caesar, the die was cast.

Martin was from Halesowen in Birmingham, he was tall and strong with a Roman nose and a love of surfing. I was very sexually inexperienced and he taught me everything he knew which, being several years older than me, was a lot.

Whilst not a virgin, I knew nothing of the female orgasm, oral sex or the joys of spending the night with someone. As he enjoyed the higher rank of silver-service waiter, Martin had been allocated a small private room in a block of ten purpose-built staff quarters and it was there, during the summer of 1975, that I experienced a full and magical sexual awakening.

We would organise our days off to coincide and I would often spend most of my precious free time under a bin liner on a rainy Fistral beach, watching him surf when the tide was full. Flasks of tea, towels and bottles of warming brandy were my domain and although I tried surfing a couple of times, not being able to grasp the rudimentary skills immediately, was enough to make me petulantly throw in the towel.

I certainly became expert in reading the mood of the sea. An offshore wind would hold up the wave and if the swell was good, it could create near perfect conditions. Cool crisp swollen lines of liquid that would glide towards the shore in sets of seven or eight, each wave bigger and more powerful than the last. Thick glassy perfect curves several feet high creating exquisite question marks all urgently reaching for the sky and racing toward the sand. Up at the top, the lip of the wave would be thinner which allowed the wind to blow out great bursts of spray, creating droplets of rainbow-coloured spume in the air. For the surfers to catch a wave at the optimum point is to harness the full energy of the question mark and hurtle through its glistening tube, man and board outrunning the break a fraction of a second behind them and cutting through the fluid as if it were solid matter. Make a mistake and the wave will take you over with it, crushing you under the full weight of thousands of gallons of water and bringing the surfboard down on your head in the swirl of raging water. A punishing lesson you'll be keen not to repeat.

Martin had a bicycle. On the days when there was no surf, he would cycle the hilly country lanes to keep up his fitness. It was a Raleigh Sport hybrid road bike with pimped handlebars and as he was six-foot-four, was way too big for me. I couldn't afford a bike but longed to whizz around with him on our days off and would wistfully watch him leave for his lone adventures. Finishing my shift one morning, I noticed a grey, battered ladies' bike with one black and one white tyre leaning against the staff block entrance. Two days later, it was still there. It wasn't locked and although a bit of a boneshaker, looked pretty solid. I kept my eye on it for several more days and when it hadn't moved, gently pushed it to the back of the staff block where it was out of sight. I wasn't taking it, merely putting it in a safe place so it wouldn't be stolen (or seen again by whoever it belonged to).

In my head, the bike was now mine, but a period of grace and possible owner reclamation was needed before I dared ride the thing.

On our next day off, Martin purchased a can of pink spray paint and affected a clever disguise on the already hand-painted, peeling grey frame. We had no idea of the make or model of this beauty, but everything worked brilliantly and once we'd changed the white rubber tyre it looked pretty unrecognisable. I promised everyone who knew of this deceit, that if challenged, I would willingly return the bike to whoever laid claim.

Trying to keep up with someone of Martin's size, fitness and gear capacity on a three-gear pink-painted boneshaker was a challenge, but one I relished and I would long for the surf to be flat so we could escape on the very much not flat country roads to Perranporth, St Agnes or Padstow. Quite how we managed those hills must have been sheer exuberance and reckless youth, but the sun always shone, we would stop for pasties and beer and it was truly one of the happiest times of my life. I had a boyfriend, a job, a community AND a bike. My life was filled with riches.

My needs in a relationship were few as I had no experience or idea about what was available. To be desired was mistakenly viewed as being loved and cared for which felt good enough to be going along with.

The staff at Bredon Court were all pretty cosmopolitan; there were Australian pot washers, Spanish and Italian waiters, German bar staff, two French patissiers and a South African receptionist. I loved hearing about their lives and felt my entire summer was a brilliant education that taught me so much of worlds I had little knowledge of.

Many of the summer season workforce were nomadic creatures, saving money for world travel. With food and board covered, this was pretty easy to do, as long as you were able to stay out of the bars and clubs of the town where your wages could disappear in a single evening.

Martin was keen to save money so we led a pretty frugal existence. Travelling on our respective two-wheeled machines to local beauty spots or further afield in his battered Renault to surf beaches and coastal oddities, before spending the evenings enthusiastically practising carnal oblivion.

The summer rolled on in all its blissful glory and I vowed to return the following year with a job upgrade of silver-service waitress.

As the summer season drew to a close, I managed to cadge a lift back home with one of the kitchen porters. The car was packed to the hilt with surfboards, six months' worth of three people's sun-faded clothes and no room for my lovely pink-painted bicycle. As with all the bikes I have owned, a relationship of sorts had been formed with this collection of wheels, gears, brakes and tyres. That they had all taken me on adventures and kept me safe even when I had been drunk or careless, ridden too fast or taken needless risks, I always felt as though I somehow owed them a debt of gratitude. How could

I leave Pinky when we had journeyed so far together?

Leave her I must and I begged the hotel groundsman to allow Pinky to winter in the greenhouse until the following April. It was an emotional goodbye. The bike had come to me as an unexpected gift and facilitated many gruelling but joyous adventures. It felt no different bidding adieu to her as it did to the many hotel staff I had loved but would almost certainly never see again.

She would be safe, we would be reunited. There would be further adventures.

The winter of 1975 saw Martin and I journeying back and forth to see each other, love held us together. He got a job in Oxford and I would hitch-hike from Bletchley on Friday evenings after whatever temp job I had secured that week. I was aware that hitch-hiking could be dangerous, but I would dress smartly in hat and gloves and quickly engage the drivers in conversations about their families and children. The psychology being they were less likely to rape and kill me if we had shared personal details. I was growing and changing and so was Martin, but we still laughed constantly and agreed we would save money during the following summer season and then spend the winter travelling the world together. Life was good.

Silver-service waitressing meant a significant pay rise at Bredon Court, my own room in the purpose-built block, a considerably heavier workload and promotion from the lowly land of bed-making. Wherever one lands in life, there will always be hierarchy.

One of my first jobs arriving back at the hotel after a long winter, was to go and get my bike and give her an overhaul. Pump tyres, oil chains, check brakes and so on. I sought out the garden groundsman who had vowed to keep her safe. He was nowhere to be found. Further enquiry revealed he had been 'let go' after a physical altercation with the hotel caretaker resulting in a nasty glassing and ten stitches in hospital for the hapless caretaker.

I managed to gain access to the greenhouse, now filled with soon-to-be planted bulbs and garden produce ripening for the season ahead. The corner where Pinky was stored was now home to several coiled garden hoses, four stacked buckets and a window-cleaning contraption.

The bike was gone. In much the same mysterious way it had come to me, it had disappeared without trace. Martin tried to console me by telling me we are only ever custodians of our possessions and that I should be happy someone else had the opportunity to enjoy riding her in the same way I had. That all just sounded too hippyish. I was happy to embrace the hippy ideology until it affected MY things.

'You must be philosophical about it,' he said. I didn't really know what that meant and wanted to tell him to fuck off and stop being patronising. 'What does philosophical mean?' I asked. 'It means Que serra, serra, whatever will be, will be,' he said with confident authority.

The restaurant was so much busier than making beds as a chambermaid and there never seemed to be enough time to keep on top of the workload let alone think about carefree cycling excursions.

I was given six tables of six, began work at 8am for breakfast service, would be finished by 11, had an hour off before lunch, then would be free from 2.30 until 6.30 when we would prep for dinner service. Dinner was tremendously posh, all mood lighting and a la carte splendour. It was hard graft and took me a fair while to master. I learned words like 'mise en place', 'sommelier' and 'pears belle Helene', but I also learned a lot about human interaction and the benefits of a guileless charm.

I began the season in the up-market end of the restaurant, a vast room with full-length windows along two sides revealing views of the golf club nearby, the sea and horizon beyond. The sunsets were spectacular and romantic. Martin and I shared a station, where all condiments, cutlery, napkins, and so on, could be laid out for service.

It was also used (by me) when the weight and awkwardness of carrying six or seven heavy plates became too much for my tiny hands and I knew I wouldn't make it to the guests' table without mishap. There were also silver tureens, trays of vegetables and potatoes to be managed, which all had to be served using a large spoon and fork at the table onto each plate in turn. It was a lot to contend with and the heavily laden walk from the kitchen proved increasingly tough.

Martin complained that I was messy and untidy and didn't like having to share a station with me as he felt it looked amateurish. We were serving food, not performing the Ring Cycle. I was new to the whole thing and felt he was being prissy and unsupportive.

That he also revealed his thoughts to the pompous head waiter really hurt my feelings. My position in the restaurant was moved. A blow to my pride and our relationship, but tables nearer the vast swing doors of the kitchen would be easier to navigate and I would have my own station to do with as I wish. To prove a point, I kept it as clean and tidy as a whistle and settled in to serve each week's guests in a 'not so upmarket' area of the dining room.

Within weeks, I had got the hang of things, the work was extremely hard, the hours long, but the rewards if you judged things right were plentiful.

My wage was £25 a week, the average tip was £5 a week per table. On a good week I could make the full £30 in tips alone. These amounts seem ridiculous now, but at eighteen years old, it was a small fortune. Further enhanced by the fact I was beating Martin on the tip front. Like a lot of the food I hastily scrambled to the tables, revenge was a dish best served cold.

The song from the film *Mahogany* by Diana Ross was in the top ten at the time and it became my theme tune in the restaurant. I would lay up my tables singing,

Do you know where you're going to?
Do you like the things that life is showing you?
Where are you going to?
Do you know?

Summer season work is by its very nature temporary and transient. It attracted itinerant lost souls who had yet to find out or know who they were and what they wanted from life. This for me was part of the appeal. You didn't have to explain or pigeonhole yourself into a mode of life or employment that defined you. It was a holding pen, a state of limbo that needed no explanation or apology and for me it was a pivotal period of learning about the world and my place in it. Where WAS I going to?

The staff at Bredon Court in 1976 had sex ALL the time. Not only with each other but also (although strictly verboten) with a selection of guests.

This seemed to me like another element of the transient existence. No strings, no ties, no questions asked. The sun shone, alcohol was in plentiful supply and sex was fun and free.

The seductive sounds of 'If You Leave Me Now' by Chicago would waft out of staff rooms into the humid night air of the hottest summer on record and everyone was horny and happy.

The prolonged heat caused drought and Dutch Elm disease swept across the United Kingdom. Simultaneously, gonorrhoea swept through the staff rooms and corridors of our tiny love commune in Cornwall.

We were a decade before the horror of AIDS, and 'the clap' as it was then called was easily treatable with antibiotics, but the shame and the knowledge you would have to inform all sexual partners of this nasty malady and necessary clinic visit was mortifying.

I felt quietly smug because Martin had been and was my only sexual partner. We went out for a drive one afternoon after lunch service, to picnic on one of the estuaries leading to Falmouth, we were tanned and happy and laughing about one of the guests, who had stormed into the kitchen complaining about his undercooked steak. The chef, who was Italian and renowned for his cliched chef's temper, had threatened the guest with a meat cleaver and the police had been called. It was high drama indeed.

On the way back, Martin became serious. He told me in a faltering voice that he had slept with one of the waitresses, a blousy girl from Hull, ten years his senior with a wide sweaty moon face and a thin wispy bob. He had contracted gonorrhoea and, almost certainly, so had I.

She had slept with a barman from the local pub who had infected her before she then slept with Martin. She went on to have sex with the head waiter who had given it to the Australian receptionist who was also sleeping with one of the bar staff. He was in a long-term relationship with one of the chambermaids. The list went on like white noise and my eyes became blurred by tears.

Not only did I have some nasty disease rampaging through my vagina, causing possible infertility, but my lovely, loving Martin had broken something between us that was way more important and my life was now over.

We had an almighty row, shouting, crying and slapping from me and pathetically lame excuses from him. Before I knew what was happening, he had pulled into a layby and pushed me out of the passenger seat where I landed in a heap on the parched mud. He drove off at speed shouting obscenities and 'to find your own way back then!'

I was on a tiny side road, at least 20 miles from home and it was 90 minutes before evening service. He would come back? It was just a temper tantrum? He couldn't possibly just leave me on the side of the road after telling me he had given me gonorrhoea? Apparently, he could.

The only option was to hitch-hike. Sobbing, looking distressed and like an escapee from the local asylum is not a good way to catch a lift.

Hastily rearranging myself and affecting my best non-threatening smile, I stuck my thumb out and hoped for the best. After half an hour a kindly man in a white Cortina stopped. It was a bit out of his way but he could drop me nearby and I was beyond grateful. We chatted gaily about the weather and I told him I had become separated from my friends and needed to get back for work.

What I really wanted to tell him was that I was riddled with the clap and would possibly end my life later that day.

By the time we reached Newquay he was in full flow about how tourists were spoiling the beauty of his hometown and I nodded in full agreement. He was kindly and very concerned that I made it back in time, so he took me directly to the hotel.

Rushing in to evening service in my un-ironed uniform, wet hair and puffy tear-stained cheeks, I was dreading seeing Martin and the sweaty, wide-faced waitress. Feeling as I do that the older we get the stronger and more emotionally capable we become, I have a great deal of compassion for my eighteen-year-old self, who dug deep that day and pasted on a bravely defiant face.

The days that followed were very sad. Antibiotics were taken and explanations were made to all who needed to know that me and Martin had gone our separate ways. He was contrite and made efforts to repair the damage, but my idealistic younger self rejected all such overtures.

One of my tables the following week was a young couple from London. They were with a male friend who was alone. The woman worked for Harrods in the beauty department and they asked me to join them in town one day for a drink. They were all extremely kind and generous and I often think of them and wonder what became of them. The lone man who was with them had a red MG sports car and, one afternoon, he asked if I would like to go out with him for a spin. A good ten years older than me, I was not interested in him owing to my mashed-up heart, but he was very attractive and funny and I was flattered.

As we roared out of the car park and onto the open road, sunglasses on and roof top down, I spotted Martin walking into town. This couldn't be better.

I knew he had seen me and as we sailed past him, apropos of nothing, I threw my head back and roared with laughter to demonstrate in no uncertain terms that I was living my best life. The man driving was quite taken aback by this as he hadn't been speaking at the time and my maniacal laughter came out of nowhere. It mattered not a bit. The timing could not have been more perfect and in that simple moment of extreme fakery, I had clawed back a modicum of pride and dignity.

Six-year-old Jekyll and Hyde.

Back from Mass
with decapitated
parents.

Holy Communion sisters and cousins 'smirking for Jesus'.

Very, very holy with sisters Clare and Teresa.

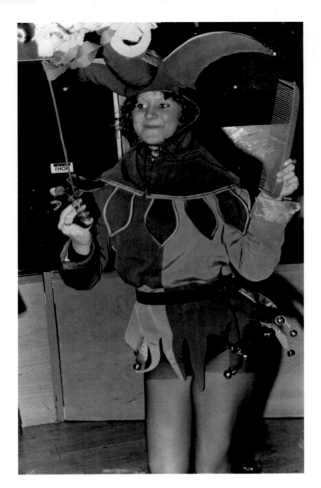

First job after drama school, 'The Jester Performs'. They could have given me sheer tights?!

Promotional work! 1979.

Hitting the big time! 1979.

Late 70s album cover when pics were developed at the chemist. L–R: Jackie Baxter, Angie and John Gardiner.

Promotional work post-drama school, 1982.

Edinburgh Festival, 1986. Fluffy Girlies (fake bosoms) Me, Steve Frost, Janet Prince, Amanda Symons.

A Virgin and a Queen, 1987.

Edinburgh Festival hit show *Thirty Somehow*. Julie Balloo, Jenny Eclair, me. Written and performed by us, 1987.

Assorted Things in Tins, Edinburgh Festival with Johnny Immaterial stand-up show.

Gary Lineker. First night in play of same name. The West End!

Six Thirty Something. Channel 4, 1992.

Spoofing the Ferrero Rocher
ad on a '90s sketch show.
Ate a LOT of chocolate.

New York stage dancing.

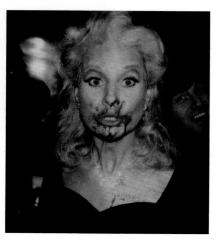

Channel 9,
*The Fast
Show*, 1993.

Several weeks after they all left, a parcel arrived at the hotel for me. It was a large gold and green Harrods box filled to the brim with make-up samples, perfumes and pots of creamy unguents. Everything in the box was SO expensive and overwhelming, I happily shared it with the other waitresses, with the obvious exception of 'sweaty wide face'.

The heat throughout August was almost unbearable and the dining room floor of vinyl tiles began to sweat and buckle. Walking was perilous and walking while carrying multiple plates of hot food was positively dangerous. We all 'scored' the soles of our shoes in order to give us more grip and stop the possibility of slipping; it helped, but not for long. Our uniforms for breakfast and lunch were purple cotton dresses tied around the waist with matching cummerbunds. For dinner, a slightly nicer orange dress. Both dresses needed to be washed daily as they would be drenched in sweat after each service. The heat was so intense that I started to eliminate underwear, a not unreasonable decision, but I hadn't factored in the slippery floor. So it was on that fateful day, forcing my way through the double swing doors of the kitchen, hands and arms piled high with plates full of goulash, my feet danced from under me and the slow motion of seven goulash-filled plates being tossed into the air in the middle of a busy service is now etched onto my brain forever.

My legs shot out and up from under me and I remember the shocked faces of staff and guests alike as I landed heavily on my back, with my dress somewhere around my middle, exposing my lady garden and bottom for all to see. The crashing noise of plates hitting the floor brought the hubbub of the dining room to a stilled and deathly silence, with 120 sets of eyes focused on the culprit. I realised three important lessons that day:

1. That everyone loves slapstick.
2. That catastrophic mishaps can sometimes work in your favour.
3. ALWAYS wear your pants.

It was, as the head waiter later told me, the best entertainment he had ever seen during service.

As I scrambled to my feet, covered in spicy goulash and shards of broken crockery, there was nothing I could do but style in out and make an enormously exaggerated curtsy. The entire dining room burst into applause and I made more in tips that week than I ever had previously.

The season drew to a dusty close, none of us could remember what rain felt like, everyone was exhausted as we said our tearful goodbyes knowing that in all likelihood, yet again, we would all be gone forever.

I had learned more than I ever had at school, not about leaf mould, the Roman Empire or parallelograms, but about people; life, love and fortitude. The value of friendships, that differences can unite as well as divide us and that strength, endurance, humour and kindness were all in my gift.

Living in a pretty cosseted, hyper-religious home had become detrimental as I started to form my own opinions of the world.

I'm not sure what the crazy brainstorm was that led to me messing up my exams, but it may have been a deep sense of rebellion. There was an urgency about being set free into the wild and a feeling of stiflement and suffocation about staying put.

I have no qualms about folk remaining in the family unit until they're 30, 40 or even forever, whatever suits you. I just know that for me, there was a raging curiosity about what I would find in the greater beyond and how I would fare.

The answer was that I would find everything. 'There is no cure for curiosity,' as my grandma used to say, and while school subjects held little interest for me, other people, who they were and how they got to be who they were was a source of infinite fascination.

It was my education. The university of life, for want of a better term. There were no exams or grades, just a centre of learning in real time, a little commune of nomadic folk all finding their way and working out what to do next. I learned the rewards of hard work, the intricacies of human relationships and the often necessary need to be alone.

In order to learn and absorb information, we all need to make mistakes and be allowed to mess up. Part of growing up and finding your way is by doing it alone. This is difficult for overbearing or controlling parents to take on board, but by setting a child free you are gently nudging the fledgling from the nest.

Working at Bredon Court Hotel in Cornwall remains an education like no other, it taught me how to navigate the future and was a major factor in forming the me I am today.

Chapter 5

Who Shall I Be?

My Own Bike – Hercules, God of Strength

'Let me tell you what I think of bicycling. I think it has done more to emancipate women than anything else in the world. I stand and rejoice every time I see a woman ride by on a wheel'
– Susan B Anthony

In the olden days (1960s) television shows were full of bicycles, *The Flying Nun* had one, posh ladies in films, land girls from war dramas cycled to the factories with their hair tied up in knotted cotton scarves. Midwives and nurses with wicker baskets up front containing battered Gladstone bags, nannies, secretaries and students alike.

Bikes were where it was at for girls who wanted to go places.

My bicycle love was always intense but I readily accepted that family finances could not accommodate such a luxury.

Dad always felt guilty about my unrequited bike longing and when I was ten, hoping to divert me into other avenues of pleasure, he decided to make me some stilts.

Dad (Jack) worked in the Wipac factory on a grim, post-war industrial estate in Bletchley. Not perhaps what he wanted from life, but working-class men like him got married, had children and worked in whatever jobs were available, until retirement or death, which usually followed soon after.

Jack liked to sketch and was a gifted artist. After he died of

Parkinson's disease aged 72, we found books of his written poetry, some quite sad and reflective.

He had briefly been in the army and had worked as a medical assistant in the western desert of Benghazi in Libya for the very last part of the Second World War. Benghazi featured in many stories when we were young; tales of being taken prisoner by the baddies, buried up to his neck in sand in the noon day sun and having his head covered in thick honey.

As the sun grew ever hotter, the giant ants marched over the sand dunes in their thousands, lured by the sweet sticky substance. While he awaited his fate, the heat and the fear caused him to slip into unconsciousness where he dreamed of a happy life in a place called Sycamore Avenue, marrying a beautiful woman called Jean who gave him three angelic daughters. We would listen to this story repeatedly and would shout, 'Dad! It wasn't a dream, we are here, we are real! The ants didn't get you!'

For reasons unknown, but arguments eavesdropped, the preparation and construction of my stilts seemed to take weeks. Mum wouldn't allow me to question when they would be ready for fear of the offer being angrily withdrawn, so after my initial enthusiasms about acquiring new and impressive skills, the stilts were quickly forgotten.

One hot summer day when I returned from school, there leaning against the bedroom door were two planks of wood with nailed on blocks as footrests. I can only attribute the unbridled joy to the fact that Dad had made them for me and they were all mine. The sort of pleasure a baby would have for a cardboard box once the annoying toy had been removed.

From a slow start, falling off repeatedly, managing just a few steps like a toddler learning to walk and getting blisters on my hands, those stilts quickly became the intended extension to my own tiny legs and I learned to dance on them, run, jump, hop on one leg, high-kick and stilt up the stairs two at a time.

Wearing Mum's long 1960s dirndl skirt to cover extended

wooden legs was a firm favourite; a six-foot child who walked like the war hero Douglas Bader was a questionable party trick perhaps, but determined to be at one with my wood, I rehearsed a stilt dance routine to the tune of 'There's No business Like Show Business'.

Regrettably my overly lipsticked first performance was cut short after the first two bars, when it was reported on the news that Robert Kennedy, like his brother President John Kennedy, had been assassinated and everyone huddled round the telly. A great tragedy for America and something of a dampener on my positive and solid ambition of a life in the circus.

Annoyingly the stilts were removed after one too many splinters and a trip to the doctor's for painful treatment of a badly infected thumb. Would it have killed Dad to have sanded them smooth? 'Sure, the Devil is in the detail,' said my grandma.

In our house, anything deemed dangerous, outgrown or unsuitable was 'disappeared' without comment. A raggedy white fur lamb I dragged around as a toddler suffered the same fate when it became bald and blackened by filth. Crying about its disappearance provoked the response, 'You don't need lamby anymore, you're a big girl now.'

Joy of joy though. Stilt walking and the passing of time caused a massive growth spurt. On total tippy toes and enduring a small amount of pain in the front bottom along with a bum twerking motion on each pedal push, Dad's green ladies' Raleigh that he rode to the Wipac factory was finally conquered and my two-wheel love affair began in part-time earnest.

It would be several years before I would acquire my first bike, but I could read about them! I had found a copy of Frances Willard's *A Wheel Within a Wheel* at the local library in Bletchley. It was first published in 1895 and was quite a revelation. Having moved on from the Bobby Brewster books by HE Todd, I was constantly searching for new and exciting information.

Frances Willard was an American feminist who first learned to ride a bicycle aged 53 in a time when it was thought most improper for a woman to be at wheel. She wrote about the potential freedoms, small and large, allowed by 'this uncompromising but fascinating illimitably capable machine'.

My interest was piqued and women on bikes became the subject of a school project aged thirteen (when I was still a model student.)

It was difficult to find out information as all I had was the library and access to their encyclopaedia, so along with some copied-out writing for my project, I drew a lot of penny farthings and sketched women in the new-fangled outfits that were frowned upon by the clergy and society of the day.

A woman called Alice Bygrave patented the 'Bygrave convertible skirt'. The fashions of the time for Victorian women were all about modesty. The usual full-length skirts were entirely unsuitable for cycling, so Alice designed a system of ingenious weights that could be sewn into hems, which would then be attached to a pulley system that would bring the skirt up and away from the wheels and were attached to buttons at the waist. It could be easily released when no longer cycling.

This design was so successful that Jaeger purchased it and went into production. The sight of a woman's legs also caused outrage and necessitated the invention by Amelia Jenks Bloomer of . . . See if you can guess?

When I was asked to appear on *Celebrity Mastermind* some time ago, I rather madly chose Women on Bikes as my specialist subject and spent some time (alright, a week) boning up on these fabulous women who made it all possible. So here's a potted history.

The Suffragists were early adopters of the bicycle and faced a massive backlash. Quite why this caused such controversy in the late Victorian age seems almost entirely to be about fear and control of the fairer sex.

Doctors and physicians also held wildly opposing views. The fierce anti-cycling lobby came up with an exhaustive list of hazards for a woman on a bike. Unsurprisingly it was the reproductive system that would suffer most.

Pelvic inflammation, pressure on organs, absorption of harmful vibrations, Uterine displacement, inflamed fallopian tubes, infertility and chronic onanism through the massage of bicycle seats.

So sitting atop a bike may cause you to experience PLEASURE in the front bottom.

There was also an entirely invented condition called 'Cyclemania' which was defined as a chronic psychosis with symptoms similar to hysteria or kleptomania.

These included an addiction or intoxication that left women dishevelled, shamed, lacking self-control, likely to engage in risky behaviour and purporting themselves in an unladylike fashion, not dissimilar to a chronically drunk woman.

This describes so many pleasurable elements of my own life and I consider them all to be thrilling benefits of a life well pedalled.

The other pseudo medical condition physicians warned of was 'Cycling Face'. This included a pinched face, pointed nose, slack jaw, a wild and haunted look in the eyes and a frazzled expression. The perfect description of the Wicked Witch of the West in the *Wizard of Oz*, or a pointy-nosed woman having an orgasm.

The patriarchy really did not like it up 'em! Pioneering women of the Victorian era, I salute you.

Moving to the big city of London aged 19 was a reckless indication of my further need for independence and wider horizons. London was where it was at and anything was possible. A couple of summer seasons with board and lodgings thrown in had taught me a lot, but now I needed to find a flat, a proper job and to create a grown-up life.

While working in Bletchley as a temp for the photocopying company Rank Xerox, one of the visiting technicians had told me of a house in North London where his chum was looking for tenants.

He offered to drive me there the following week and effect an introduction. This involved a stop off at Biggin Hill flying club where he was a member, me glugging nervously at a rather too-strong gin and tonic in the club bar and a firm but insistent refusal of any funny business from the technician.

Clambering back into his white Rover SD1, which he drove way too fast, I had to dig my nails into the palms of my hands to avoid being sick. Despite being a boiling hot day, I had worn an old mink coat of my Auntie Lily's in order to give a good impression and to look posh.

Coming from a three-bedroom council house, the five-storey Victorian property off Highbury Barn, was palatial. It was owned by Humphrey Tizard, a charming and suave devil of 28 who introduced me to the other residents; his sister Jane a doctor, another doctor called Stephen and an archaeologist called Mike. I never managed to establish quite what Humphrey did, but I think he was a spy.

I was way out of my league on every level, but they seemed to like me despite my sweating profusely and refusing to take off my fur coat. The room was mine if I wanted it.

My London life was up and running.

Strolling around my new neighbourhood of Highbury and Islington, I happened upon a dusty, musty, filled-with-treasure junk shop on the Balls Pond road. There, propped up on the back wall, was a black, pre-war Hercules bicycle. It was priced at ten quid, but necessity trumped shyness and with hitherto unknown chutzpah, I managed to barter it down to £7.

Hercules: Roman God, famed for his strength and his numerous far-reaching adventures.

He was battered and chipped, had a dented rear mudguard, broken pump half hanging from the cross bar, an old, cracked, leather saddle bag with a rusted buckle, and a still working but filth-clogged Sturmey-Archer gear system. Hercules was the very definition of an old man in need of a dedicated carer. This old fella had certainly seen some action, suffered collateral damage and in all probability been left in a shed to rot for several decades.

Determined to bring this broken god back to life, I set about replacing the tyres, changing brake cables and blocks and squirting liberal amounts of oil on every conceivable moving part. The once shiny, brown Brooks saddle was faded, cracked and had borne the brunt of many a wartime bottom. Neatsfoot oil (made from the shin bones and feet of cattle) was massaged into its chapped and parched surfaces and its springs cleaned and polished to a shine. Hercules would ride again, let the far-reaching adventures begin.

London, like any big city, has always been treacherous for the two-wheeled warrior.

Once, a kindly cabbie selflessly positioned his cab between me and an articulated lorry whose driver had failed to see me – quite a selfless act and one for which I am eternally grateful. Tragedy avoided, the cabbie drove off, but not before shouting from his window, 'As long as you remember that everyone is out to kill you, you'll be fine, luv!' Wise words.

The exposure and vulnerability of our easily breakable bodies is never more apparent than when drawing alongside a vehicle whose multiple wheel sets are several feet higher than your head.

None of the dangers deterred me.

It's difficult to explain to a non-cyclist the pleasures of propelling yourself from A to B, or on a good day from C to D. Nose only for navigation, exposure to the elements, prevailing winds, one's own fluctuating pedal power, heightened senses, the ease of observation and complete blissful independence. You can lose yourself on a bike, any worries and troubles eased by setting them free in the breeze.

Life for me has always been lived fast. More haste, more speed, being an apposite motto. Why walk a 25-minute journey when it can be greatly reduced by leaping aboard this humblest of mechanisms and hard pedalling until your cheeks are a fetching shade of crimson? The bright lights of London Town were entirely new to me and with Hercules as my companion, we explored from Seven Sisters to Dulwich and Hackney Marshes to Ealing Broadway.

Next, I needed gainful employment.

Hemdale film company was owned by John Daly and the actor David Hemmings, their plush offices were based in Mayfair complete with a sumptuous basement cinema. Hemdale were involved in film production and distribution but were also known for a variety of tax avoidance schemes. Investing in films being one of them. (In the 80s, Hemdale went on to achieve huge success with *The Terminator* and *Platoon*).

When I arrived for a job as the front-desk receptionist, I was to be interviewed by the head honcho Mr John Daly. He was a blond, rascally, East End boy who looked me up and down, told me I could be pretty, and then said with a smirk, 'You'll do.' It was the late 70s, they did things differently then.

My pedal to work was 20 minutes, using short cuts, roads with the fewest sets of traffic lights and side streets too small for buses and lorries. Hercules would be hastily chained to a lamp-post and I would race in to fix my hair, face and levels of 'could be' pretty before answering phones, serving coffees and flirting my way through the day. The actors Albert Finney and Julian Holloway were frequent visitors to the offices. They would tease me by asking, 'Will you be joining us for lunch today, Maria?' Naïve as I was, it seemed that Hollywood was only moments away.

My job was not in any way glamorous, but it was a film company and through a process of osmosis, surely I could learn about the industry and slide in the back door? The closest I got, sadly, was as a hand model in a blink-and-you'll-miss-it added shot where I played Farrah Fawcett's hands. I dined out on that for weeks.

In the private screening theatre in the basement we would often be invited to watch new releases or snigger through risible films they had invested in like *Sunburn* with Farrah Fawcett Majors (my hands) or *Harlequin* with Robert Powell (loss makers both).

It was in the screening room in 1979 that I saw the life-changing piece of work by Michael Cimino called *The Deer Hunter*. One hundred and eighty-four minutes of brilliance that made my head explode. I adored these after-work screenings and would clamber on Hercules afterwards and ride all the way home, propelled by the sheer joy of cinema and how it could make you feel.

Joan Collins was also a frequent visitor to the office. She had just filmed *The Stud* with Oliver Tobias and had the natural entitlement of someone who truly believed she was a star. Always impeccably turned out in wide-shouldered suits, high heels and massively big hair, I used to marvel at the amount of make-up she wore and remember thinking that her pillows must be an absolute mess, covered in foundation and false eyelashes.

One day as she swanned through reception, all Harmony hairspray and clackety stilettos, I asked her if I should call up to John Daly and let him know she was here? 'Not any of your business, little girl,' she spat and clacked on up the marble stairs. We all have our off days.

Some years ago at a Lady Taverners lunch to honour my old mate Graham Norton, I sat next to her at the top table and she was charm personified. As the old saying goes, 'one minute you're treading the grape and the next you're drinking the wine'.

During my time at Hemdale, I would often take off on my bike during the lunch break to cycle around the wonder that was Hyde Park, pedalling happily up to Marble Arch, left to Kensington Gardens and back along Horse Guards Parade where I would see the majestic horses in training or out in their polished livery in readiness for a state event.

Hercules was with me for a magical four years. Day and night we covered hundreds of miles and he became a necessary and much-loved part of my life. It is peculiar to have such an attachment to an inanimate object, but together the adventures and animation were made possible.

His departure was silent and swift.

A moment of amnesia saw me leave him outside a tube station unlocked for a nano second in time, and that was all it took. Whoosh! An opportunistic scallywag seized the unattended moment and he was gone. Standing where his mighty presence had been only moments before, it was inconceivable to me that this was possible – we belonged together.

Finding a tiny voice, I pleaded with a nearby newspaper seller for some sort of reasonable explanation, but like a character in a film with their own busy life to lead, he just stared at me and folded another paper as life sped past around us. I stood for a full ten minutes in bewilderment, hoping to spot him, willing myself to produce a logical outcome and that it was probably just a silly mistake.

Walking back home from the tube filled with misery and dread, my teary eyes searched left and right, hoping for a brief final glimpse of the battered Black God of travel, all the while knowing that our adventures together had concluded and I would never see him again. I had yet to experience the pain of deep loss. From the moment we are born losses begin. The comfort of a mother's milk, teeny tiny baby teeth, much-loved toys, all departures a small inconvenience, essential to our growth and understanding of what it is to be human.

The outrage of loss for a bike can never be replicated. It is both real yet ridiculous. I was swept back to Cornwall and the mysterious disappearance of Pinky. That I cried for many days seems utterly ridiculous, but Hercules represented freedom and confidence. I had learned about both with his help. When I first acquired Hercules, he was a broken prisoner, glory days behind him, left to rot in that musty dusty warehouse. I had tended his wounds and found spare parts and shiny new accessories. The hours of attention to sand, rub and polish him back to his former glory were significant and my devastation was real and piercing. I hoped he would go on to further adventures, but I never stopped looking for him.

Something of an old hand to theft these days, it has been a hard lesson to acquire the skill of letting go. Understanding quantum physics or dialectical materialism would be easier, but time and the loss of greater things has eroded the sharp incandescent fury to a slight shrug of inevitability. In much the same way as broken relationships, hard edges get worn down to a softer ache and an ability to pack it all away in the mind box of injustice.

Nothing lasts forever and most things can be replaced.

Chapter 6

London Living:

Dawes Lady Racer

As my treasured Hercules weighed as much as a small family car, the next two-wheel relationship felt like dancing with Nureyev. It was a pink Dawes ladies' tourer with drop-handlebars, sixteen gears and a triumph of modern engineering. It also necessitated the purchase of cycling shorts with chamois leather bum lining, Day-Glo waterproofs and fingerless cycling gloves.

It was on the brand-new pink Dawes machine that I suffered my only (thus far, touch wood) mishap that left me scarred and bloodied.

Along with new wheels, I had also acquired a fancy London boyfriend who worked in public relations and was also mad about cycling.

Christopher was something of a fogey, he wore herringbone jackets and smoked a pipe. It's hard to remember whether I even fancied him or not, he said he found me 'bubbly and fun', although I knew I was still under construction and hadn't yet decided if bubbly and fun was where it was at. I longed to be a clever academic bluestocking.

A deliberate attempt to lose any trace of my regional accent had been quite successful. My housemates in the Victorian mansion (terraced house) were all middle-class professional folk, with an additional Sloane ranger who had been at school with Lady Diana Spencer. People treated you differently if you had a posh voice, and it gave me a sense of entitlement. A façade, of course, that wouldn't stand up to scrutiny, but useful nonetheless.

My origins were resolutely working class, but I took the decision to reinvent myself as many folk seemed to. It was an anonymous new world and I was a blank canvas waiting to be daubed with beautiful vibrant colours. I watched and listened intently to everyone I met and soaked up facts, jokes and anecdotes to be repeated as my own. I learned about nuance and sarcasm, how and when teasing was acceptable and the right times to employ such wonder. It was rather like someone who had been raised by wolves being introduced into polite sophisticated society and I quickly understood that the most important aspect of who you were, was to be interested and interesting.

The interested part came naturally and was essential in creating my new self. I learned physical mannerisms, the power of understatement, humour, empathy and self-deprecation.

Christopher's father was a prominent professor of English at a major university and his mother was a psychotherapist. My mum and dad were a factory worker and a housewife. Meeting his parents was traumatic. I had nothing to offer but my own endless questions about their lives.

It quickly became apparent (in general) that most folk like nothing more than talking about themselves and can happily leave a conversation feeling it's been a great success once they have relived their own triumphs and victories. It was when I was asked about my own life that things got tricky. The answer I should have used was that I was a work in progress, who wasn't fully formed and had only a vague idea of the me I wanted to become. I'm not sure that would have played out too well.

Christopher the fogey lived in a flat in West Hampstead which he shared with another girl. Her name was Jackie Baxter, a food stylist with a shock of bleached blonde hair and a rapier wit. Where I was mousy and quiet, Jackie was loud, hilarious and bursting with joie de vivre.

We hung out a lot together and in small incremental bite-size chunks, I borrowed all her best personality traits. She had many pieces of the jigsaw puzzle that I was missing. Like the tin man, the lion and the scarecrow from *The Wizard of Oz* who were all looking for a part of themselves that was lacking, Jackie Baxter taught me confidence, the vital element that I needed for my new creation. I am forever in her debt.

Would that it were that easy to acquire confidence in its truest sense. No, what I learned from Jackie was the power of pretend. We are all quivering wrecks fearful of failure, of being found out, of looking foolish, but if you present a confident front, people are inclined to believe you. They will take you at face value. You will be popular because those who claim shyness are bloody hard work. I have a friend who scoffs at the word 'shy', preferring instead to call it being touchy and vain. Harsh perhaps, but I know what she means. Life in all its forms can be difficult, social functions may be trying, but being a wallflower is not going to get you anywhere and is no fun for anyone, least of all the wallflower.

I watched Jackie in earnest, yes, she could often overplay her hand (especially with one too many) and she wasn't to everyone's liking. There were times when flowers would need to be sent to the previous evening's hostess, along with cards of apology for bad behaviour, but what I most respected about her was that SHE liked who she was and she was never dull. To paraphrase Oscar Wilde, it is better to be insulted than ignored, to be memorable rather than forgotten.

Confidence without knowledge though can be a dangerous thing. Aged 21, I spoke out at a dinner party quoting something I had read by the French writer Proust. Pretentious, moi? The problem was that I pronounced it Prouwst, as the spelling suggests, rather than Proost, the correct pronunciation. Seeing the sniggers around the table saw my confidence dribble away and is a terrible memory that makes me sweat. A valuable lesson that confidence can only take you so far.

Fogey Christopher and I shared a mutual love of cycling. Weekends would see us hauling our bikes onto trains, checking the wind direction, going as far as we dared into some form of countryside, and then cycling back with the breeze through parks and leafy glades. For one such excursion and knowing we would be returning after dark, I bought new flashing lights, which the boyfriend offered to attach. The front basket held our picnic lunch and left little room for anything else, so he opted to attach the light to the front right fork that held the wheel in place. The rear light slotted onto the saddle post and off we went.

Twenty minutes in, I was hurtling down Kilburn High Road at some speed when I was suddenly and inexplicably thrown over the front handlebars, landing hard and heavy on my chin.

The lunch basket was strewn across the road, chicken and coleslaw sandwiches now inedible, fresh strawberries pulped.

In a state of incomprehension and shock, I knew things were serious by the copious amounts of blood dripping onto my dove-of-peace CND T-shirt.

The boyfriend arrived panting and white-faced by my side, a kindly shopkeeper brought out a blanket and I shunted myself up onto my elbows to check out the damage in the reflection of the silver hub cap of a parked car.

This was not a wise decision. The convex nature of a hub cap produces an image similar to the hall of mirrors at a funfair. Twisted and distorted.

My face, already swollen, looked twice the width it had been that morning, it was smeared with blood and had a large four-inch chunk of flesh flapping free from the chin. The blood was gushing like a comedy geyser and I became lightheaded, barely acknowledging the paramedic who gently cupped the flesh flap to my chin, as I was ferried into the ambulance where I passed out.

At the Royal Free Hospital, the boyfriend was hovering at the end of the bed, looking sheepish as the surgeon injected my bloaty face with local anaesthetic.

'If you were Princess Diana, we'd have a team of plastic surgeons here!' he said.

'But I WANT a team of plastic surgeons,' I mumbled, as my face began to lose feeling. 'I'm an actress!'

The boyfriend and the doc exchanged an indulgent grin, both knowing that this disfigurement would mean never playing Juliet and that the best I would get would be comedy goons or sad, fat friends of the female lead.

Where once the screws attaching the front light to the front fork was fully secure, my speed of travel, coupled with heavy vibrations on the poorly maintained Kilburn High Road, meant they were loosened at an alarming rate. Like an old Western where the wagon train is being chased by angry 'injuns' (native Americans) and the camera pans back endlessly to a close-up of the wheel slowly coming away from its axel.

The wretched front light had slammed into the bike spokes jamming them to an immediate halt and propelling the comedy goon over the handlebars and onto the tarmac.

'It could have been worse,' said the doc, before he noticed my bleeding ears and the fact that stitches were also needed on both hands. 'You may have lockjaw for a few days, but I'm pretty sure it'll just be bruising.'

'I think my boyfriend tried to kill me,' I said to no one in particular.

The scar has faded but remains visible and a little bit lumpy. The opportunity to have it properly fixed by plastic surgeons has come and gone and it now rests amongst the other lines and imperfections as part of my history.

Bikes have been receptacles for both emotional and physical baggage as I've pedalled my way through the last 40 years. Carrying grief, joy, laughter, a 26-inch television, a microwave, suitcases and dogs. In a far-flung land and a different life, I am that woman overloaded with water, chicken and grain balancing her way along the dust track.

The simplicity of cycling will always bring me joy. Aside from exercise endorphins, or the relief that fatigue can sometimes bring, the greatest pleasure is in what lies ahead. As Albert Einstein said, 'Life is like riding a bicycle, to keep your balance, you must keep moving forward.'

At the top of an unknown steep and painful climb there may be a blissful descent or it may be an even higher hill. You've just got to keep pedalling to find out what's round the next bend. As in life, the wheel goes up and the wheel goes down and we are just freewheeling through, hanging on to the handlebars and sailing into the future. As Diane Ackerman said, 'When I'm on my bike, the world is breaking someone else's heart.'

The process of my reinvention was deliberate and calculated.

It wasn't that I knew I would undergo this metamorphosis, rather that circumstances required me to become something other than the wishy-washy, half-finished painting that I was.

Learning to be someone else was a gradual process and I wouldn't now be able to identify any of my original self. It was just a way of chiselling down the edges to fit in the boxes that seemed the most likely to suit me. Along with how to behave socially and in the workplace, my ideology and morality. It was just a way of becoming who I needed to be in order to get the best out of the life I was living at the time.

Throughout this process, the person I was while riding my bike, all the adventures enjoyed on two wheels was who I am. I was the little girl seeking freedom and her own individuality. My true, spiritual self has probably never really altered that much and that is reflected in my love for this simple, self-propelled, two-wheeled contraption.

Whoever you are and whatever your origins, there is nothing to say that this must define you for the rest of your life.

Wanting to be someone else was always an ambition, a difficult one to fulfil as I didn't know enough about life to have a clear picture of who that should be.

Arriving in London in order to become a fully-fledged grown-up was the biggest adventure and one that was filled with many nutty incarnations as I tried out a range of different personas. I was ashamed of my origins and wished to erase them completely. It took a long time to realise their importance and to embrace the oddities of my humble beginnings alongside my newer more sophisticated self (as I saw it).

Life is constantly changing and the trick is to change with it. Much like fashion, nothing stays the same, but if you wait long enough, the 'look' will come around again.

My early years in London were filled with almost all the mistakes I've ever made. Important and necessary errors that retain their ability to make me cringe in shame.

There is little wrong in appearing gauche and uninformed as long as you take on board those failings and attempt to correct them.

Mum and Dad did their best for me, for all of us. They repeated what they knew until all of a sudden we knew more, or perhaps different ways to live and thrive and be. This is the way the world works.

The one constant in my trying on of different personalities has been my enduring love of cycling. The feeling of being 'at wheel' hasn't changed at all, perhaps the only thing that has remained innocent and pure. It brings me as much joy now as it did as a child.

The pink Dawes was lent to a friend who was late for a date with a new girlfriend. He promised to look after her and that he would return with a spring in his step and a week's supply of chocolate. Lusty testosterone saw him fail to lock her up properly (if at all). He was given the brush-off by the object of his desires and had to walk four miles home. While he was engaged in the art of seduction, an opportunistic scallywag spirited the bike away in plain sight. My kind and altruistic act taught me that no good turn goes unpunished and that horny men who promise chocolate, are never to be trusted.

With the unfortunate disappearance of each of my trusty steeds, I have picked myself up, dusted myself off and found a way to resume the journey. Even now, at the first sign of trouble or difficulty, everything can be resolved by jumping on my bike, oxygenating my blood and tossing my woes onto the open road. All of life's knots and kinks can be straightened out with a prevailing wind, a good set of pedals and a bicycle pump, but most importantly, a sturdy thief-proof lock.

Chapter 7

A Dangerous Obsession:

Peugeot 1976 Drop-Handlebar Tourer

'Be happy for this moment. This moment is your life'
– Omar Khayyam

Where does body dysmorphia suddenly appear from? An always slim child, overeating was never really possible as there weren't any spare food stuffs available. Fridays would often be white-bread toast and lard for tea, meaning end-of-week poverty.

On one of our final family holidays in Blackpool, I remember venturing out alone to peruse the wonderful stalls and cabins on the South Pier; Madame Petulengro could tell your fortune, Count Edward de Coello would 'Cut out your profile silhouette in the style of a Victorian lady or gentleman', while a nameless rogue who couldn't afford the signwriter could 'Guess your age with 100% accuracy' and the promise of a cheap fluffy toy, should he guess wrong.

Having stopped some yards away to observe the 'Uncle Phil can Guess your weight' sideshow, I watched in quiet fascination as old ladies gasped in horror while a weight guess was made, before they all screamed in mock disbelief when, in order to confirm the guesser's outrageously high number, they were forced to step onto the scales as proof of both their heft and his extraordinary gift.

'15 stone 8 pounds!' he would roar victoriously to the baying crowd as the rickety scales finally stabilised. The recipient of this news now wishing for the planks of the pier to part and her hulking mass to crash into the Irish Sea below.

It seemed the most humiliating past-time but caused much mirth, real or otherwise for the friends and families of those taking part. The loudest laughter was reserved for fat ladies, that was where the fun was at. The type of ladies who could also be seen on cartoon dirty postcards, with rosy cheeks, large bottoms and heaving bosoms, spitting out some dubious double entendre at a weasly little man. 'I asked you to squeeze my LEMONS George, not my MELONS!'

Uncle Phil spotted me lingering and beckoned me over, the crowd having now dispersed. 'Come on blondie, I'll give you a free one!'

Having never weighed myself I was certainly curious.

He sized me up and down, did some pretend magic by closing his eyes and clutching his head between his hands 'YOU, are 8 stone 4 pounds,' he boomed.

I dutifully got on the scales and indeed the magic man had got it right.

'Thank you,' I mumbled and hurried off before conversation or payment might be called for.

As a literal child, I imagined that what the man told me I weighed would be my weight for life, like having blonde hair or green eyes. I am five-foot-five, I weigh 8 stone 4 pounds and my star sign is Sagittarius.

Too young perhaps to have any knowledge of hormonal fluctuations, societal norms and expectations, or that hunger can be about so many elements of life rarely to do with sustenance.

Being alone in London was an education in all of the above.

Singularly ill equipped to actually 'cook' anything, I survived on sandwiches, booze and copious amounts of chocolate.

Affection and attention often involved sex, so it was that the contraceptive pill entered my life. It certainly evened out mood and chronic period pain, but also made my clothes extremely tight and my face rather moonlike.

Pregnancy may have been more extreme, but this new look didn't sit well with my vivacious gal-about-town expectations. People treated the 'fat' me differently and I didn't like it.

Food was making me chubby so the best approach was surely to stop eating food?

There is a Japanese word: 'Kuchisabishii', which means that you are not hungry but you are eating because your mouth is lonely.

Days would go by without solids. Weary from starvation, I would often arrive home from work, get straight into bed with my coat on and stay there till early light.

By morning, hunger pangs had disappeared and clothes were significantly looser which was sufficient reward to do it all over again.

Unsurprising then, that I became depressed and lethargic, but also aware that abstinence eventually led to excess and that a binge would soon be upon me. This would include chocolate, crisps, bread and butter, ice cream, fizzy drinks and biscuits while avoiding all foodstuffs with any nutritional merit. There were late-night shopping expeditions to replace food I had stolen from the fridge belonging to flatmates, strictly verboten.

Unhappy and helpless, I was stuck in this cycle for over a year until a friend who knew of my destructive behaviour suggested I join her for a dance class, exercise being fundamental to wellbeing and weight loss.

Eating disorders were rarely spoken about. Anorexia nervosa was seen as an unfortunate wasting disease with little knowledge of the cause. Only extreme cases with tragic deaths were ever reported. The myriad of other food- and control-related maladies were brushed under carpets like unwelcome crumbs.

My introduction to exercise came at around the time of The kids from 'Fame' and when Pineapple Dance Studios opened all over London. They were awash with brightly coloured leotards, matching leg warmers and waists cinched with elastic belts which skimmed the hips over high-cut legs and cellulite-compressing spandex tights.

Aerobics classes became my salvation and a new addiction. A

day missed made me angry and irritable and meant greater control was necessary on the eating front.

It also brought more anguish. Spandex leisurewear is unforgiving to the larger shape and there was a Jane Fonda body type that we all aspired to. That we were becoming strong and fit mattered not a jot if bulges were visible, legs were too heavy, bottoms too wide and thighs too thunderous. I would often see tiny ballerinas with bodies like ten-year-old girls, smoking incessantly while sipping scorching cups of black coffee. Tiny, strained faces fighting hunger and their natural curves. For almost every woman of my generation there have been difficult and psychologically painful relationships with food.

And all for the loss and gain of the same 14 pounds.

The very definition of futility.

Writing this now gives me a physical pain in my heart at the days lost, the time wasted, the damage done both mentally and physically over a period of 30 years.

It was through these daily aerobics classes that I learned about nutrition. Mainly that protein filled you up for longer, vegetables and fruit were the carriers of protein to muscles and bones and that carbohydrates gave you energy. 'Think of your body as a car that needs petrol,' said one woman in my dance class. 'Your car will work way better if you fill it with good fuel.'

This seems like common knowledge in these enlightened times but was truly something of a revelation to me back then. Knowing about the benefits and necessities of good eating doesn't make it any easier to follow, if you are steeped in a world of feast and famine as I was.

With ALL other addictions you just eliminate the drug of choice. Alcohol, cigarettes, drugs, gambling, each one must become something you no longer touch, take, inhale or inject. But food? You have to eat to stay alive so it's about controlling what you eat. Eat when you're hungry, stop when you're full.

But what are we hungry for?

Love, affection, comfort? Do we eat to dull pain? To erase the unspeakable? To numb oneself from anxiety? To avoid confronting difficult emotions? Sadness, anguish and loneliness are all pretty strong reasons for any addictive behaviour and for many of us food is a treacherous addiction to navigate.

So, discovering exercise was my new way out of the starve–binge cycle. My new 'positive' addiction.

Life was exhausting and it was clear I lacked the willpower to keep my eating in check. One of the dancers at Pineapple happily recounted that she had lost 18 pounds by using slimming pills. Gaunt of face and with ribs clearly visible, I thought she looked fantastic and sidled up to her to enquire further.

A private doctor in Harley Street was mentioned: 'He gives prescriptions to all the dancers without even weighing them!' she giggled.

That first visit to Dr Avani's immaculately minimalist surgery was a mix of terror and thrill. There were ladies sitting around with recently blow-dried Farrah Fawcett Majors hair that fell around their tailored, padded shoulder jackets, Gucci clutch bags resting on tiny laps, while perfectly manicured fingers flicked idly through copies of *Vogue* magazine.

Who were these exquisite creatures and how did they all look so expensive?

The chairs were brown velveteen, coffee tables of brass and glass and bouncy cream carpets covering every inch of flooring.

I had arrived on my bicycle, long sweatshirt slung over my leotard and tights and baggy woollen leg warmers. If I looked like a dancer, surely I was half way toward my quest for the miracle pills?

It wasn't actually MY bicycle. It belonged to a Kiwi dancer who lived over the road. She had gone travelling and the bike was on a long-term loan.

Dr Avani was Iranian (or Persian as he referred to himself), a dapper man in his early sixties with an all-year suntan, silver-tipped sideburns and a kindly non-judgemental manner. He too had beautiful hands and manicured nails. In my other life fantasy, he would have been my dad.

He weighed me, 10 stone 8 pounds, took my blood pressure and listened to my heart with a stethoscope. That was it. The extent of my examination. He also gave me some diet sheets with details of 'good fats' – avocados and slow-release carbohydrates such as brown rice and kidney beans.

Then he wrote a prescription for a month's supply of Tenuate Dospan, a diet pill or appetite suppressant that was to be taken at 9am sharp every morning. Hallelujah.

So began the next addiction, one that would last 15 years.

If you have ever taken amphetamine sulphate or 'speed' you will know something of the effects of slimming pills.

Energy in abundance, barely contained mania, dry mouth, short attention span and difficulty sleeping. Also headaches, jaw clenching, dizziness, increased heart rate, constipation and breathlessness.

Side effects could have been head shrinkage, incontinence and a slow, painfully premature death at 30, and I would still have considered the risks worth it. At least I would die thin.

During the first month of my newly assisted regime, I lived on endless cups of black tea and coffee, half a chicken breast a day, undressed salad leaves, seven apples a week and occasional pots of low-fat cottage cheese, but only IF I was feeling weak. I lost 16 pounds and was thrilled beyond comparison.

I bought clothes two sizes smaller, felt confident and sexy, but now the little pills were gone and I had to once again rely on my own willpower.

This was where the success and failure conundrum kicked in. Triumph or shame. Being thin represented discipline, restraint, desirability and denial; whereas being fat was weak of will, greedy, lazy and ugly.

It is shaming to recall and to confess quite how deeply ingrained in my psyche this mantra became.

There was a beautiful marketing manager called Sheridan who came to work at Hemdale films where I had been manning the reception for two years. She had glowing skin, jogged daily, was model thin and always wore monochrome outfits. She survived every day on cans of TAB (precursor to diet coke) and I never once saw her eat anything.

My admiration for her was almost worshipful and we became great friends.

She was very posh and had a boyfriend who ran an expensive German handbag outlet in Bond Street. One evening after work she suggested I come for dinner with her boyfriend and a wealthy German colleague at a restaurant in Shepherd Market, Mayfair, called Tiddy Dols. There was some semblance of food served but neither of us ate any of it, preferring instead to quaff the generous supply of champagne that arrived at 15-minute intervals. The men chomped away happily, each mouthful observed by the disciplined women smugly denying themselves such pleasures.

We all got extremely drunk and returned to their Kensington apartment where we drank, danced and flirted until the early hours.

I ended up having to stay the night and to share a bed with the German. He had been perfectly charming and gallant the entire evening, but opportunism and drunkenness saw him attempt a clumsy seduction.

This may well have gone his way but for my utter revulsion at his fatness.

His expensive suit had cleverly camouflaged the rolls of fat, the width of his rather feminine hips and the stomach that made his penis look like an afterthought, certainly the only area of his body unfettered by excess.

He laughingly told me that he couldn't actually see his penis as his stomach got in the way.

My horrible fascistic disgust was twofold. His obvious lack of control over his body triggered my own seriously warped view of how one should look and my tenuous hold on what was needed to achieve that goal, plus the arrogant confidence in his own desirability simply because he was male and extremely rich.

In the morning, embarrassed apologies were made and hasty

arrangements for further evenings of fun. All subsequently declined.

I was only too aware of how skewed my view on weight had become but had no way of knowing how to alter it.

Without my little pills and with my now starved body returning to its normal needs, the weight came back, the binges increased, lethargy returned, and unhappiness overwhelmed me.

I was fully trapped in the fat/thin cycle and my own self-centred destruction.

Should you have experienced any of this madness of your own, you will know that life is permanently on hold. Party invitations and evenings out are refused if you're in a fat phase and the small windows of 'thinness' become fewer and farther between. 'The tyranny of slenderness' as Kim Chernin wrote is all-consuming.

I returned to Dr Avani in Harley Street several times over the next year. Prescriptions were duly written, perfunctory health checks undertaken and the tragic charade rolled on.

Over several months, the appetite suppressants lose their power as your body cleverly adjusts but the side effects remain the same.

I was about to embark on a one-year postgraduate drama course which called for a fresh start, student digs and a big reduction in available cash. Along with feeling constantly ill, the cost of a private doctor's consultation and unsubsidised prescription meant it was simply not possible on a student grant to spend such vast amounts on slimming pills. They would have to go.

Stopping with any addiction is extremely frightening. However much you want to, there will always be that voice in your head telling you that it's not possible, you haven't got the willpower, why would you give up something that defines you and gives your life meaning?

Going cold turkey from my magic pills caused me to gain weight again. Every ounce of willpower was used to shed this hideous blubber before I started drama school. I was miserable, hungry and about to embark on something great, but all excitement and thrill was lost to the lunacy of my own perception.

The multiple years I spent taking these magic pills was a total and utter waste of time and money.

It was an effort to regain control of part of my life that needed to be controlled.

A foolish choice, a dangerous addiction, but a choice nonetheless. Eating problems were now becoming commonplace. At drama school, anorexia, bulimia and self-harm were rife. The holy trinity of punishments many of us used for not feeling good enough.

Forty years on, I wish things had changed more than they have, but with the pressures on young people from social media platforms, these damaging illnesses seem more prevalent than ever.

To be involved in the entertainment industry needs rhinoceros levels of skin-thickness and an Elsa-like ability to 'Let It Go'. Everything that seemed so important as a young impressionable woman is laughably meaningless now.

If I could go back and have a chat to my younger self, ALL our younger selves, I would advise that every action has a consequence, that health must be taken seriously and that the body has a remarkable memory.

Chapter 8

An Actor's Life for Me:

The Gunmetal Grey Falcon Tourer

Drama school meant becoming a student. I was a student! I had a student rail card and student sensibilities, I never had any money and lived on cauliflower curry for four days. It was brilliant.

I shared digs with another student during this time, an American called Phil. Funny, clever and eccentric. Like magnets attracting, it quickly became apparent that Phil had once been a chubby boy and had food issues way worse than my own. A bowl of ice cream gobbled down in an unguarded moment would see him pull on his running shorts and head off on a six-mile hike at 11pm in order to burn away the needless calories.

Together we tried to manage our collective disorder by endless talking and poring over cookery books and fat content. We would make elaborate meals with hardly any carbs, season everything with chilli and eat endless amounts of cheap, bruised fruit before class to keep the beast of blubber at bay. A tragic little pair held together by abstinence and denial.

I needed another bike. The Peugeot tourer was returned to its Kiwi owner after over a year of use. I was extremely grateful but it never felt as though it had belonged to me so our parting was painless. It was ridiculous to be a student and not have a bike, but where to look for my next machine on a student grant?

The digs I shared with Phil were in a large Victorian house owned by Carol and her husband Ian, who was much older than her. He was a radio producer and worked for the BBC in their classical music department. Carol was his second wife and they had two small children. Ian had kids from his first marriage and didn't seem that keen on the second batch.

He sent me to see his mother who was selling her bike. I had calculated that she must be a million years old given Ian's advancing years and the bike would likely be pre-war. Still, beggars can't be choosers, so off I trotted around the corner to a 1950s bungalow. The whirling dervish who greeted me at the door was a tiny bird-like creature in slacks and pearls with a very severe, dyed-black bob.

Miriam had worked for MI5 during the war, didn't really like men, had given birth to Ian after a one-night stand at 40 and married an old colonel who died of malaria on their honeymoon. Miriam swore like a trooper, which was incongruous to her frightfully posh voice.

'I'm almost certainly a lesbian,' she laughed, 'but I didn't know how to go about it all. Besides, it wasn't really done.' She looked sad.

We had tea from chipped mugs in a book-filled room with overflowing shelves, a threadbare sofa covered in throws and a lovely but moth-eaten Persian carpet.

'I brought this carpet back with me from Persia in the 60s,' she told me. 'I had three of the buggers and sold two in London which paid for the trip! Of course, they call it Iran now. It's only a matter of time before it goes to the dogs!'

Knowing little about Persia other than Dr Avani of the diet pills, I swerved the topic and cooed about the delicate intricacy of the rug, then picked up a corner for a closer look. Underneath was a scrap of newspaper. I think it was the *Daily Sketch* and it was dated June 1970. I marvelled at the eccentricity of this but then remembered my grandma used newspapers under rugs too, to stop the draught from the floorboards.

Miriam ignored my fumbling and whistled as she searched for her train of thought. 'Ah, now, the bike, that's it,' she remembered. 'Now, I bought this bloody bike five years ago to go around the world.'

This information was relayed with nary a mention of the fact she was almost 80 and round the world was very far indeed.

'I was to go with two other old farts from Cambridge, but one of the silly bastards died.' She sighed. 'Then I got bloody cancer of the rectum so that put paid to that.'

Miriam had been at Girton College and could easily have stepped out of an Evelyn Waugh novel. I wanted to find out everything about her but she was now on a mission to show me the bike.

The garage was filled with canoes, climbing crampons, a potter's wheel, artists' easels, camping equipment, which left me in no doubt that this was a woman who had embraced life, taken on the world and wasn't about to stop anytime soon.

There in the corner of the garage stood an almost pristine 1970s Touring Falcon with drop-handlebars in gunmetal grey.

'Oh, she's lovely,' I said, 'and what a shame you never got to use her.'

Miriam looked a bit cross. 'No use moping!' she said. 'Now, I was going to ask for 60 pounds, but as you're a student and paying rent to my son, you can have her for 25! How does that sound?'

That sounded very good indeed and I handed over hard cash from my first term's grant money.

The Falcon tourer was a bargain and Phil was extremely jealous. I think it was one of my favourite two-wheeled companions. Every time I rode it, I would calculate the mileage in an attempt to go around the world.

Miriam lived way into her nineties and spent her final years cruising around the world to exotic locations accompanied by a lovely lady companion – the sole beneficiary of her will, as it turned out. Poor Ian and Carole.

Drama school was a mixed bag. Peer pressure, lack of confidence, money worries and the relentless need to qualify for the best parts took up a lot of space in our brains. We had a teacher in charge of 'stagecraft', a very broad term and it always seemed he had never prepared a class but would invent something on the spur of the moment.

One week it was kissing. How to convincingly kiss a fellow actor on stage while still acting.

This produced much tittering in class. We were to improvise a love scene which culminated in a slow, unselfconscious kiss.

I was paired up with Chris, an attractive Canadian of such height and sex appeal that very little acting was called for.

Several couples performed before us with varying degrees of cringe and embarrassment. One pair had to stop mid-kiss when a violent coughing fit took the poor girl down. The boy tried to stay in character, but the moment was gone, lost in a hail of phlegm.

Finally, our turn. We spent longer than was necessary on our improvised scene, attempting waspish put-downs in a low-budget style of *Who's Afraid of Virginia Woolf?* Then the kiss. Chris hovered before me, his face only inches away, letting me be the one to instigate. We were very much in tune with each other and I moved forward to gently let my lips brush over his. There was a magical pause, a moment in time when everything and everyone was still, then he cupped his hand in the crook of my neck and pulled me into him with great tenderness. Stage kissing requires no tongues to enter the mouth, but we forgot ourselves and our acting. A beautiful, sweet-tasting, sensuously sexy moment that I didn't want to end. It was brought to an abrupt halt by the jeers and wolf whistles from the rest of the class. We pulled away, both going beetroot red at what had just taken place. Applause and the next couple stepped up. Something stirred and I found it impossible to look at Chris or concentrate for the rest of the afternoon.

The stagecraft teacher complimented me after class. Told me our scene was 'very believable', then went on to talk about a character I had played in a previous production of *Spring Awakening*. 'I would like to work with you on Wendla's big speech,' he said. 'There was more you could have achieved.'

Flattered, I said as nonchalantly as I could, 'OK, when?'

'I am staying in town this evening at the hotel on the corner. I will meet you outside at seven,' he said and turned to leave.

Now, I was young, quite naïve and he was a teacher, but I knew. Somewhere deep in my solar plexus, I knew.

We all went to the pub after college and I ruminated on whether or not I should go to his hotel.

Just before seven and still undecided, I made my farewells in the pub and clambered on my bike. As I neared the hotel on the corner, I could see him standing outside, leaning against the entrance with a cigarette in hand.

He spotted me just as I pushed down hard on the pedals and he waved frantically to get my attention. I waved back, one hand on the handlebars, gaining speed by the second and shouted what was meant to be a cheery 'Goodnight!' as I whizzed past him. It came out more jeery than cheery, which was not my intention, but it felt appropriate. A power versus control moment that I was delighted to have won.

Not tonight, Satan.

I got together with Chris the sexy Canadian from the 'kissing class' and we had a lovely college romance. Thank you, pervy teacher, who must remain nameless. I hope you got your #MeToo moment.

A few months into my acting course, I sustained an injury after a careless stage fight with Chris involving an albeit modified rapier and dagger. This necessitated registering with a local NHS doctor and a butterfly stitch over the left eye. The doctor asked if there was anything else she could help with? Unable to stop myself, tears dribbled from my eyes and it all came tumbling out. The lack of control over life, the weight gain and the subsequent unhappiness.

A very diligent doctor, she sat me down and asked me what was at the root of it all. This was way too big a question and impossible for me to answer. Kindly words were given, yet further diet sheets offered, and the prescription pad scrawled upon. Two months' supply of appetite suppressants. The merry-go-round began again.

Launching oneself into an acting career with an already shaky hold over self-esteem was the fate of almost every student in my year.

We were spewed out into the real world having learned the rhythms of iambic pentameter, a good few songs from *Cats*, the wonders of period dance and that things would never be quite so easy again.

One of the first open castings I attended was for the director Franco Zeffirelli, who was in London to cast the film *Cavalleria Rusticana*. It was to be filmed in Sicily and needed many girls, was all I was told.

These castings are often referred to as cattle markets or cattle calls, as it is rare you get to speak or do anything in the first elimination rounds.

Hundreds of beautiful girls were gathered in a hall in Westminster. Much excitement, reapplying of lipstick and nervous hair flicking, each girl waiting their turn to enter a large audition room where a panel of 12 men were seated behind a table.

I had worn a Rara skirt, (named after Rasputin, Russia's greatest love machine) which was fashionable at the time. It had white polka dots, a high waistband and three frilled tiers finishing six inches above the knee. Strappy sandals over bare legs and a cutesy low-cut blouse were topped off by back-combed and hi-lighted big hair which was very much an 80s look.

The brief was to 'look sexy' and frankly that was the best I could do.

My outfit and general demeanour was more tart with a heart or busty barmaid, not quite the sophisticated look Mr Zeffirelli may have had in mind.

The walk into the room was a long one. Sandals clacking on the parquet flooring, I was told to stop in front of the table. Twelve sets of eyes appraised this hopeful vision in front of them. Was I the right sort of sexy? A mere flicker and the eyes quickly returned to their notebooks. A resounding No. The spokesman waved his hand to indicate they had seen enough. Dismissed and rejected, dismayed and dejected.

Two chums from drama school were also at the audition, one a sultry Welsh beauty, who made it to the next round and was required to writhe around in a bikini trying to seduce a man in a bear suit. Her journey ended shortly thereafter.

The other girl, a Titian-haired, six-foot model was asked to meet one of the executives later that night for dinner at the Dorchester Hotel in Park Lane. She dutifully slept with him but didn't get a part. This enraged me but she was philosophical and told me, 'Look, he was cute, dinner was amazing and he was a very good lover. I probably would have slept with him anyway!'

There were to be many mass castings that would steal your soul and cast an air of dejection for many days.

The New End Theatre in Hampstead was the venue for my first paid job. A comedy sketch show with three other actors. The comedy was hit and miss but we all worked hard to make it better. I was described as 'an adorable bubble haired blonde' in one newspaper review, praise indeed and I got myself an agent.

Getting a job where you have to be someone else is bonkers. Largely because you have to second-guess what and who the 'someone else' is, to the director, writer, producers and casting agents, who will all have an image in their minds.

You may read the script beautifully but could be too tall, too short, too fat, too thin, too old or too young for their imaginings.

Often you will need to match up with other actors in various roles, which is also part of the equation. Knowing the infinite number of variables as to whether or not you land the job, doesn't make it any easier to take when your agent says, 'Sorry, not this time.'

Each rejection a tiny wound.

A particularly gruelling television audition saw the director playing the part of a medic who had to relay the news of a husband's death to a distraught wife who was six months' pregnant.

A difficult and challenging task for a Tuesday afternoon to repeatedly convey such anguish, and one which reduced both me and the director to snotty tears.

Vomiting one's emotional guts in front of strangers is never easy, especially when you have to gather them all back into your skirts, politely say your farewells and get the tube home.

'They loved you,' trilled my agent some days later, 'but they have gone with someone who IS actually pregnant, so don't feel too bad about it. Ha ha!'

Whilst I loved performing, the brutal audition process took its toll. Punishment for any failures saw the binge–starve cycle hurriedly mobilised.

Thinking back, I was never really fat. The power that I gave to 14 pounds of adipose tissue in order to determine happiness or misery, confidence or fear, remains a ludicrous, self-indulgent state of madness.

I recall this period of my life being dominated by 'waiting'. Waiting for the phone to ring from my agent with news of a potential job, waiting for the scales to show the optimum weight for happiness, waiting for my next prescription after the magic number on the scales spelled out failure, or waiting for the results of yet another questionable audition.

It wasn't all bad. Jobs DID come my way and they were always fun and pleasing. Those moments when life is good and you are getting paid for what is essentially mucking about were sustaining, although once the job was over, you were back to square one, on the bottom rung of a greased ladder, or floundering in a multicoloured ball-pit of perfectly voice-trained wannabes. There is an art to acing auditions and that is simply not to care.

Having performed in a few fringe plays, done my fair share of promotional work – skimpy outfits and lairy, bad-breathed businessmen – and given my all in medical training videos, an Oscar-worthy rectal cancer patient and a post-partum puerperal psychosis sufferer who gets sectioned, things weren't really on course for Hollywood.

I needed something regular that paid proper money and having left my lovely Highbury house share for student digs, I also needed somewhere to live.

I spotted an ad in the rental section of the *Evening Standard* that read, 'Free board and lodgings in large central London location to attractive woman 20–30 in return for some light house keeping'. Call me naïve, but this sounded perfect.

The ad had caught my eye because the space between light and house had been missed out, thus reading 'lighthouse keeping'. This made me laugh and produced visions of being dressed up in oiled yellow waterproofs, aka Grace Darling, rushing around with a massive lamp and saving salty seamen from being dashed onto the rocks of a London lighthouse in the middle of Piccadilly.

Wearing Auntie Lily's trusty old fur coat to look chic and respectable and eccentrically arriving by bike, I was already hot and bothered as I rang the bell of a Victorian townhouse in Albemarle Street, Mayfair. Two men in their late forties with grey complexions and a sweaty demeanour greeted me on arrival and led me up the stairs into a very swanky apartment. Marble floors, lots of starburst gold mirrors, pop art on the walls, fur throws and a Joan Collins in a *The Stud*-type of window swing.

The men had a certain unwashed smell, noticeable if you got too close.

I listened politely and intently as they told me how they liked to throw parties every weekend and that quite often everyone walked around naked and filmed each other.

'Would that bother you?' one of them asked.

Stifling a small amount of sick, I lied, 'Not at all!' adding what I hoped was a sophisticated, worldly laugh, but in reality was a nervous get-me-outta-here squeak.

Enquiring about the 'light housekeeping' and the number of hours required, they looked a bit shifty and said they would let me know the details once I had moved in.

We shook hands and an image of my mum swam before my eyes, wagging her finger and saying, 'Don't ever do anything to make us ashamed!'

Escorting me towards the door as I clucked about how pretty

it all was, a skinny, pale girl with greasy hair and what looked like chicken pox scabs on her arms was letting herself in.

My soon-to-be-flat-mate, perhaps. I smiled.

She didn't make eye contact with any of us. No one introduced me or paid her any attention at all.

In that moment, I knew for sure that the 'light housekeeping' required was a little more involved.

I stuffed Auntie Lily's fur coat in my tote bag and cycled away, letting the air rush through me to cleanse my mind. I had just been exposed to something very unpleasant. I had choices and I thanked the universe that I was in such a lucky position.

One of the sleazeballs phoned me later that night.

'Hello, Maria. We think you'll fit in very well, so yes, we'd like you to join us in the house.'

I mumbled some semblance of fake gratitude. I couldn't take on the response that I should have given because I just wanted to hang up. The sleazeball continued, 'Oh, one other thing I should mention, can you lose a little weight?'

What?!

'I'm ten stone,' I spluttered.

'Better if you were nine,' he said.

'Better for what? Light housekeeping?' I asked, and hung up.

I was saved from the baddies, potential heroin addiction and a career in porn!

For weeks after my ordeal, I worried about the poor naïve soul, who had maybe just arrived in London innocently trundling her suitcase and who was now recruited into the sordid, naked, weekend parties and beyond.

Yes, I had dodged that bullet, but the sleaze bags' 'Can you lose a little weight' request had cut deep and had confirmed that I wasn't even thin enough for porno movies.

I had kept in touch with my lovely Highbury landlord, the assumed spy Humphrey Tizard, while I was at drama school and met him for drinks one night. He asked me the dreaded question, 'How's the acting going?' I recounted my near-miss porn opportunity and lamented my search for somewhere to live. He told me that his sister Jane was leaving London for a research post in Cambridge and that I was welcome to return to the Highbury house, take over her old room in return for some fully clothed 'hardcore housekeeping and sexual favours after dark.'

Serendipitous joy. The old saying has it that you should never go back, but I loved the house in Highbury and while the inhabitants changed, it felt like my little London home. I was sharing with a cameraman from America, a neurotic doctor, an archaeologist who always looked as if he's spent the night on a dig, and Humphrey who was back from a mysterious posting (spy mission) in America.

A disparate collective who all rubbed along nicely and brought in others to group social events and parties. Humph's chums were all as mysterious about their source of income as he was and had names like Gilbert and Persephone. Larry the cameraman knew other behind-the-scenes film folk who could apply gaffer tape to any household appliance at a moment's notice. The archaeologist didn't seem to have any friends at all but was always game for a drink and a laugh. The doctor was a scream and was always looking for sex. He had many friends who were also always looking for sex. I attributed the sexual urgency of the medical men down to the fact that they saw a lot of death. Sex and death are intrinsically linked so their needs seemed entirely justified. My chums were all slight show-offs, which meant guitars were produced constantly and warbling around the fireplace was a common occurrence. Ailments could be hastily diagnosed over a beer and as my chums weren't averse to helping out with the horny doctors there were several reciprocal arrangements.

The entire house sat down to watch Bob Geldof's Live Aid in 1984. It was a terrific achievement that made us all feel that anything was possible to save the world from starvation, especially when pop music was involved.

In between castings and part-time waitressing jobs, I returned to all my old haunts and resumed my daily aerobics classes in order to retain some sanity in the topsy-turvy love/hate world of showbiz.

Working with Brad Peterson, my then teacher at Pineapple Dance Studios, I decided to train with him as an aerobics instructor, attending all his classes and undertaking tutorials. Also enrolling at the YMCA to understand the physiology of the body.

I bought books on muscle function, had large, laminated posters on my wall detailing the whereabouts of quads, lats, abdominals, pecs, gluteus maximus, adductors, deltoids, trapezius, biceps, hamstrings, obliques and their multifaceted function in relation to the bones of the body.

It is fair to say that this was quite an obsessive period of my life, which is in no way the same as interesting. People often wandered away from me at parties.

I also took up swimming, getting up at 7am to swim an hour every day at our local pool in Clissold Park before unlocking the trusty Falcon and cycling to aerobics in Paddington. While certainly very fit, my eating was still wildly out of control. Looking back at photographs of that time, I am reminded of a hard-bodied javelin thrower, muscle-bound and solid. How I longed to be long of limb and slender. My dad, who had in his youth almost become a professional footballer, once remarked that from the waist up I was 'very dolly bird', adding the rejoinder that 'waist down I was Nobby Stiles!' (a famous footballer). If only he'd known how much these words hurt. Of course I laughed along with everyone else, mindful of the oft used phrase in Sycamore Avenue, 'Don't come down here with your la-di-da London ways, lady!'

Brad the aerobics instructor pulled me aside one day and asked me if I wanted to cover someone's Legs, Bums and Tums exercise sessions. The teacher in question was flying back to America for six weeks and needed a stand-in for his twice-weekly classes at the Queen Mother Sports Centre in Victoria. I jumped at the chance. The studio was a very large space with a subsidised rental of £9.80 an hour.

That weekend saw much desperate cassette tape recording and

frantic cycling to record shops for the perfect records in order to fit my hastily arranged routines.

I had written out all the exercises I would be using, including which areas of the body they would benefit, before practising them obsessively in the mirror, to make sure I had all the placements correct and that I looked like I knew what I was doing.

The warm-up consisted of regular beats but not too fast. I chose Diana Ross's 'Chain Reaction', 'Kung Fu Fighting' and 'Like a Virgin' by Madonna.

This selection covered stretches, breathing and arm exercises neatly packed into 15 minutes. Next came the running aerobic part which required something a little faster and more up-tempo: 'It's Raining Men' by the Weather Girls, Bonnie Tyler's 'I Need a Hero' and Donna Summer belting out 'I Feel Love'.

This was all timed perfectly for the 14 minutes of a routine where I would shout over the music to 'KEEP BREATHING! HOLD THAT STOMACH IN! AND SMILE!'

It also involved me having to actually do the exercises myself, with excess enthusiasm, while simultaneously shouting out the beats 'FIVE AND SIX AND SEVEN AND EIGHT! ANOTHER SET, YOU CAN DO IT! ONE AND TWO . . .' etc.

This section of the class would finish on five sets of jumping jacks – 'BEND THOSE KNEES!' – then a short break to glug water and get my breath back before leg exercises, sit-ups and abs work.

Soft Cell's 'Tainted Love', 'Sexy Thing' by Hot Chocolate and Dead or Alive's 'You Spin Me Right Round', chosen as the perfect motivation for a flat tum and a toned bum!

The first class went very well, I arrived early and introduced myself to nine women and two men. That I didn't look like the ideal Jane Fonda, lithe-legged, poster girl, didn't seem to matter to anyone. The routines went down well, I charged £2 per person, covered the room rent and made twelve quid.

The second class that week, I had 20 expectant faces. The energy in the room picked up, we chatted and laughed. It seemed as long as I made the class fun, instilled confidence that I knew what I was doing and smiled a lot, everyone went away red-faced and happy. Plus, I made 40 quid profit.

By the second week, I had recorded another tape and bought some new togs; matching headband and leg warmers, a shiny spandex leotard with Ziggy Stardust orange lightning bolts and a satin bomber jacket to stay warm after class.

The first session on Monday saw 22 people. Mixed ages, weights, and four of them men. I started to enjoy myself and began remembering names to personalise any comments. 'Keep that back straight, Janice!' 'If you want abs of steel, push your back into the floor, David!'

Some of the girls came to chat after class, all with their own personal hang-ups over undetectable flaws and 'problem areas'. The men on the other hand seemed pretty happy with their bodies or at least unprepared to admit otherwise.

The following weekend I had a call from America. Brian the instructor wasn't coming back to London. He had been offered a place teaching at a football college in Michigan and felt it impossible to turn down. He tentatively asked me if I would like to take over his classes? How could I not?

Virtually running to the printer's to get leaflets with class times, inspirational pictures and feel-good quotes, it was now my very own class. If I could increase numbers, it would give me regular money to pay the rent and still take acting jobs along the way.

As a one-woman marketing team I posted leaflets around all the offices in the Victoria area, stood at the train station handing out flyers to my imagined demographic and took an ad out in the local paper. Over the next six months, the numbers built steadily until it wasn't unusual to have 35 people per class. I was having to turn folk away in order to avoid overcrowding. I spoke to the booking department at the Queen Mother Sports Centre in an attempt to rent the studio on other evenings and to spread my classes across the week.

Whilst all other nights were taken up with judo, trampoline lessons and taekwondo, I was offered another hour on both Monday and Wednesday in order to do two classes in succession. Quite a tough gig to maintain energy and sustain the momentum, but it seemed the best option.

The control over food was still erratic, often existing on chocolate, air and willpower. One of my dancer chums at Pineapple confided that despite her heavy training schedule at Ballet Rambert, she survived on diet sodas and cigarettes with occasional bags of carrots and broccoli. It can only have been the resilience of youth that got us through.

Not once did we contemplate the damage we were inflicting on our bones and organs, or that our future selves may have to pay the price for this nutritional shortfall.

The lovely thing about being young is the totally blinkered view that we may, at some point, have to get old.

Often I would lay in bed all day, hungry and depressed, rising only to collect my tapes, pull on an often unwashed leotard, grab a chocolate bar and make my way to the sports centre to teach two one-hour-long sessions.

On one such occasion, my heart started to hurt during the second class, a stabbing tightness in the chest. Class completed and money collected, it seemed like a good idea to take myself off to A&E at the Royal Free Hospital.

Many tests, monitors and manipulations revealed that there was muscle strain around the heart, nothing too serious but an indication nonetheless that my body was being pushed beyond its capacities.

Teaching was fun and I was good at it. Being something of a performance, I was able to quell my desires to show-off. It wasn't acting per se, but I had an audience, it would do for now and I was earning a bit of cash. I occasionally tried out jokes during class which would momentarily ease the pain of exercise and went down well with my pupils.

My class seemed to like the fact that I had heavy thighs, was a bit of a clown and often smelled less than fresh. Never underestimate the power of self-deprecation.

During the days I continued the rounds of auditions and castings. One of my final commercial castings made me realise how emotionally costly those ghastly charades were.

It involved me being paired with a male actor in a dingy studio in North London. We had to serenade each other with the Hot Chocolate song 'It Started with a Kiss', although the ad agency had cleverly changed the words to 'It started with a crisp'.

Ironically I can't remember the brand of crisps but do remember the male actor being very agitated and looking as though he was going to either throw up or cry.

First we sang to each other, 'It started with a crisp, I never knew it could end like this', etc. The agency boffins seemed to like this and we were then given a crisp each to hold in front of our faces and to sing again, this time singing to the actual crisp.

At this point, the actor had something of a flip out.

'I can't f***ing DO this anymore! . . . What the hell am I doing? Where's my self-respect?! Why are you making me sing to a f***ing crisp? . . . I am classically trained . . . Three years at the Royal Academy! You are doing my head in! I swear this will send me over the edge! I am hanging by a thread here, I'm . . . Sorry, I just can't, I can't . . .'

And then he started to cry. Not just screwed-up face of anguish but proper full-on sobs with snot and spit and tears and heaving shoulders. The room became icy cold. Silent. Shocked. I gingerly put my arm around him, but he shrugged me off and ran from the room wiping trailing snot away with the sleeve of his frayed jumper.

Everyone stared.

Then the writer piped up with, 'What does he mean he can't do it? It's just a commercial for a crisp?'

The director chipped in, 'I mean it's not as if it's a difficult thing to do. We changed one word, ONE word! 'Kiss' to 'crisp'. It's a well-known song, fer Christ's sake! What's so bloody hard?'

The creatives all startled babbling at once, each one talking over the other, justifying the reasoning and sense behind this genius commercial, each worrying that their part of the process was to blame for what just occurred.

Nobody seemed overly concerned that some poor guy had just demonstrably had a major existential meltdown, was obviously in psychological distress and needed help and assistance. The agency babbling continued. I glanced across at the casting director hoping for some sort of signal as to what I should do. She looked pained and did the walking sign with her fingers along with a nod of the head towards the door.

No one noticed as I crept away, as they were too busy screeching amongst themselves. Earlier justifications now being repeated in raised voices and wild gestures. I was torn between worry for the poor, broken actor, and feeling annoyed that along with his melodramatic breakdown, MY chance at being Mrs Crisp in the commercial had been well and truly kiboshed. Actors can be very selfish.

They say you get one in 13 commercials you go for. Some folk have the right faces for commercials: non-threatening, cheery, relatable, Mr or Mrs Everyman/woman. I didn't have the right face but had a bit of comedy on my side, so got a few of the 2Cs in a K type of advert. That is (or was) advertising parlance for Two Cunts in a Kitchen. Yep, you read that right.

I would often be cast as Mary or Barbara and would often be found in the kitchen with another actress discussing washing powder, kitchen appliances, nappies or particle theory (I made the last one up). We would both be similarly clad: jeans, wifey-style paisley shirt, pastel jumper slung around the shoulders, and she would be called Jackie or Anne or Mrs Average C*** trapped in a kitchen with me, the equally average C*** who lived next door.

The more of these castings I went for, the greater my understanding of the Crisp Breakdown man.

When my agent rang and said, 'Yes, darling, it's another commercial casting for ketchup and they want you to dress up as a dancing tomato!

I think it could be great fun!' I knew it was time to stop and to try something else. Preferably something that wasn't tomato-based.

One evening, after a full 30 minutes of intense thought, I decided to give stand-up comedy a go. It would be perfect. I had body dysmorphia, a serious eating disorder, was periodically unhinged, had no idea how to write jokes and was even more clueless about where to perform.

An inspired choice.

'Believe in yourself,' one of my teachers at drama school told me. 'If you don't, no one else will.'

I'm not sure I realised quite how difficult things would be, going from drama student to working actor. It was a slog.

We can all fake self-belief, but the little voice that keeps you awake at night, whispering, 'You'll never make it, you're no good, give up now before you make a fool of yourself,' never leaves. Even the most accomplished and successful of actors will tell you of their constant self-doubt.

Frankly I think it's a good thing as it shows humility and sensitivity, but I'm the first to admit that it takes a will of iron to keep pushing forward. I quickly learned that if you say YES to everything, other opportunities are bound to arise. Who you meet, the connections you make and what you learn along the way. It's important to diversify. To take things on that don't seem in any way related. All experience can help you towards your goal.

Some of the jobs I had were mortifyingly embarrassing, but they all led to other possibilities.

When some of my fellow students left drama school, they had lofty ambitions and proclaimed, 'I'm really only going to work in film.' Oh yeah, how did that work out for ya, buddy?

I learned to be humble, to never take myself too seriously and to carry out the work to the best of my abilities – even while working on a sitcom with the glove puppet Roland Rat. Cringing at every line I had to utter, it was important to do the job properly and to banish negative thoughts.

An actor's life is not for the faint-hearted and there may come a point when you've had enough, but there's absolutely no point in trying if you don't give it your best shot. Even when you're despondent, you've got to keep getting back on that horse!

Chapter 9

Boom, Tish!

The Falcon Tourer Lives On

The late great comedian Barry Cryer once said, 'Analysing comedy is like dissecting a frog. Nobody laughs and the frog dies.'

Writing a 20-minute stand-up comedy routine shouldn't be that hard, I thought, as I sat down to scribble some ideas. This new adventure was going to give me back agency, fed up as I was of waiting for jobs, for the phone to ring and for some semblance of a career.

Comedy is subjective, what one person finds funny can leave the next cold. I figured that if I found it funny, it would be an easy sell. How little I knew.

The first attempt was tried out on my friend, the producer Victoria Pile (*Smack the Pony*, *Green Wing*, etc.). She was kind. Well, you have some interesting topics, but where are the jokes?

I looked at her blankly. Is it not enough to have a funny train of thought, be a bit off the wall and a little near the knuckle?

No. She sighed. That's an actor taking on a character for a monologue. An audience needs to feel secure that your ramblings are going somewhere, that there will be a pay-off to whatever you're talking about and then they can feel relieved and laugh when you leave a pause after the punchline.

Of course, she was right, and I returned to the drawing board.

The results of my second attempt were brash and raw. The first five-minute open spot was upon me (new acts can try out their material but don't get paid). I was excited and petrified by the hundred or so people drinking and smoking in the cosy basement with a makeshift stage and a lone mike stand ready for my entrance.

'Hello!' I proclaimed. 'I'm Maria Callous and this is my first go at stand-up!' A rookie error. They hadn't paid good money for an amateur who didn't know what the hell she was doing. The only way out of this was to launch into my patchy and hastily written five minutes.

Some gags worked, others fell away to awkward silence and embarrassed fidgeting. I ad-libbed a bit, chatted to the audience about what needed work and owned up to my fear and dread. That seemed to go better, largely because it felt natural and spontaneous and that I wasn't attempting to fool them.

The manager of the club seemed singularly unimpressed but surprisingly booked me for the following week. A full 20-minute slot with a share of the door takings. In truth there weren't many women on the comedy circuit: Jenny Lecoat, Jenny Eclair, Donna McPhail, Hattie Hayridge, and Jo Brand who had just started under the name 'The sea Monster'. Rather than seeing any comic potential, we were all just something of a novelty and an inclusion box to be ticked.

To stand up in front of a group of strangers believing you can make them laugh and keep them entertained involves both a massive amount of ego and high levels of kamikaze energy.

The nothing to lose element has to be strong. It's certainly no place to be timid or apologetic. 'What's the worst thing that could possibly happen?' was my pre-show mantra, as I bounded onto a stage armed with dubious quality gags and an actor's unshakeable confidence.

The main points in my favour were that I was not unlikeable, was just self-deprecating enough, and was never threatening, as a lot of comics felt they needed to be. Honesty compels me to confess, though, that my joke-writing was poor to non-existent. Something of a drawback in this particular line of work.

My first 20-minute set felt like the longest exam I had ever taken.

Expectant faces of the audience and the judgemental gaze of other comics who had all been performing far longer than me, waiting to see if I would fail and become that evening's sacrificial lamb. Again, it was a mixed response, some gags hit and others bombed hopelessly. Any momentum and audience approval quickly disappeared with two dud gags on the trot. This was clearly a craft that needed a lot of performance time to hone the bare bones (which was all I had) into a cracking, surefire set. A solid set that could build the laughs on a gentle incline with an 'as yet to be written' supremely funny banger of a punchline.

The biggest thrill of my first evening was being given an envelope containing 40 pounds with the promise of another gig in a month's time. An audience member told me, 'Yeah, not bad, needs a bit of work, but yeah, you're quite funny.' Praise indeed.

I vowed that I would go away and work hard on the material, write more jokes and generally be better.

This was absolutely my plan after each gig, but life, other work, fear and sheer laziness somehow got in the way and the day of the next performance would roll around to find me scrabbling about, adding bits of nonsense on the hoof and being generally ill prepared.

Phoning around other comedy clubs and venues, it was always nice when someone had heard of you and that they would take a chance on a booking. For others the dreaded open spot was suggested. It seemed that I should take anything I was offered if I was going to get good at this game.

Stand-up and the search for potential jokes became my life. At the time I had a not very funny opening joke where I played the guitar. I played it very badly and could amuse myself (if not the audience) by stretching out the discordant twanging to see how long it took for the crowd to get restless. A risky strategy but a good litmus test to gauge their kindness levels and patience.

Me and the guitar would set off most nights on a selection of buses and trains to whichever new venue had booked me, where I would chat nervously to the other acts and attempt to insert new, untried material. My childhood, Catholicism, questionable boyfriends and sexual peccadillos all raked over in search of elusive laughs. The guitar meant I couldn't cycle to venues as it was too unwieldy. This was one of the main reasons the opening material was dropped. I liked being able to whizz away on two wheels, pedalling speed dependent on how well the gig had gone. I also started to include cycle gags, the fact that cycling wasn't seen as cool and wasn't going to get me a boyfriend. There may have been jokes about the saddle shape and usefulness, but I have erased this from my mind for being too cheap.

I was performing with people like Jo Brand, Eddie Izzard, Jack Dee, Paul Merton, and Julian Clary with his then canine companion Fanny the Wonder Dog. The other comics became friends and were always supportive with encouraging words and helpful advice. I can remember only warmth from a disparate group of people who had found themselves pursuing a crazy dream.

Paul Merton once told me, when I was wondering why a new gag had fallen flat, 'Try it out three times and if it still isn't working, drop it and move on.' He was absolutely right, of course, and I would soldier on, from venue to venue, changing the wording and rhythm until it worked, or I was forced to finally ditch it.

So much of stand-up is finding the right approach and/or character. Jack Dee started as not quite a cheeky-chappy, but worlds away from the deadpan misery he became. On the point of giving up, he performed one night in the way he was feeling and suddenly found his comic persona.

I would often got booked to compere an evening. Some promoters saw having a woman in this role as a way to keep the evening civil and relaxed. Compering involved coming on at the beginning of the evening to warm up the crowd for ten minutes before introducing the first act. I would then reappear throughout the night, topping and tailing the comedians, calming things down after the interval and thanking all the performers after the final headline act.

Compering was a good ploy. If I could get the audience onside, they would relax and trust me. I could chat with them and mess about, often discovering new material that I could use at a later date. If things go well, the compere keeps the evening moving, dovetailing acts and maintaining the energy. If the night is rowdy or someone bombs, the compere needs to rush on and pick up the pace, deal with hecklers and get the rabble back onside before letting the next performer onstage.

This became more of a psychological battle and taught me huge amounts about how and why an audience can turn from charming and receptive to angry and unforgiving. If an audience takes against a particular performer the atmosphere can turn on a sixpence and is an uphill struggle to settle things down. Akin to reasoning with a room full of furious toddlers.

I loved compering and was thrilled when the *Guardian* wrote of me, 'one of the best comperes in the business'. My actual 'act', however, continued to be entirely average.

Some clubs were harder than others, and two in particular – The Comedy Store midnight show in Leicester Square and the Tunnel Club in South London – were both soul-destroyingly difficult.

Hecklers were commonplace and as a woman you would certainly have to deal with your fair share. 'Get your tits out', 'You're shit', and 'You're too ugly to be fucked' being some prime examples. A long way from being witty, they were specifically male and designed to intimidate or undermine. We were very much in the 'women aren't funny' territory.

At the Tunnel Club, the audience had worked out an ingenious way to show their displeasure. If an act was starting to struggle or the crowd had picked up the faintest whiff of fear, a small, almost imperceptible noise would begin at the back of the hall. You would see in the comic's eyes when instinct told them they were losing the crowd and he or she would speak louder or faster as if trying to outrun an avalanche; changing their routine and cramming in surefire gags to win back momentum, all to no avail. The sound at the back would grow louder and spread quickly as the audience all began to join in with the monotonous and chilling clamour that would soon overwhelm the room and become deafening.

Humming. It was HUMMING. A group of people who had come out for a comedy evening was capable of a silent and collective decision that, for whatever reason, they didn't like the act and they would join forces and hum them off the stage, hum them back into the dressing room and hum them home in disgrace.

I saw and heard it happen many times and the malignant din would ring in my ears as a very clear warning that this was a crowd who took no prisoners.

Another tough set of gigs where you would certainly earn your money was on the university circuit. Students can be bastards. That I loved the process of clambering into someone's car with two or three other comics chattering and trying out gags all the way to Hull or Manchester was not in question, but the sheer terror of a massive hall filled with baying, half-drunk adolescents was an experience I never fully enjoyed. Incoherent heckles, bottles used as flying missiles and even fights breaking out with an act and a member of the audience were commonplace. If ever you find yourself in need of an adrenaline boost, go and perform at a university hall and you will be awake for days.

The journey back to London could be spent dressing wounds – metaphorical, and on one occasion with a young, male comic, literal. Convincing ourselves that we had done our best, that 'not even the best comics in the land could have turned it around', and swearing we would never return to that particular hellhole, until we did.

In the late 80s, alternative comedy had caught the eye of the dreaded television executives and you could often find yourself approached after a gig by some oily oik pressing his card into your hand and telling you about a new concept sketch show you would be perfect for.

I shouldn't knock it as, in truth, I did very well with the arrival of the television comedy scouts, but it changed the circuit from a mad place filled with misfits and oddballs to a fully-fledged industry. It quickly became the survival of the fittest and competition was rife.

I had loved the fact that when I first began performing I could be on a bill with someone who heaved a massive chunk of ice on stage. His entire act was to carve it into some recognisable artwork or object. There was also a chap who would make the sounds of jets taking off, marching military bands or a baby sneezing. Magicians, ventriloquists, vaudevillians all fell by the wayside in favour of the quick-witted gagsters who all upped their game to get onto the small screen and make 'loadsa money' à la Harry Enfield.

I did TV shows with Jo Brand, Paul Merton, Jack Dee and Jeremy Hardy, Sean Hughes, Ann Bryson of the Flaming Hamsters and countless others. I even made it onto *Have I Got News for You.* It is a truism that work breeds work and before you know it you are being offered jobs on a regular basis which is, as you would expect, very pleasing.

It was after a show at the Meccano Club in Islington that had gone pretty well that I was happily cycling home, a drink or two taken that I got flagged down by the police. I had my lights on and wasn't at all sure why I had been stopped? A routine check perhaps, had I spotted something on my travels that may be of vital importance? No. I was stopped on a potential charge of 'furious cycling'. I had never heard of this and felt myself to be a careful and considerate cyclist, so I was tempted to laugh. The policeman told me, 'You were wavering and weaving through traffic in an unsafe manner, have you been drinking?' I told him that I had only supped two half pints of lager over a period of three hours. He looked doubtful and asked me to lean my bike against the wall.

The other officer got out of the car and they both began to look over my bike as if I may have stashed drugs or diamonds beneath the saddle or in the handlebars. This was clearly a slow crime day. I asked him to explain this furious cycling law that I was unaware of.

'Wanton or furious cycling,' he said with some authority. 'Cycling in a fashion that may cause danger to others.'

I told him about the comedy gig that had gone well and that any exuberance may have been as a result of adrenaline at this happy outcome. We chatted for a bit, I was half expecting them to ask me to walk in a straight line or recite the alphabet backwards, but no.

'Were you just on *Have I Got News for You*?' the second policeman asked.

'Why, yes, officer, I was,' I replied.

The temptation to slur this in a Southern drawl, in the style of Blanche DuBois from *A Streetcar Named Desire*, was almost too tempting, but I resisted. This information seemed to please them. They put away their notebooks, having scribbled down my details for any future misdemeanours, before one of them asked, 'What's Angus Deayton like?'

'Oh, he's lovely,' I said, 'very funny, very sharp, but a bit tight. The last to the bar!' They both smiled and nodded their approval at this news, told me to slow down for the rest of my journey and gestured for me to clamber back onto my bike.

Chastened, I did as I was told and gave them a cheery wave of acceptance before wobbling off and giggling my way home.

My first and, to date, only two-wheeled felony and one which provided five minutes of material.

Leaving stand-up comedy after four years was a conscious decision when other work began taking up too much time and energy. I was lucky enough to be asked to write for myself and others, and in my heart of hearts I didn't have the killer instinct needed to continue as a comic. Neither did I have the talent.

I learned more performing live gigs than I ever did at drama school and will be forever grateful to all the people who booked me, helped me and for all the fabulous comics I met during that time, many of whom are and will be friends for life. I salute you all.

Acting is a ridiculous profession and if you are thinking of it as a career you'll need to toughen up and batten down the hatches.

Always take the work seriously but NEVER take yourself too seriously or believe your own importance. It used to amaze me working with big, successful stars that they would spend a lot of their time bemoaning the fact that this actor or that actress had got the job THEY wanted or that they hadn't been seen for something that undoubtedly they would have been perfect for.

Despite being cast as the lead in whatever project we were engaged in, there was little time for happiness and enjoying the moment, instead worrying about which of their contemporaries was doing better, earning more money or being noticed by Hollywood.

The very nature of the business is uncertainty and unless you take that on board it will make you at best very unhappy, and at worst bitter and twisted. For me, the fact that I have made a reasonably successful living by 'mucking about' astounds me still.

'There is nothing in the world so irresistibly contagious as laughter and good humour' – Charles Dickens, *A Christmas Carol*. I couldn't agree more, but boy is it harder than it looks!

Being the master of your own destiny means having no one else to blame.

Stand-up comedy was one of the most difficult jobs I have ever undertaken, yet it gave me total autonomy to write material, book my own gigs and market myself as I saw fit.

It was a crash course in self-belief, promotion and public relations.

There was no greater training in life and yet there WAS no training. It was all picked up along the way and on the job.

In retrospect, I was not very good at it. That I could have got better and approached the writing of new material with a greater sense of urgency is a failing I now recognise.

I didn't have the requisite discipline and it showed. Never has the term 'failing to prepare is preparing to fail' been more relevant to my stand-up career!

Did I take it seriously? No, not really. I was quite interested in getting away with it and not being found out (as a chancer).

That I DID get found out, when the gigs went badly and my jokes went down the toilet, should really have spurred me on to do better, write more, be daring with new gags, but the truth was that I was frightened of writing, didn't really know how to do it properly and judged everything I did write to be rubbish.

Being a stand-up comic was never really part of the master plan, rather a means to an acting end. It was a lucky coincidence that during my time on the various comedy circuits I learned a huge amount about performing and understanding an audience. Watching others who had honed their craft with beautifully written rhythmic jokes that flowed into cracking punchlines was the best apprenticeship I could have ever had.

The lessons I learned from my brief stints alone on stage are still being put to use even now, both in performing and in life.

The most valuable thing I learned was fortitude.

If I could go back and do it all again, knowing what I know now, I'm not sure I could.

Chapter 10

Real Life Hits:

The Falcon Tourer

For me, at 28, when my partner Mark died, it was and still remains a catastrophic implosion of my fiddly dee, will-o'-the-wisp, Peter Pan existence. As I now understand it, Real Life.

Mark suffered from Marfan syndrome – a genetic disorder affecting the connective tissues, a mutation of the genes that make fibrillin. People with Marfan tend to be tall and thin with long arms, legs, fingers and toes.

The most serious complications involve the heart and aorta, with an increased risk of mitral valve prolapse and aortic aneurysm. You are now imagining a spindly spidery creature with a sickly demeanour. Mark wasn't especially thin, but tall and handsome with freckly Polish pale skin and the blackest hair that curled into bobbles like a poodle.

While playing rugby at Oxford, he literally felt a ripping in his chest area and was rushed to hospital for what was, in 1982, pioneering surgery. His aortic valve was replaced with a synthetic version; it went surprisingly well. He came round asking for Coca Cola and was seen by his surgeons as a back-slapping 'didn't we do well' success story.

A daily dose of Warfarin (blood thinner) and the occasional beta-blocker were the only medications needed as his life returned to normal.

Four years on, he was running the Meccano comedy club in Islington, London, and promoting up-and-coming talent to television spots.

A routine hospital check-up revealed the replacement aortic valve had begun to fail.

Having cheated death once, now his options were limited: do nothing and get progressively weaker as his heart became enlarged before eventually failing, OR, have another operation to investigate the damage and hopefully replace the defective valve – an operation not without risk.

We discussed it at length. He was only 28 – there was really only one option.

We talked of death, we laughed and joked. I asked him to come back from wherever and tell me about the afterlife if there was one and if there wasn't he must find a way to let me know that too; a contradiction in terms. Discussing death with someone who is very much alive is hard to get your head around. It was an abstract concept that we struggled to make real.

We also started planning where we would go for Christmas, whether to buy a new kitchen table and/or get a tiny puppy.

Scared and optimistic in equal measure, life still had to be lived. A week before the operation was scheduled, we took a holiday to Italy with his family. We had both been performing in a show at the Edinburgh Festival and caused more than a little consternation with the other actors by leaving them in the lurch with a week left to go. It was hard for them to understand that this could be Mark's final huzzah. In Rome, we threw coins into the Trevi Fountain, visited the Vatican and cried at Michelangelo's *Pieta*.

On our return, we arrived at Hammersmith hospital tanned and in good spirits. When the surgeons, anaesthetists, intensive-care nurses et al. gathered around the bed to discuss the process, our positive outlook dimmed somewhat as they all seemed shifty and uncommunicative.

We told ourselves it was probably hospital policy to err on the side of caution. Aside from the heart defect Mark was a young, healthy chap. His glass was half full! Of course everything would turn out well.

Over a smuggled-in Big Mac later that evening, Mark was teary and frightened. He would switch from laughing to looking at me with terror, asking, 'But, what if I DO die? My mum is still in Italy and I haven't said goodbye.' I told him he would see her in a few days when he was feeling better.

The following morning, in the muddled-thinking period after the pre-med, Mark asked for the last rites. As a fellow Catholic I understood but still managed to tell inappropriately crass jokes: 'The doctor says there's bad news and good news. The bad news is you're probably not going to make it, but the good news is the man in the next bed wants to buy your slippers!'

The on-call priest was summoned remarkably quickly, almost as if he had been hovering in the shadows waiting for his moment. He reminded me of a Dickensian character; rather round, a little obsequious and full of pained righteousness. He anointed Mark with sweet-smelling holy oils on his head, hands and heart while muttering with a practised boredom the exit incantations.

The compulsion to laugh overwhelmed us both and I couldn't make eye contact with Mark for fear of unacceptable hysterical explosion.

When the priest left, we both shrieked with helpless giggles that stripped away some of the unbearable tensions. It was agreed that, however silly, what had just taken place was probably a good thing. A form of insurance and one in the bank of Jesus.

He was called down for surgery. I walked with the trolley and the porters through the ward to the lift, holding Mark's hand all the way. I described delicious food stuffs and sweetmeats that he would soon be able to gorge on for a rapid recovery. His nil-by-mouth status caused him to salivate and drool, which made the porters smirk and tell me off.

Just before the lift arrived and when I had to let go, we kissed and I whispered, 'Sweet dreams, Bubba, I'll see your silly little face later!' He looked momentarily stricken and said, 'I'd better tell you where I parked the car, otherwise you'll never find it.'

I wouldn't and couldn't let him tell me and simply told him we'd find it together.

The damage to the back of the heart from the operation four years previously was greater than imagined, there was a problem with the anaesthetics, but they managed to replace the valve.

His surgeon was brusque when I spoke to him. 'We'll see in a couple of hours.'

See what?

In intensive care Mark wasn't coming round, I talked to him, babbled at him, sang songs, outlined *Eastenders* storylines, what I'd had for tea, and told him Julian Clary had rung (an old school chum) to tease that it was an extreme way to avoid giving him a gig at the Meccano comedy club, ha ha ha!

I squeezed his hand, he squeezed back, didn't he? The medical team were concerned that he wasn't regaining consciousness.

As afternoon turned to evening his best friend Jim visited. He walked onto the ward to see me chattering madly at an inert figure on the bed, hooked up to tubes and drips and bleeping machines. He just stared, looked frightened, then burst into tears and left. There was no energy in me for the comfort of others.

I stayed in the ICU for three days, sleeping on the floor of the family room and waking as every emergency bell rang out. You quickly get to know the crash teams and as they rushed onto the ward, their overtired faces always told me that the emergency bell was yet again for Mark.

He had a stroke, his heart stopped, he began fitting, he remained unconscious. I spoke to his mother by telephone and told her they feared lower-body paralysis.

'I will just adapt the house for wheelchair use,' she assured me.

We were all hoping for something good.

On day four he was massively sedated to avoid further brain activity. The staff nurse gently suggested I go home. 'Nothing will happen tonight, come back in the morning.'

At 4am the phone rang at home. I refused to answer it. It kept ringing and ringing until Bill, an old drama schoolmate who had been staying with me, answered it and said, 'Maria, you have to come to the phone now.'

Mark had died. That can't be right? I wasn't with him? How? The world stopped turning. My beautiful boy was gone. There was no boy.

The following morning I went to see Mark in the chapel of rest. En route I collected our holiday photos (the olden days). There he was smiling out at me, chucking a coin behind him into the Trevi Fountain, grinning as he emerged from Lake Bracciano wet and suntanned, covering his willy with his hands when I surprise snapped him early one morning in the shower.

His family were already in the chapel. His sister Monica, her girlfriend Barbara, his mum and Polish-only-speaking great aunt with her long, grey, winding bun. They had flown in from Italy that morning. Understandably deeply distressed, I couldn't muster the same energy and could only gaze on as if watching a scene I didn't need to be involved in.

They cut off locks of his hair which was bewildering, but I nevertheless found myself following their lead and snipping off a lock of his beautiful poodly curls.

There was a small graze on his upper lip where a medical tube had been hastily removed; I remember thinking, 'Ah, now that will never heal.'

The power of my reaction was surprising. Having never experienced anything remotely similar, there was nothing to compare things to. The death cliches became a reality.

When I heard those words on the phone my body became disconnected, it was as though my bones had crumbled and movement was no longer an option.

I couldn't understand how the shops could still be open, how time could become wrong, how something could not be done to rectify this obvious error.

Speaking once to Ivan Massow, whose partner had killed himself, he told me that on hearing the devastating news, his first reaction was to reach for his cheque book, i.e. everything can be solved with money.

It is one of the truisms in life that money really cannot buy you everything.

I always felt the 'grieving' process or reaction to a death would somehow be filmic, I would look inexplicably beautiful, there would be a wind machine and everything would be in slow motion with a suitably poignant soundtrack. If you've never experienced something, the only clue is from others who have, or from films and TV.

The reality was pain like no other, a physical ache impossible to locate. A hole in the solar plexus made by a cartoon cannonball. A punctured lung, the inability to take breaths, a dull constant throb.

Pleasingly, there was a bit of slow motion. Walking the long hospital corridor to the chapel of rest my hair became Harmony-hairspray-slo-mo-bouncy and my skirt swished around my knees at the wrong tempo. Also other people slowed down. Children laughing in the hospital gift shop, a man on crutches pretending to dance, all at the wrong speed like a broken film acetate on a now slowing reel.

It was a space between the awful reality, it was extra time to process, to catch up and grasp this new dimension.

Coming home from the hospital, I was acutely aware of everything that Mark had touched.

He had left his shoes splayed out near the front door, the shape of his feet imprinted on the leather.

The leftovers of his favourite snack – Hula Hoops and soured cream. A Hula Hoop on each finger dunked into the sour cream and hastily crunched before globules of cream could fall to the floor. Moving anything was not possible. The mould built up on the sour-cream bowl and the shoes remained how they had been kicked off, profound and banal. The kicker would kick no more.

The first few weeks after Mark died felt like another person had inhabited my body. My reactions were different, my view on life skewed, I was, if not pleased, then certainly smug when the Zeebrugge ferry disaster happened and many people died. It was a shared suffering.

I went to see a spirit medium, something I'd never have dreamed of doing previously. Alas it only made me more angry, as did most things.

Dreaming of Mark was comforting and constant, usually involving magic potions that could be administered to return him to life, powder that could be sprinkled into his ashes to rehydrate his being, or potions that would restructure his body.

I'd wake most mornings and think, 'Oh, thank god,' before the cartoon cannonball of realisation. I still couldn't help but look for him everywhere. Once, utterly convinced he was a bird reincarnated, following my train.

There was a promise made. He was meant to let me know what the fuck was on the other side?

The subconscious struggles to make sense of something that will never make sense.

How can someone be there one minute and then disappear?

Suicide was definitely an option, to put an end to the sheer fatigue of grief. The choices were stark and simple: to continue with my life, or not to continue.

One day I had a bath, the next I bought a pint of milk, and so it was I clawed my way back to some sort of, if not recovery, then haphazard continuation.

There were so many beautiful heartfelt letters that I've retained in an unopened shoe box, along with the lock of hair and an old answer phone tape too painful to hear. Some letters were perfunctory guff, others mesmerising for their intimacy and compassion. Those that resonated were raw and unafraid, stripped of artifice.

When my friend lost her husband some years ago, we laughed bleakly on reading a letter from Harold Pinter which read:

I happen to know that John recently went to see a production of my play the Birthday Party, which he thoroughly enjoyed. Love Harold

One of the things which did give me comfort came from the late theatre critic Jack Tinker who lost his daughter aged 16. He told me something that he had found helpful: 'Try not to see it as a life ended but a life completed.'

None of us know how much time we have or when the bell will toll for us. Some are given 90 years, some only 16. That Mark had completed his life at 28 gave me a small amount of peace.

Organising a funeral is both a final act of love and a lesson in tedious organisation that one has little appetite for. I was tasked with booking some of the acts who had appeared at the Meccano Club to play songs and add cheeriness to the day.

The wonderful singer and comedian Ronnie Golden arrived at the church late to set up. He looked at me sadly and said, 'Which side of the stage shall I put the mic on?' It would have made Mark smile. Stage or altar, it's all showbiz really. Ronnie sang a song by Nat King Cole, 'There Was a Boy', a beautiful rendition which destroyed everyone.

I hadn't yet found the car. It had seemed unimportant, but a few days after the funeral I set off on my bike to search the streets around Hammersmith hospital. That I had been with Mark when we parked the car should have given me some inkling as to its whereabouts, but sadness had wiped all recollection. I cycled around endless roads that all looked the same, I was tired, exhausted and had lost weight without trying. 'Every cloud has a silver lining,' as they say.

I leaned my bike against the front garden wall of an unimposing 1950s house, put my head down and rested my hands on my knees to stop the dizziness. The lady from the house appeared, bringing her bins out. She asked if I was OK? I half blurted, half cried the words, 'My partner has just died in the hospital and I am trying to find his car.' She stood for a few moments, not saying anything, then came towards me and gave me a tentative hug. 'Perhaps have a little break,' she said. 'Why don't I make you a cup of tea?'

She picked up my bike, wheeled it into the front garden. The British insistence that tea will make things less unbearable is a peculiar one, but it had never seemed more apt.

I followed her into the living room, a small, pink paradise of cushions, antimacassars, tiny ornaments on cluttered shelves and swirling patterns of every combination covering walls, carpets and curtains. This working-class cliché of hideous overload had driven me mad as a teenager, but in that moment I found it comforting and familiar.

In the corner there was a bird cage and a tiny yellow canary that sat forlornly on its wooden perch, staring intently at this unwanted visitor. There was a mirror that hung from the top bars of the cage and an array of half-pecked cuttle fish scattered around the sawdust-covered base.

'I'm Jenny,' said the lady, as she flicked the switch on an already filled kettle. She was a tiny birdlike woman with unfeasibly small hands. 'Sit yourself down.' It felt as though I was in a play or a sitcom on a set where I didn't really know my lines.

'What's the little canary called?' I asked, caring not a jot what the answer might be. Jenny brought in a tea tray and a plate of pink wafer biscuits, the type that taste of nothing and turn to mush in your mouth. 'Janet, she's called Janet. We had Jimmy too, but he went soon after Geoff.'

The 'we' and the 'Geoff' were kind of obvious, but I knew what was needed.

'Was Geoff your husband?' I asked.

Geoff was indeed Ginny's husband who had died eighteen months earlier from a quick and aggressive form of pancreatic cancer. It was only seven weeks from diagnosis to death and an end to 42 years of marriage. 'Janet has been my lifesaver,' Ginny told me, nodding towards the bird.

For some reason, however inappropriate, this made me laugh out loud. A tiny yellow staring bird sitting in a wire cage was keeping Jenny alive.

We had tea and chatted, she told me I looked very sad. 'I recognised distress as soon as I saw you. I think I'm sort of attuned to it,' she said. Then she laughed at herself. I told her that I had noticed it too. Grey-faced people on tubes and trains, in the middle of their own hideous journey of sorrow.

To break the mood Jenny said, 'You've just gotta get on with it, haven't you? Hey, you could do worse than to get a canary, Maria,' she laughed. 'It's the relief of having something nearby with a heartbeat!' and with that, as if to demonstrate the existence of a heartbeat, she got up and set Janet free from the cage.

Janet fluttered around, landed on the net curtains momentarily and made a few squawking sounds which Jenny assured me were the words 'Pretty baby', then she flew towards us and settled on my shoulder. 'She knows,' said Jenny mysteriously.

I have never forgotten Jenny's kindness, nor indeed the odd reassurance of a ball of yellow feathers with a heartbeat, perched on my shoulder.

As I left, Jenny said in a serious voice, 'Just remember what my vicar told me: death may end a life, but it doesn't end a relationship.'

I clambered back on my bike, waved my farewells and set off. The very next street I turned into, I spotted the car and cried with relief. I would return with the keys to collect it and some chocolates for Jenny. Cycling back, the alliteration of Geoff, Jenny and Janet made me chuckle all the way home. A slightly hysterical sense of elation caused by car, kindness and canary.

Feeling ill, tired and sick seemed to be a physical manifestation of grief that I hadn't anticipated. The very thought of food made me nauseous and the smell of my flatmates' breakfast bacon caused me to physically heave.

I was still losing weight and looked 'dog rough', as a comedian friend told me. Under pressure, I went to the doctor's and was secretly delighted to find I had lost 16 pounds. There was part of me that hoped it was some form of wasting disease and that I would shortly just cease to exist. The doctor came back with blood test results:

'Well, your bloods are all fine, so no need to worry, but did you KNOW you're pregnant?'

Two months before, Mark and I had been in Italy, relaxed, suntanned and enjoying ourselves. Despite knowing about the operation to come, we were extremely happy and Mark had certainly been pretty frisky. Given that his oxygen levels were low, it made me laugh that he was acting like the lead character in *The Stud*. We had joked about him being 'Mr Ever Ready' and one morning before breakfast he had chased me around the bedroom shouting, 'I WILL impregnate you before I die!' which made us both laugh. I was now questioning the pre-death biological imperative, in light of this bombshell news.

Stumbling out of the surgery in a fugue state, I sat on a park bench for what seemed like most of the afternoon. Holding onto a part of Mark felt like the most essential act. A wonderful gift that would return him to me. How delighted his mum and family would be, a beautiful and magical fuck you to the ugly finality and pain of death. There was also a tiny nagging fear that it would be too much. Too precious, too impossible, too great a task. Feeling so broken, I had to question if I could actually do this, alone and in grief? When a Hollywood ending seems implausible, it's because it usually is.

I resolved not to tell a single person of this news. I couldn't cope with anyone's advice, however well-meaning, and did not want reactions of joy, horror or concern. It all had to be processed and understood by me alone.

I remained in bed for 24 hours, morning sickness became morning, noon and night sickness, and rational thought seemed out of reach.

In the middle of the second night, I woke up sweating. Marfans. What about Marfans? The disease that resulted in Mark's death at 28 years old? It hadn't crossed my mind, until now. In the morning I called Mark's consultant and made an urgent appointment.

In his office, the stupid tears began. Seeing him again was agonisingly painful and imparting this massive news made my hands tremble. Our conversation that day must remain private, but his kindness and concern touched me very deeply.

Marfan syndrome is caused by an abnormal gene, FBN1. In three out of four cases, the gene is inherited from a parent. A child of an infected parent has a one-in-two chance of having the disorder.

In 75 per cent of cases, Marfan syndrome is inherited from one parent. The syndrome is autosomal dominant.

I stared at the statistics while the consultant talked me through them. The list of possible symptoms was long, the severity of each varied massively.

Abnormal facial appearance, eye problems, tall thin body, abnormally shaped chest, crowded teeth, laxity of joints, curved spine, poor healing of wounds or scars, dilation of the aortic root, mitral valve prolapse, pulmonary disease, it seemed endless.

Medical advances since 1986 have made Marfans infinitely more treatable but there is still no cure.

We discussed all the options at length, but both of us reached the same conclusion. Looking back, it was almost certainly evident to Mark's consultant that I was not capable.

There would be no more grief. The simple fact was, that this embryo was not viable.

At the clinic, after the pre-med I allowed myself a small pat of my tummy and the words 'not this time kid', then I was wheeled to theatre and the deed was done. There were no more tears left, I was empty and now I was empty inside too. This was the right decision and there would be no recriminations.

The body can sometimes work independently from the mind and after a drunken New Year's Eve one-night stand with a most unlikely and unsuitable candidate, I was pregnant again. This time round was a bit more difficult. A ridiculous and foolish mistake and one that I am not proud of. My body really wanted a baby but this was not the way. Two terminations in such a short space of time made me deeply ashamed. I vowed that there would be no more. If I were lucky enough, the next pregnancy would bring me a baby.

We held a memorial for Mark at Jongleurs in Battersea with lots of acts, lots of laughter and copious amounts of booze. There is a great need to keep the dead alive with memorials, benefit nights, films, books and any medium available to stop them slipping from our grasp. An impossible and futile attempt to delay the reality that they categorically no longer exist.

Some months later I popped back to Hammersmith to visit Jenny and deliver a book I had found on canary husbandry. She was delighted and ushered me in quickly. Sitting on the sofa in carpet slippers was a portly gentleman with a shiny bald head and a kindly face. Ginny blushed like a teenager as she introduced me.

'This is my friend, John,' she said.

The little yellow canary was sitting on its perch in the cage chirruping happily.

'Wow, Janet's very vocal today,' I said.

'Oh no, that's not Janet,' cut in Jenny quickly. 'I'm afraid Janet died . . . this is our new canary, Jilly.'

John smiled and said quietly, 'I thought Janet needed a friend, much like Jenny did.'

Of all the events in my life, the death of Mark had the most profound effect. Having never had to confront mortality, the ramifications were immense. As Joan Didion said, 'Grief turns out to be a place none of us know until we reach it'.

Imagine a tablecloth on a long trestle table that has been lovingly laid up to create a beautiful picture. Each item having been placed carefully for full effect. Every place setting beautifully symmetrical, cutlery polished and shining. Sweet smelling freshly cut flowers in tiny vases dotted at intervals and your most treasured possession as the centrepiece to complete the scene.

This is the arrangement of your life, how you have ordered it, lovingly treasured each aspect and the way you understand your existence to be. It is the furniture of the self.

Then a magician enters the room, you are intrigued but it has taken you up until the age you are now to build this tableau and you are understandably nervous. He is full of showmanship and while you know his act is a well-rehearsed piece of theatre, there is a gnawing doubt, but you have no choice. He is going to perform his magic trick on your conscientiously coherent life where every object has its status that builds a table of perfect harmony.

All will be well is the last thought you think as the magician positions himself at the top of the table. He makes three overly theatrical fake attempts to pull at the tablecloth in order to build the tension as he has been taught. He pauses momentarily and with great gusto, goes in for the fourth attempt. Yanking away the starched linen as you silently hold your breath.

He is not a good magician, he is a charlatan and you watch helplessly as all the long-prepared, carefully curated order descends into comic mayhem. Plates smash, glasses tumble, knives and forks clatter. The vases spill their water and fragrant cargo and the fully lit candles from the candelabra begin to burn the fluttering napkins from each placement. Everything is chaos on the floor around your feet and you wait for the bad dream to be over.

Then the magician is gone and everything is silent.

This is death.

Unable to comprehend, you douse the flames and gaze at the rubble. Days pass before very slowly you begin to move amongst the debris. Heirlooms destroyed, precious memories from much-loved trinkets shattered into tiny pieces. Your most treasured possession is nowhere to be found, it has been spirited away by the uninvited magician.

Slowly you collect each part of your life and replace them on the table, many are beyond repair, but you put them back anyway.

It is a pitiful scene, but you will painstakingly mend everything possible and recreate the continuity as best you can remember.

It will never look the same, there is a wonkiness that wasn't there before, the fabric of your linen tablecloth is now frayed at the edges and burned, but you will repair and disguise the damage in the hope no one will notice, but it will never again be how it was.

Chapter 11

Famous Folk:

White Mountain Bike – Built to Own Specification

After working on the second series of *The Fast Show* for BBC One, I decided to reward myself with a custom-built bike. This would be the most money I had ever spent on a bike (or anything really) and I spent many hours in the Battersea cycle shop choosing a lightweight frame, comfortable handlebars, high-tech wheels, gear system and a super comfortable leather saddle.

I had never been interested in the intricate workings, latest gadgets or fashions of bikes, but I loved putting together this personalised machine, even if it did cost over 600 pounds and an extra hundred on the super-duper 'you can't steal this' lock.

Setting up your own preference for the fit of a bike is extremely important. Being comfortable with the position of weight on saddle or handlebars and how you like to extend your legs on the pedals will make all the difference. I often see cyclists with saddles way too low, meaning bent knees, twice the effort and a sore back. For myself, I like a full leg extension on the pedals and a straight foot, tippy toe contact with the tarmac when stationary, in the manner of a ballerina on point.

The Fast Show enjoyed great success and people began to recognise me, quoting various catchphrases and snippets of dialogue as I queued in the Co-op. A not unpleasant experience, although I always felt compelled to be funny in order to justify my existence. An exhausting and impossible side effect.

Being famous is not all it's cracked up to be, elusive, transitory and alienating for those on the outside. When you belong to others you are always on show and that precious anonymity to carry out life's normal function is lost to you.

A couple of my close friends are famous and I'm not entirely sure the benefits outweigh the tough stuff.

I first met Graham Norton on the comedy circuit in the late 80s, early 90s. We went on to record a programme together called *Carnal Knowledge*. It was a show rather like *Mr and Mrs* where you need to demonstrate how much you know about your partner, except the subject matter was sex.

Frankly it was pretty awful, out there on the edge of acceptability. We filmed 20 shows in five days.

Without Graham and his funny, charming and calming influence, it would have been a lot worse. We were both a little green around the gills, but it was a good telly break and despite signing terrible contracts that allowed it to be shown forever, it felt like we should be grateful.

Graham became a good friend and has remained so for almost 30 years, although he may say otherwise.

When he began his Saturday morning BBC Radio 2 show in 2010, he asked me if I would like to come on and do a segment as an agony aunt with him. We were both big fans of 'other people's relationship' analysis and would happily hold postmortems on an evening out or a dinner by discussing the guests and their lives at length. Being agony aunts was a natural extension of our mutual nosiness and a way of understanding how we all tick. Besides, it's so much easier to sort out other people's problems than your own.

There were a lot of big famous guests on the radio show and our producer Malcolm Prince suggested that I should hang around after my slot to chat to the guests, make sure they had coffee etc. and warm them up before their time in the studio.

The Radio 2 green room is not terribly glamorous, a couple of sofas, a coffee machine and kitchen area and a shiny black lacquered grand piano donated by Elton John. It's more of a wide corridor extension from which offices and studios can be accessed.

It was over the next ten years, chatting and shooting the breeze with a whole heap of celebrities, that it became clear that this fame game can be problematic for some people. By being in a job where a lot of people see you in their living rooms, on their televisions or big screens, and in theatres or music venues, it means you have got quite good at what you do, which is a reasonable goal for most of us. Then being good at your job brings fame and fame separates you from the rest of us.

My observations have shown me there are three distinct kinds of famous folk:

Type A: Those who don't really want to be famous and feel a bit embarrassed by it all.

Type B: Those who quite like it but don't want you to behave any differently towards them, and,

Type C: Those who are gonna milk it for every ounce of prestige and advantage they obviously deserve.

This latter category can be tricky, or as Graham's mum Rhoda would say, 'When they lose the run of themselves'. Meaning they start to believe their own publicity, that they ARE truly great and that they can be unkind to the little people when things don't match their exacting standards.

When my friend Nigella married her second husband, the quite rich former ad-man and art dealer Charles Saatchi, I was lucky enough to be included in fabulous swanky dinners and trips abroad on boats and in posh hotels.

Charles liked a famous person and would often invite whoever had taken his fancy to supper. As Harry Enfield once said of him, 'He sees us on the telly and thinks, I'm SO rich and influential I will make them come to dinner!'

If you are with a famous person or part of their group, you will be treated as though you are in the famous club, although don't expect anyone to ask you anything about yourself. It is an unspoken code that as you clearly qualify to be there, no further enquiry is needed. I often felt my role was to be amusing and to help oil the wheels of conversation. A role I was happy to play as it allowed me to see a world I was unfamiliar with.

Once, when arriving at a restaurant for dinner (I never knew who would be there), I was seated next to actor and comedian Steve Martin. 'Charles tells me you're one of the funniest women in London,' he said. 'That's right,' I replied, refusing to rise to the challenge. We went on to have an interesting chat about the writing he was doing for the *New Yorker* magazine. 'They just always want funny,' he said. 'They are really not that keen on my serious stuff.' He was with his girlfriend who was a fact-checker on the same magazine. 'The funny is good,' she said, 'save the serious for when you're old and not funny anymore.'

Another such dinner at the Ivy and I was seated next to Cilla Black (very much category C). I felt she didn't like it when I called her Cilla, despite that being her name. I was sitting at a table with her. Was I meant to say Miss Black? A not unpleasant woman but from a different time perhaps. She seemed a bit sad and really only came alive when the conversation was about her. I never mentioned that I had seen her at the Winter Gardens in Blackpool when I was ten and had scurried backstage to wait for autographs. She swept out of the stage door wearing a massive fur coat and got into a gold Rolls Royce. Things were different then. I don't think I ever got her autograph.

A famous actor who shall remain nameless once confided, 'My old friends don't ring me up anymore because they're convinced I will be doing something exciting with other actors, when in reality I'm eating Pot Noodles, watching telly and feeling a bit lonely.'

It's often assumed that one changes on attaining fame and money but it's other people who suddenly see you achieve success and behave differently around you.

On holiday in Italy with the Saatchi Lawsons, Michael Douglas dropped in for lunch. I liked him enormously and asked him about this over our seafood linguine. His response was interesting having come from an acting dynasty and grown up amongst big stars. He said, 'Nothing changes at all. We have the same problems as everyone else. Marriages break up, jobs come and go, people carry on dying, but it is somehow not meant to touch us because we have the fame privilege, as if we live in fairyland.'

There were some very rich men at lunch that day and I loved hearing them talking about deals involving vast amounts of money. It seems that when you get to a certain level of wealth, it's not about the actual money, rather getting one over on the other guy. It's more of a complex game. A dick-swinging exercise, if you will.

I used to take my little Maltese puppy into Radio 2 and had a laminated risk assessment form to prove she wouldn't wee or poo, chew through any wires, or give anyone rabies. Bold claims all and I can't honestly vouch for any of them, apart from the rabies.

The dog was a good icebreaker with guests and she would happily greet all comers with a lick and invariably jump on laps or perform zoomies in the corridor.

I got into the habit of taking pics with the guests holding the dog with half an idea of compiling a book for charity. Dogs are great levellers and don't care a jot who you are. I like to think she was a 'fame therapy' dog. To relax the sometimes uptight or self-important stars who were often surprisingly nervous. When Tony Bennett came in beautifully dressed in a very classy three-piece suit, he held the dog and sang, 'Fly me to the moon and let me live among the stars!' to her, telling me how much he was missing his own Maltese terrier. Tony laughed easily, was proper old school and very, very sexy.

Bradley Cooper was charming and came in with a massive entourage, manager, publicity agent, the whole shebang. He scooped up the dog and was about to pose for a picture when his publicity wonk said, 'No! He is doing his own dog book for charity.' Bradley looked apologetic and shrugged a sorry at me. I guess everyone has to justify their salary, although I've yet to see the Bradley Cooper charity dog book on the shelves.

One of the nicest and funniest chaps in show biz is Richard E Grant. I interviewed him on a magazine show called *Sixthirtysomething*, back in the early nineties. He invited me and my co-presenter Ann Bryson to see him in *The Importance of Being Earnest* in London's West End. Then he took us to dinner at Joe Allen's and regaled us with funny stories about Maggie Smith who had played Lady Bracknell. Because Richard was in the classic film *Withnail and I*, he would get a massive round of applause at the curtain call, irritating for the other actors but not really his fault. Richard was also on the Saatchi Lawson supper rota many years later where I got to know his lovely wife Joan and daughter Olivia. He is a force for good.

There are some famous folk who are, as they say in the business, 'never off'. Always having to entertain and be the centre of attention. While in New York with Graham Norton, we had drinks in a beautiful town house with Carrie Fisher. Graham had become friends with her after she appeared on his television show (something he rarely does, viewing his chat show as his job rather than a social directory). Carrie was charming and gracious, extremely funny and told great stories about her mum Debbie Reynolds, her dieting tribulations and *Star Wars*. Any attempt at conversation or interruption for further enquiry, however, was met with an awkward silence. Carrie was the main speaker, that's what she did and she was extremely proficient at it.

Robin Williams was another who never seemed to want a day off from being Robin Williams. He came into Radio 2 and was a brilliant on-air guest.

Even sitting in the green room with him was exhausting though, as he would rattle through a selection of funny voices and maniacal impressions until you either wanted to give him a hug to stop the madness or yell, 'Shut up! Just be normal, there isn't an audience here!'

It is the permanent show-offs that probably find it all very hard. I imagined him going back to his hotel room and staring at the wall in morose existential terror.

My brief window into the world of fame came when I was on TV a fair bit in the mid-90s. People would ask for autographs and photographs and I always felt a bit fake and that what they had seen on their living-room TV screens was not what they were getting in real life. I think I understood the drink and drug conundrum then. Booze and barbiturates alleviate all that pressure and give you back some agency over who you are. So many young folk want to be famous and it can be extremely lonely and frightening up there on that hallowed cloud. The trick is to hold on tight to who you are and keep old friends around you to tease out any pretensions. Easier said than done, I know.

Some of my favourites during my window to the world of celebrity at Radio 2 were Armistead Maupin; funny and clever, Roger Moore; very wry sense of humour and utterly charming, Olivia Colman; exactly as you see her, Sarah Lancashire; down to earth and easy to laugh, James Norton, sexy as hell and super nice; and Annie Lennox who played the piano and chatted about fripperies in between songs.

There were only a few divas and it would be ungallant of me to name names. Everyone has an off day and sometimes the pressure can get to you.

The stars and celebrities of today are generally more humble than yesteryear and are fully aware that everyone will take away a memory of good OR bad behaviour. Besides, it's really not that hard to be kind, is it?

Chapter 12

Daniel:

Mountain Bike

'If you tell the truth, you don't have to remember anything'
– Mark Twain

In 1991 I met Daniel.

The Girls from Quimley Lodge was the name of a television pilot I was involved with in 1991. It was written and performed by Jenny Eclair, Julie Balloo and me. Early on in the shoot I became aware of a very kindly floor manager.

He was called Daniel; was six-foot-four and more than a little handsome. I had shied away from all relationships since Mark died because my heart was a little bit ouchy and, whilst there had been a few contenders, the cancel clause became my modus operandi at the first sign of anything vaguely serious. *The Girls from Quimley Lodge* was something of a budget production with a lot of filming taking place in hastily arranged locations and a minimal crew. Daniel was the only member of the unit who had a mobile phone (unthinkable now), which was the size of a house brick and a battery that weighed the same. I would often tease him about this piece of modern technology before one day noticing that my teasing had turned into flirting. An almost imperceptible change indicated by a fluttering butterfly tummy.

It was certainly not a glamorous shoot. One role was a female gangster with a fake scar covering my right cheek from eye to mouth, it took so long to construct using liquid collodion that I went out to dinner after filming with it still in place for the following day. We also imagined a day in the life of the Bronte sisters. A pitiful trio with scraped-back, greasy hair, period costumes, failing health, hideous make-up and coughing up small bloodied body parts. Hey, you never know when you're gonna pull.

One day while filming in Richmond Park, full Bronte outfits and make-up, I was chatting to comedian Nick Hancock who was playing Bramwell Bronte, about the fact that I had spent the night with a man who was ten years younger than me. I was feeling and certainly looking very old. 'Do you think it's got legs?' I asked Nick. He looked at me dressed as Anne Bronte and said, 'Look, you can fuck yer mum once but there's no real reason to go back.' Harsh but fair.

It was at the cast and crew screening, while glammed up to the max, that I made my move on the cute floor manager. It wasn't hard and D gave me a sweet, lingering kiss before I clambered, grinning into the taxi home. A few weeks later in my shared apartment in Hammersmith, we threw a Champagne/Perrier party.

This was the early 90s, many chums had been to rehab or Alcoholics Anonymous and this was a way for folk to bring their drink of choice without being urged or tempted to fall off the wagon. The 80s, for those who don't remember, was a time of excess, 'Loads of money' and drink and drugs in plentiful supply.

D had been invited and arrived clutching both Perrier and Champagne, wearing a suit and looking slightly awkward. It was a successful evening in every sense, much fun was had and D spent the night. He had just got out of a long-term relationship and while caution should have been employed by both of us, we threw ourselves into a passionate love affair. We were from very different tribes and friends were surprised by this union.

D liked fast cars, had a penchant for gold chains and was a fan of the cowboy boot. I drove a classic 20-year-old BMW, thought gold was gaudy and mainly wore Doc Martens. Whatever the alchemy needed for two people to click, it seemed to work. Only now with the benefit of hindsight do I know that often we find chameleon partners who mould themselves into what they think is expected of them in order to make the coupling work.

D and I used to mud lark on the Thames when the tide was low and rejoiced in finding objet that may or may not have been Roman pottery, Victorian bracelets, unidentifiable bones or murder weapons. We laughed a lot and took lovely holidays; Ibiza, the Greek islands and frolicked in balmy seas.

On one such occasion, we spotted a man who buried his belongings every night on the beach. Towel, snorkel flippers, blow-up pillow, etc. He would leave a small stick at the exact location then dig it up the following day to resume his water sports. One evening after a cocktail or two, we decided to dig up his possessions, move them 20 metres to the left and re-bury them complete with locator stick. Childish and silly, it made us helpless with laughter. There was no malice intended, we just wanted to mess with his head.

D and I settled into a happy routine back in London and after a year or so began looking for a house to buy. At 34 there was no personal urgency for children but I had a longing to nest and build a home. There was a child in D's previous relationship but questionable paternity had led to the split with his then partner. He was a little cagey about the details so, naturally, it was brushed aside for cheerier matters.

The rundown Edwardian house we settled on in Acton, West London, was once three flats, had been mangled by a selection of builders with dubious credentials and needed gutting. We planned to return it to its former glory with the enthusiasm of folk who have never undertaken such a project before. Restoration was not high on my list of skills as choosing three complete fireplaces from a reclamation yard many miles away proved. Delighted with myself for managing to barter successfully, load them all into my car and position them over the boarded-up chimney breasts for D's return from work, my 'Ta Da! Aren't I clever' moment evaporated fast when

D revealed they were in fact Victorian fireplaces NOT Edwardian and were quite wrong for the house.

We both continued to work, D as a floor manager and me in increasingly better jobs. House progress was slow but life was good, we were having fun and images of children began to creep into the bigger picture. After six months without protection, I sensed something may be amiss. Tests revealed very poor motility in D's sperm. He received this news very sadly and went into a dark place. It was puzzling to me that his mother THEN decided to impart the information that as a baby, D had been diagnosed with undescended testicles.

On doctors' advice, he had undergone an operation to release them. This did not go well, infections and complications had caused considerable damage to his vas deferens (the piping that takes the sperm to be ejaculated) and there had been concerns about his future fertility.

The testicles cannot be close to the body as they get too hot, neither can they be too far away as they get too cold, so it was left to the Goldilocks surgeon to make the incision, release the balls and hope that they were just right.

This was in the olden days and clearly not a very exacting science. For some years now the treatment for this condition has been an injection of the hormone HCG, which causes the stubborn little blighters to abseil down freely to their natural and correct resting place. D was understandably devastated to find out this information at such a late stage. Did he know previously? I wasn't entirely sure, but my Pollyanna instincts took over and we set about finding out what could be done with the information we had.

We saw a specialist. D had to ejaculate into the first of many cups and his seminal fluid was examined under a microscope. We were invited to view this tiny scene and it reminded me of the Battle of the Somme. Dead and dying little chaps littered the slide. Some with no tails, others joined together in the manner of ants assisting injured colleagues back to the nest. Some had been dead a long time or maybe they had never been alive. A few were swimming around in furious circles like beleaguered Red Cross medics attempting rescue of the fallen.

The news was not good. IVF was recommended. D's sperm would be spun centrifugally to eliminate the negative and accentuate the positive. There WERE viable candidates, just not that many. I retain enormous admiration for women who undergo this invasive and heartbreaking procedure multiple times. Daily injections, hospital visits, egg extraction, egg selection, embryo replacement and the heart-ravaging wait for the oh-so-longed-for positive pregnancy test.

In the interests of sanity, our decision was to call a halt after our first failed attempt. The fertility drugs made me weep at baby ducklings and angry enough to call radio stations ranting about the importance of punctuation.

I didn't recognise myself. Life returned to normal but scar tissue and disappointment lurked beneath the surface. I 'thought' we had both resigned ourselves to the no-baby landscape and we made tentative plans to adopt at some time in the future when we were ready for the invasive process of being screened. For now, we would party on.

There was more to life than children. It was the mid-90s and cocaine was very much the drug du jour in the entertainment industry. I dabbled a little but came to the conclusion that this particular drug was both madly expensive and would steal the joy from tomorrow. If you are feeling low, lacking in confidence and need a bit of a lift, cocaine seems the perfect solution but then you need to have more. If you have never been in a room with a group of coked-up fiends, let me illuminate. The volume of noise will be high. Everyone will be engaged in animated chatter, stories will be told and hearty laughter enjoyed. Return to that room two hours later and the volume will now be at number 11.

Invariably the same anecdotes will be being regurgitated, perhaps in different groups until by the end of the evening, everyone will have drunk their body weight in booze and used up all the words in their agitated brains. There will be a reluctance to go home, dealers will be called and the party will move on to a new club that stays open till 5am. No one will remember anything anyone said in the morning or even at the time they heard it. In 1995 cocaine was £60 a gram. D got promoted to the role of producer and was working with a comedy actor well known for being a little difficult.

I knew he was struggling as his gentle temperament was not suited to this new job. You have to be pretty tough as a producer and a lot of producing involves saying 'No' to egocentric turns who can't understand why there isn't enough money in the budget to recreate the moon landings. One day when I visited D in his office, he was so distraught that he removed a large, framed poster of the aforementioned comedy actor and smashed it to the ground, sending shards of glass all over the room.

During this rather fraught period we were spending a lot of time apart as I was away on tour with a play that would be coming into the West End (it never did).

Unbeknown to me, D was taking increasing amounts of cocaine, staying out until dawn and returning to work at nine in the morning. When I returned from the tour, he looked bloated and ill, was irritable a lot of the time and too tired to participate in ordinary life.

Like a lot of couples do, we popped our problems onto a shelf, to be dealt with another day, afraid of delving too deep, confrontation and having to act on the outcome of potentially damaging conversations.

I was about to turn 40, something of a milestone apparently, and a reminder that you are no longer a young flibety gibb.

Chapter 13

Being 40:

White Mountain Bike

When Jean (my mum) hit 40, she had a light perm, purchased a selection of crimplene suits and kind of gave up on her own existence. 'It's all about my children now,' she would comment, to anyone foolish enough to ask.

For me hitting 40 was, and is, everything I had feared and it also heralded one of the craziest decades imaginable.

As 40th birthday parties go, mine was a relatively small gathering. A few years before, I attended a very grand affair thrown by TV's Angus Deayton. Angus was very famous at the time and had assembled the great and the good for a wild night atop the Eiffel Tower in Paris. It was a tremendous evening of fun and laughter, until a massive cake was wheeled out from the kitchen along with many photographers with flashbulbs madly taking pictures of the astonished guests. The cake read Happy Birthday Angus from the *Daily Mirror*. Quite how they had found out about this event I have no idea but it changed the atmosphere and everyone became very cross and guarded. Was it a tip-off or a tacit agreement with a fee to fill the paper with pics of famous folk? We never got to the bottom of it. Interestingly, the *Daily Mirror* with its fulsome greetings was the very same paper that brought Angus down some months later with its reporting of extra-marital affairs and drugs. They build you up and cut you down in the blink of an eye. As they say in the film of the same name, 'FAME costs and this is where you start paying.'

My party was in no way such a swanky affair but a glorious

celebration of still being alive. If life begins at 40, I feared I had used up an awful lot of it ahead of time.

My obligatory, 'Yay, I don't look 40!' party was held at a private club in London with friends new and old.

I was sporting a sort of half bob, shorter at the back with a floppy front (very wrong hair), a soft, sequinned, fitted shift and a satin jacket. The only relevant point of this being that I'd had some notion that you should change up your style once you're four decades in and wear age-appropriate clothes. Neither item was ever worn again.

I didn't have children but had lovely friends, an old rundown London house that was being rebuilt from scratch and work was plentiful. Decent amounts of money meant an easier life.

The sensible part of my head told me that unless you hit the big time by the age of 40, career choices thereafter would begin to dwindle. As a woman, however successful you are, opportunities are fewer anyway, owing to our obsession with youth and the fear of seeing real life and real ageing onscreen. I wasn't in the position of many of my friends and contemporaries who could command large fees, so essentially I was a jobbing actor. Nothing wrong with that.

The main obstacle to this lofty ambition of being famous at 40 was that I really wasn't prepared to make the necessary sacrifices that being famous required. I didn't want or need it enough, it certainly was way down the list in terms of importance.

The career was going OK: sitcoms, theatre, presenting jobs and voiceovers. I was unexpectedly offered Channel 4's *Big Breakfast* with Chris Evans at its inception in the early 90s, which could have been a game-changer.

My decision to turn it down was threefold. One, because they wouldn't give me financial parity with Chris Evans, and two, regrettably, for love.

Daniel was my first proper boyfriend since Mark had died. I was reassessing what was important in life and getting up at 2am every morning meant we would barely see each other.

I had also taken part in the pilot with Chris. He was a force of nature and I liked him a lot, but my instincts told me that it wouldn't necessarily be an easy ride. While it was a fantastic opportunity on many levels, my heart was still sore and I wanted to avoid further bumps in the road.

Showbiz in every form just seemed too Machiavellian, once you removed the showing-off part, the part I like most. It was all who was being paid what, deals being made with agents, where you would be placed on the credits, 'don't mention your salary to anyone else as he or she is being paid much less' type of thing.

Such tedium began to make me feel hemmed in and uncomfortable. Essentially, one becomes a product that needs marketing, PR, photoshoots and magazine articles.

There was always a lot of bottom-crawling required in order to get a writer or director to see you for a part. I was quite well known in the comedy world, but I was also known for strong union principles and didn't take any nonsense.

There were certainly women not averse to the casting couch.

Whilst it's not my place to condemn their choices (a girl's gotta eat) I also felt pursuing that particular route made it harder for all of us and it was tough enough already.

This was a long time before the #MeToo movement and one's moral and sexual behaviour was a personal thing. My own code of conduct was not to sleep with anyone on a job and never to mess with a married man. It really wasn't that hard to stick to. Yes, I often played bubble-headed blondes, made jokes and did a bit of flirting, but that little Catholic girl was still lurking inside.

My absolute favourite part of acting is the rehearsal period. Mucking about with other actors, endless lunchtime anecdotes and drinks in the pub.

I would happily and willingly spend six weeks rehearsing a play or TV adaptation on the proviso it was never to be performed or filmed. That, in my humble opinion is the dull bit, full of waiting around in tiny caravans or overpriced rooms of crazy chintz with rosy-cheeked landladies listening at your door. Climbing the greasy pole towards success is the necessary process in order to reach the elusive state of fame that so many strive for. What they find is an empty goldfish bowl and a permanent fear that they may lose their position and status. I never really wanted to inhabit that world.

My old mucker Graham Norton once told me, 'When I was young, I always used to think people were looking at me, and now, they are. That's about it.'

Graham was also at my 40th party with his then American boyfriend Scott. Scott had just applied for British citizenship and along with doctors, lawyers, pillars of the community, I had been tasked with writing a letter to the Home Office to convey the reasons he should stay. My missive was suitably flowery, filled with quotes about love, Romeo and Juliet and the terrible consequences the denial of love could bring.

Almost certainly, I had been allotted the mad actress slot. Scott's request was subsequently granted, but some years later, unable to cope with being the partner of 'fame', he returned to America to conduct 'Death Tours' of Hollywood homes.

Many friends and acquaintances lived close to our tumbledown house of horror in Acton. It became a lovely melting pot of creativity and we drank and had dinner in each other's houses most nights.

I had re-established my connection with the journalist John Diamond, a brilliant writer and raconteur. We had often appeared on TV and radio shows as 'talking heads' (anyone with an opinion who can confidently complete a sentence without the ums and ahs of doom).

John was always brilliant company, usually bedecked in some cad-about-town polo neck and pinstripe suit from the latest tailor du jour. He may not have been conventionally handsome, but the shortest of time spent in his company could charm the hardest of hearts.

I didn't know for a long time he was married to Nigella Lawson (punching) but through our Acton neighbours Simon and Olivia, we quickly became part of the West London set. (There was no such thing really, other than to our rather over inflated opinions of ourselves.)

I still rattled around on my custom-built mountain bike, but John persuaded me to buy a Vespa scooter in matt black. He also had one in the campest, shiniest baby blue and would hurtle over to the house with Nigella riding pillion. She would shake her tresses free from the helmet, smile from ruby-red lips and all the boys would swoon clean away.

We nicknamed ourselves the 'Middle Youth Club' for that is exactly how we saw things. Not yet ready to settle into a comfortable suburban existence, yet also not in the first flush of youth.

We were a group of moderately successful forty-somethings resistant to acknowledging the next phase of life. What even WAS that? Some of my mum's generation wrote themselves off, but for us the parameters were not especially clear. Even though we were all loath to leave our youth behind, older, grown-up concerns like ill health began to creep in.

John had been diagnosed with cancer some months earlier. Not getting himself checked out when a small lump appeared on his lower jaw proved a costly oversight. So far, so male.

This cancer proved to be stubborn and he was advised to have part of his tongue removed to prevent further spread.

Of all the parts of the body one could supposedly live without, for John this was especially cruel. As someone who made their living with words, no longer able to speak was devastating. It also meant no longer being able to eat.

Nigella would whizz up fantastic concoctions in the blender for him, but however you slurp it, soups and milkshakes get pretty tedious.

Ice cream, peanut butter, protein powder, milk and cream would be spun to perfection, a mix of high-calorie yumminess hard to resist.

Like most things in life though, you always want what the others are having.

I have a vivid recollection of sitting in their leafy garden on a balmy summer's day, two small children gambolling happily and

Nigella preparing dinner for ten friends. A picture-perfect scene, except that it wasn't. John was never a wallflower, loved a good discussion, employed a rapier wit and was always centre stage.

He was now reduced to a shadowy figure organising drinks and looking on balefully while the conversation whizzed around him.

He had endless moleskin notebooks that he would scribble in with some quip or other, but it badly affected any sense of timing. Salman Rushdie once looked at what John had written and instead of replying with his actual VOICE, took out a pen and wrote down his reply. Why would he do that? He could speak.

I could tell that it annoyed John enormously and I tried to mollify him by saying, 'Maybe with the fatwah, Salman feels silenced too?' He replied, 'Fuck off, I've got cancer.'

John could still speak as his voice box was intact, but it was without the essential vowel sounds that the tongue produces. This made him nigh on impossible for most folk to understand.

Nigella could decipher fairly well and I learned pretty quickly. Confident while a conversation was mid-flow, anticipation, speech pattern recognition and guesswork, but if he went off on a tangent I was lost.

It often made me laugh that Nigella would refuse to translate if there were swear words involved. John would then look to me and I would dutifully interpret. John said, 'I can't just sit around gabbing, I've got a book to write, so could you lot kindly fuck off!'

Inevitably, after one hospital checkup, John was told that his cancer was now terminal. We all knew this would be the outcome but no one ever said it out loud. It was a blow that took the wind from his sails.

While he was able to vent a lot of his fury and sadness in a weekly Saturday *Times* column, 800 words a week on your impending death, told in a pithy, dry and humorous fashion is never really going to be enough to ameliorate the injustice and sorrow.

I would often be sitting at home on a weeknight, pyjama-ed and be-slippered, before getting an email or text that read simply, 'Let's go ice skating! Love John.' Should you be foolish enough to reply, 'Oooh, can't mate, have work tomorrow,' he would fire back with, 'I'll be dead soon!'

Ice skating it was!

In fact we did ALL the things that would now be called a bucket list. Drank in London clubs till four, whizzed about on our Vespas like elderly mods, attended openings, first nights and book launches with lusty abandon.

It was at the book launch for Nigella's first cooking tome, *How to Eat*, that the wizard of a maître d' at One Aldwych (then the latest cool restaurant) taught John how to administer vodka straight into his PEG or abdominal-based feeding tube. An act of great intimacy and kindness that unleashed the beast of booze.

The Middle Youth Club decided on a trip to St Petersburg in Russia. John, Nigella, Daniel and me, our neighbours Simon a book reviewer, his wife Olivia a documentary maker, comedian Arthur Smith and his girlfriend the artist Nicola Green.

When someone is dying, immediate gratification is kind of all there is and we grasped every opportunity.

St Petersburg was very badly broken. Which seemed apposite. Buses ran with broken doors and bumpers adrift, nothing worked as it should and all infrastructure was held together with rubber bands and the tourist dollar.

Daniel adored John Diamond, they were good buddies. They both went together to the tattoo parlour and got ridiculous inkings and then decided to bleach their hair blond. John had a no longer treatable cancer and was cavalier about such fripperies so Daniel happily went along for the ride.

We bought military uniforms, vintage babushka hats of rabbit fur, overpriced tchotchke, 1970s fashions, rose-gold jewellery and teeny tiny Russian dolls with increasingly miniscule contents.

Pole dancing clubs were everywhere. If you couldn't afford the entrance fee you could visit a pole dancing 'training' establishment that mainly operated in the afternoons and were very popular with

Russians. The girls may not have been as hot and would often fall off the poles, but they were full of goodwill and laughter.

The Middle Youth Club had a very clear division of those wanting trips to the Church of Blood, Hermitage, culture, etc. and the deadbeats who stayed up till five at clubs, bars and casinos. Breakfast was usually a charming history lesson from the smugs and a hazy recounting of the previous evening's drunken escapades from the vodka enthusiasts. I was in the latter camp.

On our return John was back in hospital. To give Nigella a break and time to spend with her husband, Daniel and I often had the kids for the weekend. An opportunity to gain insight as to the kind of parents we would have been.

D would be in the garden with boy child, pulling out weeds, kicking balls, daubing a snail with children's blue paint and chucking it over the fence. The amazement on a tiny face when said snail arrived back in the flower beds the following day was priceless and has yet to be replicated (trickery may have been at play).

Girl child and I would be upstairs cutting up purple suede dresses or long abandoned bell bottoms. These would be turned into small miniskirts and bandeau tops. Old 80s shoulder pads came in useful as pretend bras which are extremely important when you're six. The makeshift outfits would then be worn in front of the six-foot (picked up at auction) triptych shop mirror where our multiple selves could spend hours dancing and singing in the style of Bananarama. Dressing up at 40 is exactly the same amount of fun as it is at six.

Dinner would involve zooming off for pizza in the battered old Saab convertible with commands from the tinies to 'Put the roof down!' Despite the freezing wind turning the children blue, they revelled in this newfound exhilaration. They called it the 'Coolie car' and it certainly was. It seems kids don't mind chattering teeth and hypothermia, as long as they are going fast and squealing themselves hoarse. Seeing them so happy made me want to stop time, knowing as I did, the loss that lay ahead for these tiny beings.

As John's health began to deteriorate, some of the middle youth club relationships also began to crumble as we all contemplated where we were in the world. John didn't have much of a future and it forced us into examining our own. Lives looked at in sharp focus reveal hitherto unknown fractures.

The six-mile cycle from Acton to Soho was a great way to mull things over. I still preferred to cycle rather than use the Vespa as it gave me a greater sense of achievement and was easier to park.

Along with remembering that all car drivers are out to kill you, a bicycle will remind you of possibilities and freedoms. A chance to order your thoughts as you negotiate the terrain. A 40-minute cycle involves in all probability a thousand split-second decisions. Did I indicate? Is that lorry turning left, can I get out in time, what's that wanker doing? Why is that car in the bus lane? Ooh, Debenhams have a sale on! That's a nice bike he's got. Oooh, hello handsome! Lights! Please stay green, please stay green! These feckin slippy gears! Think my front tyre maybe soft. Ooh, sorry! Squeaky brakes, didn't mean to make you jump. He's gonna open his driver's door without looking! Why are my legs ouchy today? Where am I gonna lock this boneshaker? What's going on in my life?

Travelling on my bike was always a good place for self-examination and to work through the problems of the day. Being preoccupied with safety was just enough of an activity to allow a sidebar of analysis. Aided by the necessary intake of oxygen to the lungs and body, dilemmas were quickly dealt with. Even now when life gets tangly, I will take myself off for a 40-minute cycle which never fails to make life sweeter.

John and I had begun writing a play for the Edinburgh Festival, which I was planning to perform. A venue had been booked and we would meet most afternoons to work on the content.

It was a good distraction for John, but we were both very easily sidetracked from the actual task in hand by gossip, the internet, mucking about and the endless laughter of small amusements. Whilst I never made it to Edinburgh, I value that time enormously. The play was only half finished when John became too ill to continue.

Watching someone as vibrant as he was, becoming small and sick and knowing that nothing could be done seemed to be a process of delusion for everyone involved. Encouraging words were all we had which were necessary to maintain the important and necessary sense of hope.

There was a car crash coming that would impact everyone in the vehicle.

John was holding onto life with every ounce of his being, he researched new and outlandish cancer cures that would hold back the growth of these killer cells, all the while knowing that time was running out. To the outside world and anyone who asked he presented a seemingly unshakeable belief that the next treatment tried would be the one to fix things. It would have been heartless to disagree. Early one morning, without significant warning, John's carotid artery ruptured and he was rushed to hospital. There was talk of surgery, which carried ridiculous risks but nothing could really be done. Time was up.

We all rushed to hospital to say our goodbyes. A ridiculous notion for all concerned. He was laughing and joking and told me he had bequeathed his stockpiled morphine to me in his will. I like to think it was the morphine in his drip which gave him hope and humour in those final hours.

John died at the beginning of March 2001 surrounded by his wife Nigella and friends. It was a room filled with love and laughter and just what he would have wanted, other than to have been joining in and leaving hospital.

Even though it was clear that John would not be having a happy ending to his cancer journey, the effect of his death was devastating, like a hand grenade had been chucked into everyone's lives. That's what death does. His is not my story to tell so I will leave it there.

Hitting 40 is a point in life where you take stock.

It is the beginning of middle age.

Many years ago when I wrote a piece for the *Sunday Times* about 'The seven ages of man', I went out on a date with a series of men in their 20s, 30s, 40s, and so on, into the 80s.

It was an illuminating exercise but faintly predictable. The only fella that troubled me was the chap in his 40s. Having much of his life and ambitious plans mapped out ahead of him, it was all going according to plan until he hit that difficult age of 40. His marriage broke down, he lost a very good job and his life looked bleak.

He was forced to go back to the drawing board. It was for him, as it is for many of us, a time for reinvention. Dissatisfied with how the future is panning out, the urge to tear up the blueprint and undertake something crazy is very tempting.

It's not called a mid-life crisis for nothing.

For me, with no children on the horizon decisions were needed. I didn't want to retrain as a therapist, learn to speak Russian or relocate to an isolated croft on a remote Scottish island, but I DID want to live by the sea.

Once the idea had popped into my head, it wouldn't leave and I knew I had to make it happen.

Chapter 14

Daniel Goes Mad:

White Mountain Bike

We had all been floored by the death of our lovely friend John Diamond and were trying our best to help Nigella deal with her sadness and the bewilderment of the children. Life goes on but grief sits like unwanted indigestion in the solar plexus; ever present. Daniel was not in a good way, staying out late, almost certainly hitting the drugs and masking his own obvious pain.

One evening he came home very late and clearly high. His pupils were dilated and he was shielding his left eye. I asked him to show me what was wrong with his eye and he revealed a deep two-inch gash just above the eyebrow. It was still bleeding and dripping down into his eyes and his cheek.

'God, Daniel! Have you been in a fight?' I asked. Horrified that he could well have been blinded.

'No. I did it myself,' he replied.

'What?'

'I did it myself.'

'How? How did you do that?'

'With this knife.'

He showed me a now bloodied Swiss Army knife that was congealing around his fingers. This was above my pay grade. He seemed almost triumphant. I didn't know what to do.

'Why don't you go and clean it up and I'll pop out and get us a couple of beers,' I said, trying to stay calm and rational.

'No, don't go out,' he said. 'You should stay here.'

'Look, I'll be five minutes and I'll pick up some plasters at the shop.'

I grabbed my purse and ran to the little off-licence.

Ahmed our local shopkeeper could see I was in distress.

'I'm really sorry,' I gasped, 'but can I use your phone? I'll pay you, it's an emergency.'

I rang Daniel's mum.

'Can you come over! He has cut himself, above his eye, it looks really bad, I don't know what to do,' I garbled into the mouthpiece.

'Oh God, really? Yes, we'll be there in 15 minutes,' she said.

I hastily picked up some cans of beer, left a tenner, forgot the plasters and thanked Ahmed in a manner that would indicate he had just rescued a drowning dog.

When D's mum had said 'we', that meant she would be bringing her husband, D's stepfather. Not a good plan. It wasn't a social occasion, rather an urgent need to understand the cause of this action of self-harm.

I was back at the house in five minutes. D had not bothered to clean up the wound but was sitting on the sofa watching *Newsnight*. I whizzed to the bathroom for cotton wool and antiseptic, thrusting it at him along with the just purchased can of Pilsner.

'Daniel, what's happened? Why have you cut yourself like this? Are you in pain?'

Asking the obvious is never really a good idea.

'I don't want to talk about it,' he said, before adding, 'Paxman is on REALLY good form tonight!'

The doorbell rang. I ushered in his mum and bemused stepfather, hoping in some way we could resolve this and make it all better. Daniel remained seated and didn't look in any way surprised at visitors showing up just before 11pm.

'Daniel has cut himself,' I announced to everyone who could see or feel for themselves.

This pointless remark was ignored.

'Oh, I LOVE what you've done to this dining room,' said his

mum. 'The blue and yellow work SO well together.'

I stared at her.

'Did you manage to get the bathroom finished? I can't wait to see your freestanding bath.'

With that Daniel got up and said, 'Yes, it's finished. I'll show you.'

I watched the three of them traipse up the stairs to the newly finished bathroom and shouted weakly after them, 'I'll make some tea!'

Unable to comprehend this weird sitcom I had found myself in, I wondered if I was overreacting? A man had slashed his face and now all the actors had gone off-script and there was blood dripping on the stair carpet.

It really didn't seem funny at all.

We had tea, there was small talk, it all seemed so insane that I wanted to cry.

Newsnight finished and his mum and stepfather said they had better go.

As I saw them out, I hissed, 'But nothing has been said!'

His Mum just whispered, 'Let's just stay calm, I'll meet you in town tomorrow and we'll talk about it then.'

Daniel was washing up the cups when I returned, dried blood now caking his brow.

'I'm going to have a bath,' he said, before adding, 'It's nothing, don't worry about it.'

That night I dreamed of counselling sessions in NHS mental institutions. The other patients were the cast of the *Good Life*. Margo (Penelope Keith) kept trying to talk about her stolen kaftan while Tom, Barbara and Jerry claimed that she had made a mistake, she had probably just mislaid her kaftan. Tom said, 'Anyway, Margo, kaftans make you look fat!' and Barbara (Felicity Kendal) said, 'Oh, Tom!'

I met Daniel's mum Helen in a coffee shop in Soho the following morning. She affected the same air as the previous evening.

'Helen, he is SELF-HARMING! Something is very badly wrong,' I said, rather too loudly.

'You have to understand he is not strong,' she said.

And she told me a little bit about her life.

Daniel's father, Brian, a left-wing writer, had, in the 60s, worked at the BBC writing plays and one-off dramas. His plays were often compared to those of John Osborne in the 'angry young men' bracket, but his success was fleeting. The commissions dried up somewhat as Brian's politics became too troublesome for the then rather staid BBC commissioning editor.

She told me that Brian had been given away by his mother at birth and placed in a never-ending selection of institutions. He had never found out why and had no interest in trying to trace her. This had obviously had a massive impact on his life.

I met Brian many times and found him to be an interesting, clever man, but troubled. He was extremely argumentative, often just for the sake of it, didn't like women and could often be nasty and spiteful both to me and Daniel, then act as if nothing had happened. Despite this, Daniel adored him.

Brian would apparently disappear for days on end; once being returned to the house by the police in a panda car with hay in his hair. Another occasion he painted his entire ground-floor office black, including the windows, and refused to come out for weeks. He would creep out when everyone was in bed to get food. Daniel and his younger brother Simon would often go into the garden and attempt to peer through the blackened windows for a glimpse of their beloved dad. In today's world Brian would almost certainly have been diagnosed with some form of personality disorder, but in the 60s everyone just got on with it.

Helen struggled when she recounted that Brian was a violent and controlling man.

When Helen and Brian married, they quickly had two boys but the marriage was very turbulent. Brian's rage at his inability to have work performed was a major factor. Although Helen worked, money was always tight. She told me she became used to the beatings and whilst she tried to protect the boys from the full reality, she was sure they knew.

Daniel told me subsequently that he would put his hands over his ears to drown out her screams, never knowing if he would wake up in the morning and she would be dead. He told me he lived in two realities. One was the horror of the late-night beatings and the other was a return to normality the following morning, where his mum would set out the breakfast cereal with a bruised and battered face and act as if nothing had happened.

Brian's control and violence only got worse. There were affairs with other women, mental cruelty and Helen was hospitalised on more than one occasion. She would often be forced to send the boys away to stay with their grandparents until her wounds had healed.

There was the same glimmer of triumphalism in Helen's voice that I had noticed the night before in Daniel. It dawned on me that these behaviours, however unpleasant, were in themselves addictive.

I tried to put it to Helen that there was clearly some level of co-dependency in her relationship with Brian, and I asked her why she didn't leave? She explained; these situations are immensely complex and being a single woman with two children in the 60s was not as easy as it is in today's world. Also, she loved him.

Helen told me that Daniel had cut himself previously, it was some form of release in times of stress and anxiety. I remembered there were two silvery scars above his right eye that I had asked him about when we first got together. 'Old rugger injuries,' he had laughed, 'rugby can be pretty dangerous!'

It made me very sad and frightened that inside this lovely, kind and beautiful man there was such pain and rage, feelings that could only be released with acts of disfiguring self-harm.

I said goodbye to Helen and agreed that some form of therapy was the way forward. A safe place to unravel and confront unpleasant memories.

We all have difficult and often troubled backgrounds, but it's how we process these traumas that allows us to move forward. We can choose to be defined by unpleasant events or we can refuse to allow our past to rob the joy from tomorrow.

I rushed home and made a call to a therapist friend. His advice was to tread carefully. He emailed me this paragraph:

Cutting is a tool used for the release of anger and pain. Often patients feel their blood is boiling or fizzing and needs to be cooled or stilled. The pain of the wound is a physical one, which momentarily alleviates psychological anguish. Patients cut all over the body; arms, legs, torso, genitalia. The resulting scars are like permanent sticking plasters, the war wounds of life, forever visible. The world (others) can't physically see pain but it can nonetheless witness the havoc that pain has wrought.

I sat for an hour with my thoughts. The truth was that after nine years I didn't know who this person was. A slow and agonising realisation that I was frightened both of him, and for him.

Daniel bounded in from work that night as if nothing had happened. The slash above his eye was vivid red with the beginnings of a scab starting to form on its edges. Neither of us mentioned it. He regaled me with the latest tales of the tricky actor and how the world really needed to know what a monstrous c*** he was. We laughed, then had dinner and opened a bottle of wine.

'I'm so sorry things are difficult and unpleasant for you,' I said, 'but I think you should probably have some form of therapy.'

'Why? How is that going to help,' he said, simultaneously channel-hopping.

'Because I am frightened. Because I don't fully understand and I don't know how to make things better.'

I was trying not to cry. He could hear the tremor in my voice and suddenly looked very vulnerable.

'OK,' he said. 'I'm sorry.'

Easier than I had expected. It fell to me to try and find someone suitable, which I did and on the same day once a week Daniel went (or not) to therapy.

We only spoke about it on one occasion when I casually asked if it was helping. A redundant and impotent question. He replied that, yes, he thought it was and the matter was closed.

Life went on in all its silliness, Daniel seemed more settled, his wound healed, the job with the monstrous c*** came to an end. I went off to do a play in Ipswich (glamour) and Daniel got another job that in every regard should have been easier. He came to visit me in Ipswich for the first night, we had fun with the cast and, although a little distant, he gave the impression that all was well.

When I returned to London, he looked pretty rough. The same grey puffiness and an air of disinterest. I jokingly asked him if he had been having an affair while I was away, but he laughed and said, 'If only I had the time!'

He would stay at work very late and leave early in the mornings. Weekends were spent doing work on the house which was now becoming a tedious bore and we nicknamed it 'the house of horror'.

On a few occasions he wouldn't come home at all and would call to say he was staying in town as there was a production meeting/ recce/casting/wardrobe call/crew run-through, or some such, that was taking place very early in the morning and it made sense to stay.

Then one night he didn't come home and neither did he call. Things had been slipping, we were losing our way. I was very worried and left him endless messages. Where are you? Is everything OK? I am worried, please let me know you are safe? Nothing came back.

The following day I called the office. They hadn't seen him and he had missed a meeting. At 4pm the phone rang. I could barely make out the thin voice on the other end.

'It's me.'

'Where are you? Has something happened?'

'I'm in Hyde Park.'

'What? Why? What are you doing there? Are you OK?'

'No.'

'What's happened? Get in a cab, come home. I've got cash.'

'The cabs won't take me.'

'What? Why? Where in Hyde Park are you?'

'I'm under a tree.'

'Why won't the cabs take you, Bub?'

'Because I'm covered in blood.'

'Christ, where is the tree? I'm coming to get you.'

'My battery's dying.'

'Where is the TREE, Daniel?!'

Having established the location, I tried to pick up my car keys, but was shaking so much I didn't think I would be able to drive. I rushed to my neighbour's and begged Simon, D's friend, to go and collect him. He left immediately, looking shocked and frightened.

In the time it took to bring him back, I called Clouds rehabilitation centre. Whilst I knew nothing concrete, I absolutely KNEW it was something drugs related and needed to get him help as soon as possible. Then I cancelled my 5pm voiceover citing a family emergency. They were quite cross, it was late in the day, the studio had been booked and I was letting them down. I started to cry, to say sorry, to explain that my partner was in crisis. It all sounded so ridiculously middle-class and twattish. I hated them, myself and D. What a ridiculous cliché.

D arrived back in a dreadful state. His face looked pulverised and his shirt and jeans were soaked in blood. Simon helped him out of his clothes while I ran a bath and provided a bin liner for the bloodied garments. It flashed through my mind that we could be destroying evidence, had someone been killed? Were we now accessories? Should I just call the police, an ambulance? Jeremy Kyle?

'Daniel, is anyone else involved in this?' was all I could muster.

'No.'

We sat him down, I gave him brandy and a dressing gown, his hair was matted in clumps. I touched his face and he winced. There on his left cheekbone were two deep cuts an inch apart. Parallel lines of blood, flesh and sinew. He looked like he had been glassed. Then on his right cheek a perfect match. Two more deep, angry, bloodied gashes. What had he done to his beautiful face? Despite the shock, I remember thinking how amazingly symmetrical they were, had he done this looking in a mirror?

With neighbour Simon's help, we cleaned up his face as best we could and got him in the bath. I sat on the chair beside him and he hung his head. Large globules of blood dripped into the water from wounds now opened after being cleaned.

'We will have to take you to hospital for stitches,' I whispered.

'No! I'm not going to hospital.'

'Well, to the doctor's then, perhaps he could manage with butterfly stitches . . .'

'NO! I'm not going.'

What do you do with a six-foot-four broken man who is bleeding into the bath? Why didn't he cut his arms, legs, stomach? Why did he cut his face where everyone would forever see the scars? It looked like some form of tribal ritual the village elders would perform on a young man about to face a rival foe.

After the bath, I put him to bed, tried as best I could to hold the wounds together while I attempted to attach small strips of plaster. They wouldn't hold. Instead I told him to lay his head back on upright pillows in order to stop the bleeding and help the wounds coagulate.

With gentle coaxing I managed to glean that he had been in the park for 24 hours and had cut himself during that time, underneath a special tree. It seemed that it had been some form of cocaine psychosis, but his memory of the entire time was hazy.

Later that night I called his brother. He agreed to come over the following afternoon. I would be lying if I didn't admit that a small thing in me had broken. I didn't know what or where it was, but it was broken and I wasn't sure I could locate the spare part for repair.

Daniel slept for 16 hours. I called Clouds again and agreed he would be admitted the following day. I packed a suitcase with their approved list of essentials and disposed of the clothes from the crime Daniel had committed against himself and the world.

When he woke, he was agitated and fretful. He wanted nothing but to return to the tree in Hyde Park. This was all feeling surreal but I could think of no reason why he shouldn't be allowed to go back. I called his brother and told him to meet us at the 'special tree'. He was as bemused as I was, but agreed nonetheless.

The three of us sat in balmy sunshine under the tree, an insignificant tree in the middle of Hyde Park. We talked in quiet tones about nothing much.

Daniel cried and his brother and I looked on helplessly.

In the distance I saw a small woman coming towards us waving. She was carrying a picnic hamper and smiling broadly. Daniel's brother Simon saw her, and said, 'Oh, I told Mum we would be here, is that OK?'

Daniel looked horrified but said nothing.

The smiling lady was upon us, picnic basket plonked down and a long, complicated story was regaled about the difficulty finding the grapes that she thought would go perfectly with some brand or other of cheese that she had managed to get from somewhere or other as a special treat.

Her tone was a little desperate, I could see her distress, but why the charade of pretend jolliness?

Daniel got up and said he needed to go for a walk to the fountain but would be back soon.

His wounds, while still angry, had dried a little. They still gaped but looked far better than they had the previous day.

While he was gone, I told his mum about getting him into the Clouds hospital for some rehabilitation and that his cocaine use had gone from recreational to something a little more serious. Then I ate some of the cheese.

Again the feeling of being in some substandard sitcom washed over me.

What was I doing in the middle of a park, under a 'special tree', eating cheese with human beings unable to express any form of appropriate emotion?

Daniel returned. He had clearly been rubbing his wounds, which had now broken away from their tenuous hold on healing and blood was once more oozing from all four of them. No one mentioned it.

It was clear to me with my limited knowledge of pop psychology that they had been opened deliberately for his mother to see the full horror. 'Look at me, Mum. Look at my pain. Please acknowledge that there is something wrong here, I am hurting. Show me that you see it.'

If no one else would, I would.

'D, you have somehow opened your wounds, I think we should go home now,' I said.

We got up, exchanged some tight-lipped goodbyes and drove home in silence.

The following day Daniel was taken to Clouds.

When someone is mentally ill, you don't stop loving them but there is an imperceptible shift. You want them to be safe, to stop hurting and to be well.

You care for them.

Chums rallied round. Support was plentiful and D's boss was sympathetic and understanding. Relieved that he was in the hands of professionals, I was hopeful things could be fixed, issues dealt with and wounds healed.

Three days later, Daniel returned home. He had checked himself out of the facility and called his brother to collect him. I felt panic-stricken.

What next?

A few years previously, D and I had travelled to Eilat in Israel and had boldly decided to undertake a 10,000-foot tandem skydive.

Arriving at the tiny airfield at 7.30am on a brilliantly blue-skied morning, we were given a demonstration whereby D and I were told to lay atop an old pub table before being briefed about the necessary positions our bodies should be in while we were in the air and attached to our instructors. It was alarmingly scant.

We clambered nervously onto the tiny plane, each connected

to someone we had never previously met, looking like chubby Siamese twins. Politics dictated that we must avoid both Egyptian and Jordanian airspace, so it took some time to climb in concentric circles to the required height of 10,000 feet. This time was spent getting to know our individual instructors, in stilted sentences over the noise of the engines.

My main concern was ensuring that mine was of sound mind and didn't intend to kill us both in an act of political defiance.

Throwing oneself out of a plane goes against every piece of life advice you've ever been given about avoiding death. A visceral resistance to a plane, an open door and 10,000 feet of nothingness beneath you.

On leaving the plane, terminal velocity is reached in four seconds where you are travelling at 120 mph. Even if you've undergone the tightest face lift, your facial skin will flap around in the manner of an old, deflated balloon or a Shar-Pei puppy.

'Jump on three,' said the instructor into my left ear, as he shuffled us both to the open door of the plane. We were perched on the edge of the floor with me half sitting on his lap. The only thing going through my mind as we waited for our signal was whether or not it was an erection I could feel in my bottom or just a belt buckle.

'One, two . . .' and then we jumped into the blue nothingness, leaving the noise of the engines behind as we plummeted to the ground. Imagine the highest rollercoaster you've ever been on and the lurch you feel at the peak of the drop when you leave your stomach far, far behind you. Then multiply that lurch by 100.

For a few short moments, I was genuinely worried that I would be sick, cover the instructor's goggles in scrambled egg and render him blind and unable to see when and how to pull the parachute cord.

The body acclimatises remarkably quickly and, just like that, it became amazing. I was flying! Blue sky, mountains, twinkling seas stretched out around me and I felt invincible. I wanted to do tricks, turn somersaults, and scream at the top of my voice 'I'm alive!'

A searing pain in my groin where the straps were attached bought me out of my reverie. The 40 seconds of free fall were over and the parachute had been deployed. If you were to travel in a car at 100 mph then slam on the brakes, that is exactly what happens when the parachute inflates, and to say I felt every ounce of that braking force in my lady garden is something of an understatement.

We floated down at a leisurely pace, me attempting to relieve the pain around my groin by tugging pointlessly at the straps. The thrill was over but the adrenaline was pumping. We landed with a small bump and I momentarily didn't know where or who I was. Helping me to my feet, my instructor asked me how I was feeling. 'High,' I said. 'Like I've just taken a huge amount of drugs. Really, really HIGH!'

So it was that Daniel declared that he needed to get away. Be on his own and that he wanted to go back to Eilat and learn how to solo skydive.

Writing this now, there is a part of me screaming, 'Oh for God's sake, why didn't you put your foot down, say "NO, you are not well, this is not a good idea."'

Yes, you can get a person sectioned but how mad do they need to be?

The therapists at Clouds felt he was no longer a danger to himself or others, so that was it. Off you go, loony tunes.

His brother had paid for the stay at Clouds and I paid for the trip to Israel. Mugs. When someone is in distress, chucking money at the problem is often all you have in your arsenal.

For the entire week he was away, I was mentally preparing myself for the call. 'Yes, he had passed all the tests, undertaken the requisite amount of tandem dives, but on his final solo trip, had failed to use the parachute. We are so very sorry.'

Constant worry is not an ideal way to lose weight but it's certainly very effective.

He pulled the cord, several times, and came home clutching a certificate, 200 fags and a bottle of vodka. He was happy, had a sense of accomplishment, had clearly conquered some internal doubting force and two weeks later he returned to work. Quite how he explained the pink tribal markings, I do not know.

While he was sleeping one morning I looked at the once unblemished skin on his face and cried silent tears at what he had done. The scars would always be there, for both of us.

It's different if you have been in an accident or a fire, but to disfigure yourself deliberately with a sharp knife in such a prominent place haunts me still. I wondered if I would ever stop seeing them.

The broken thing inside me began to hurt. We had arguments and tensions were bubbling under the surface. He would seem perfectly normal and then go into crazy meltdowns; one time throwing a knife that landed at my feet and stuck with a boing in the wooden floorboards between my feet.

Friends told me I should get out. Leave him and get on with life. Hindsight is a wonderful thing, but when you have spent ten years with someone, even when they are hurting you, there is always the possibility that you will get past it and find each other again.

I never really knew if the mad episodes were real, there was a very small voice in my head that questioned this. Was it some ludicrous ploy?

I asked him if there was another woman and he repeatedly told me no. He loved me, once the house of horror was finished, things would get better.

One morning when I reached across him to turn off the alarm, he deliberately burped in my face. That I remember it so vividly seems pertinent. It was unkind, childish and aggressive. Surely we hadn't reached such a low point?

I went away for a few days filming and it felt like something of a relief. When your own life is too problematic, inhabiting the character of a pretend person is preferable. Besides, being on location with other nutty actors is always fun.

Returning early one morning after a night shoot, the house had all its windows flung open and I found Daniel in the bathroom engaged in frantic cleaning. It was 6am.

The cocaine was definitely back, he was manic and unreachable.

At the beginning of June, Daniel left for work while I was still in bed. I remember him bending down for a kiss and me protesting about morning breath.

He said, 'I love you very much,' and left.

Then he was gone. He just never ever came home again.

He didn't contact anyone about where he was. Not his brother, his mother, his friends, and certainly not me. The days and weeks that followed were grim. A Reggie Perrin disappearing act was the last thing I had expected and it felt impossible to navigate all the requisite emotions.

Sadness, anger and grief all rolled together in a great big ball of WTF?

The madness of his disappearance continued to unravel.

He had parked his car in a ridiculous place miles from the house. Why? So that we wouldn't find it? Piecing together information and searching for answers was exhausting. I wandered around the house bereft, opening drawers that may hold clues, going through coat pockets that might reveal tiny details and undertaking forensic recall of the days that preceded the vanishing.

It was while I was going through his wardrobes that I noticed several items of clothing were missing.

They had clearly been removed over a period of time, so as not to be noticed. A glitzy velvet jacket I had given him as a birthday present, shoes, summer shirts; a small childhood train set of some value, that had been stored in the loft had also gone. I wondered how long he had been planning this flit and why on earth he would need a train set?

A letter came from the building society. The house, in both our names, had been remortgaged. I knew nothing of this.

A month after he had left, his credit card statement fell on the mat. Having become Miss Marple super sleuth, I tore it open for vital evidence. There it was, the Bangkok Hilton, one night's stay on the day after he vanished. So he was somewhere in East Asia and he clearly wasn't slumming it.

Along with sadness and anger, I felt very foolish. People would look pityingly at me in social settings and put their heads to the side as if talking to someone bereaved. A few asked for details and I was unable to illuminate. I had been left in a cruel way and that can be embarrassing for everyone. He had gone and it was time for me to rattle around the still unfinished, child-free, five-bedroomed house like a modern day Miss Havisham.

That July I spent with friends in Italy, a much-needed escape and a break from the house of horror to regroup and try to move forward. It was time to put the last ten years behind me and pick up the pieces. I wasn't the first person to be left in this way and I almost certainly wouldn't be the last.

There was comfort to know that I have never been, nor would I ever be, a coward.

The twin towers in New York were destroyed on 11 September 2001. The world was changed forever and still no word from Daniel. He had gone from so many lives, not least those of his family, this could have been a moment of reconciliation, but he remained silent.

There will always remain a feeling of unfinished business and a lack of closure. We all need closure, so writing about it has helped.

Postscript:

After 16 months of silence, I put the house on the market to sell, and D suddenly contacted me for his share. It was the first time I had heard his voice since his abrupt and bizarre departure.

He returned to the house in order to sign the paperwork. I couldn't resist opening the door and saying, 'Your dinner is still in the oven.' Humour will always rescue you.

He married the woman he left me for, but sadly she died last year. I can only feel compassion because I know how that loss feels.

Dealing with a death is certainly no cakewalk but dealing with a disappearance is even harder.

When someone dies, there is a body, a funeral, grief and closure.

When someone completely disappears from your life without trace, the emotions are complex. Frantic worry and concern give way to grief and fury, then sadness and disappointment. This merry-go-round of emotions rampage through your brain 24/7 until nothing makes sense because none of it can be explained.

Of all my life's many and varied events, this is the one I have had to parcel away and put in a box in the metaphorical filing cabinet.

It was impossible to unravel, to gain closure. All attempts to put together the jigsaw puzzle, merely revealed that half the pieces were missing and it looked nothing like the picture on the box.

The cruelty of such an act must be seen to be part of the punishment. This is why, even 21 years on, events and incidents during that time remain seared onto my memory, unchallenged by any other truth. As if they have been suspended in aspic.

I would have loved the opportunity to discuss how it all unravelled, but that has not been possible.

Alfred Lord Tennyson's poem 'In Memoriam' tells us that, 'It is better to have loved and lost, than never to have loved at all', and I believe this to be true. The conundrum remains, how many times can you put yourself through loss before your heart shatters into a thousand pieces?

The protective armour has to be assembled at some point, which makes it difficult for love to penetrate. Protection from one emotion means protection from all.

There have been other relationships of deep and sustaining joy, and life goes on in all its silliness. The decision never to allow the same levels of hurt again has been a subconscious one.

Nb. Names have been changed.

Chapter 15

Copy and Print!

White Mountain Bike

A few weeks after the Daniel debacle, I was invited to dinner with the journalist India Knight in Hackney London. It was a wonderful, warm and chaotic home with two small boys chasing through the kitchen and a large selection of journos in attendance. The late Deborah Orr, her partner Will Self, the writer Andrew O'Hagan, my old pal Graham Norton, and India's ex-husband Jeremy Langmead, among others.

That I felt unable to keep up with the intellectual chit chat of this rarefied gathering saw me revert to humour as a way of not getting left behind with the fast-moving conversation. It was a very jolly evening and Deborah told an amusing anecdote about a night many years previously spent at the Eagle restaurant with questionable service, food returned to the kitchen and a punchline I can't recall.

It was only later that I found out that Graham had been the waiter at Deborah's table that evening. She had behaved appallingly, been extremely rude and he had thought less of her ever since. That he chose to remain silent through her retelling of this tale was a noble response and reminded me that, sometimes, it's best to keep your counsel. Not a character trait I've been blessed with.

I had a call some days later from Jeremy Langmead. 'I'd like you to do a column for the *Sunday Times*,' he said. Jeremy was the then editor of the 'Style' section of the paper. Instant fear. 'Whaaat, I'm not sure I can write,' I said. 'You're very funny and you just need to put that on the page,' he said, brooking no nonsense.

It was a fantastic turn of events and gave me a massive boost of much-needed confidence.

The column was to be what was then called 'a sideways look at life' – a phrase mercifully long since ridiculed and dispensed with. My debut was to be a précis of life thus far and where I found myself now. This included Daniel's departure and it gave me no small thrill to describe him as, 'My knight in shining YELLOW armour who rode off into the sunset without looking back'. I completely loved this weekly task, despite the fact I was forced to events and gatherings I wouldn't normally have attended in order to gather material for copy. I filed on time, every week, with what I hoped were vaguely humorous shenanigans and the readers seemed to like it. The bike was often featured in my columns, the back wheel being stolen outside a busy posh restaurant and another time having to cycle home without a saddle when that was nicked. Very hard on the legs and you don't want to sit on the rod!

The much-missed former *Sunday Times* writer Adrian Gill once gave me some invaluable advice on the difficulties of getting into a piece. 'You don't need to go along the corridor, just go straight into the room,' he said, before adding grudgingly, 'You have a good self-deprecating wit, Maria.'

I glowed with pride for days after that and avidly read his and other people's columns for further inspiration.

Once inside the bosom of the *Sunday Times*, I stood in for Adrian on several occasions by writing his much-revered restaurant column. The thrill of taking a chum along to a swanky restaurant to eat and drink our fill caused great joy and pleasure. I would scribble down details of the evening, what we ate, how it tasted, and so on, in a small, unobtrusive notepad at the table, before struggling bleary-eyed to decipher my drunken notes the following day.

These assignments forced me to seriously update my limited lexicon of adjectives. 'Yummy', 'delicious' and 'tasty' can only be used sparingly and even then the purists would consider it remiss. 'Delectable', 'luscious', 'scrumptious', 'palatable', 'saporous', 'voluptuous' and 'gamey', all start to get old quickly too. It's a good party game to play should the conversation cease to flow on your next gourmet outing or trip to Nando's.

I was offered lengthier commissions by the *Sunday Times*, profiles of famous folk, the changing face of the property market and various fill-ins. Gaining confidence with each accepted piece, I began to suggest possible subjects. That I always felt fraudulent goes without saying but as my editor used to say, 'You don't get if you don't ask.' I was the girl who had been kicked out of school and every other journalist I knew was really clever. Sure, I wasn't writing 'think' pieces, but nonetheless this had been a very lucky break.

I wrote for the *Telegraph*, the *Evening Standard*, the *Mail on Sunday* and *Esquire* magazine, all the while continuing with acting jobs, voiceovers and television work. Sometimes, while on an acting job, as well as trying to remember my lines, I would be jotting down ideas for another piece, outlining someone's outrageous behaviour or the madness of some dictatorial director. Everything was fair game and I quickly realised that newspapers were like hungry babies that needed constant feeding.

The editor of 'Style' changed. Jeremy moved on to bigger and better things and it seemed inevitable that I would be 'let go'.

Not so. My position on the front page was to be changed and my column was now to be called 'Health and Deficiency', detailing the perpetual difficulties of maintaining some form of exercise, not drinking too much, remaining a reasonable weight and giving up smoking. All very much within my remit.

I wrote about a weight-loss class where we were all instructed to add a two-pound bag of sugar to an old belt which would be representative of the weight we wanted to lose. This was then to be worn around our waists as an indicator of the needless and heavy amount of adipose tissue we were carting around each and every day.

By following the diet, this cumbersome belt would be reduced and eventually eliminated as the bags would be removed one by one.

It was an inelegant but effective aid to help us visualise the unwanted pounds, our bossy teacher assured us.

Making the stupid belt was a Blue Peter craft class in itself. Attaching bags of sugar to a belt being far harder than it sounded. Industrial amounts of white gaffer tape were used to secure the bulky packets to each section of belt. I wanted to lose ten pounds (always ten pounds) which meant five bags of Tate and Lyle at intervals around my waist.

The resulting image staring back at me from the mirror was of a not very bright heroin smuggler or a suicide bomber with a sweet tooth.

I dutifully lost two pounds in the first week and there was much rejoicing in class. 'You can go home and take away a packet of belt sugar!' the bossy teacher exclaimed, with as much glee as she could muster, and everyone clapped.

Releasing the heavily wrapped packet from my belt of shame proved as difficult if not more so than getting it to stay on. I took it into the living room where I picked at the stubborn gaffer tape with hungrily bitten fingernails. What a ludicrously hair-brained scheme this was.

In exasperation, scissors were brought in and before I knew it, an entire bag of white granules exploded in the air, two pounds of the stuff, over my hair, into my computer, covering the sofa, filling my shoes and snuffing out the candle on the coffee table. It was a sneezing into the cocaine moment in Woody Allen's *Annie Hall*. The resultant calorie burn caused by cleaning, hoovering and mopping an entire room and all of its contents would surely have taken care of another of the wretched sugar packets but all patience had now escaped me. The suicide belt and remaining gaffer tape were calmly picked up and ceremoniously chucked in the bin.

That summer saw the arrival of some very chubby ants.

With drinking comes smoking – and I really wanted to give up smoking. My editor sent me for a proper consultation with a famous hypnotist.

It was during the chitty chat preamble over a cup of tea that I recounted a shortened version of the Father O'Leary events in the woods many years before. I asked the hypnotist his opinion on traumatic amnesia and whether he thought it possible. This seemed to interest him far more than my 15-fags-a-day smoking habit and he suggested that we should try a form of regression back to 1968. I was a little alarmed but reluctantly agreed.

When our family holidayed in Blackpool in the early 70s, we had been to see a hypnotist at the Winter Gardens who was able to convince people under his influence that the audience were naked, an onion was a delicious apple and that one unfortunate man could sing like Elvis Presley. He couldn't. Such was this poor chap's commitment as he warbled 'Are You Lonesome Tonight' and our collective ears bled, that it was enough to convince the entire theatre that he truly believed he was Elvis.

To select those who could successfully be 'put under' as he called it, we were all asked to put our hands on our heads, which we did. Then he asked us to remove them. A small percentage of the people were quite unable to take their hands from their heads. I very badly wanted to be hypnotised, so kept my hands on my head and looked around me with fake confusion.

Off I went with the other 'hands-stuck suckers', 15 of us standing in line on the stage. One by one the hypnotist addressed each person, looking deeply into their eyes before clicking his fingers and causing previously stuck hands to fall from heads. I clamped my hands ever tighter to my head as he moved along the line. He was in front of me. I knew. He knew.

He clicked his fingers and pushed my lower back to send me packing. I kept my hands clamped and he looked at me wearily before manfully forcing my hands down to my side.

Was I the imposter or was it the seven people remaining? 'I think they are audience plants,' Mum whispered, as I plonked myself back in my chair. 'Hypnotism is showbusiness.'

Now I had agreed to be regressed. The famous hypnotist suggested I lay on a massage table before instructing some deep breathing in order to relax.

'Breathe deep into the solar plexus, filling every square inch of your lungs.

In . . . and . . . out . . . This went on for some minutes and I could indeed feel myself drifting off, then he started to speak in a gentle voice and told me that I was sitting in Father O'Leary's car and that I was excited to be going to the woods.

This would have been fine but for the fact that he was speaking in a phoney American DJ-type voice.

'Y'all are sittin' in the carrrrr,' he drawled. 'Is there a saung on the raydeeoh?'

Part of me wanted to laugh, to open my eyes and ask WHY are you speaking American? But it seemed petty and rude as he was seeing me gratis. I also had to file a column later that day.

'Is he touching you? What are ya feeling?' he continued. It was no use. Laughter threatened to get the better of me, he had been trying for ten minutes and nothing was happening.

'It's not working,' I said, apologetically. 'Perhaps we should try the smoking thing?'

I was shown some useful CBT (cognitive behavioural therapy) to help with the nicotine addiction and he urged me to return when there was more time for a full regression. I thanked him profusely, apologised and scurried off to the pub for a glass of wine and a fag.

I talked to a therapist friend.

'Do you really want to know what happened?' she asked. 'Sometimes the psyche buries things for a reason.'

I told her this sounded like nonsense. Surely if I couldn't remember anything then nothing had happened? As a grown woman trying to understand an historic incident, there would be no reason NOT to remember what had happened, lurid or otherwise. She smiled enigmatically and said, 'Maria, the mind works in mysterious ways.'

My summation of this episode is that Father O'Leary thought better of any sinister motives, if indeed there were any. He died sometime in January 2019 so the case must now be closed.

I contacted many of the parishes Father O'Leary later served, including many bishops and institutions in the diocese that may have been able to shed further light. No one ever called me back or returned my emails. That the Catholic Church likes to maintain silence on the secrets of its past is now a matter of public record.

Mum, now 94, seriously questions her actions at that time and can be sent into despairing agony at the very mention of Father O'Leary's name, which I bring up often, usually at Christmas for full effect.

After five years at the *Sunday Times* my contract wasn't renewed. It was time to move on and for new voices to be heard. I still dabble here and there if asked to write pieces and am truly grateful to Jeremy and for all I learned during that time.

Like everything else that is likely to be judged, criticised or applauded, writing and journalism are just other ways of showing off.

Acting and comedy I knew a fair amount about. This was showing off using a medium I had very little confidence in, though, having thought myself a total dunce since flunking out of school.

For that very reason, it gave me a huge amount of pleasure to see the finished product in print, but during the writing process I would often wish I had paid more attention to verbs, adverbs, nouns, adjectives, subjunctives, etc. at school. It wasn't serious journalism, rather fluff pieces that padded out the weightier columns, but it was an area I never in a million years thought I would have any chance of entering.

Chapter 16

A Difficult Age:

White Mountain Bike

The house of horror was sold a year after Daniel's departure and, when all debts accrued had been paid off, furniture was put in storage and I bid a weary farewell to Acton and moved into a one-bedroom garden flat in Marble Arch. It had high ceilings, high rates and even higher service charge.

The flat was walking distance from my favourite Soho bars and clubs, had Hyde Park on its doorstep and would be the perfect home for the next chapter of my life, whatever that may hold.

It is never easy to pick yourself up, dust yourself off and start all over again but if that's all you've got, that's what you do.

I had been diving in Antigua the previous winter and, while there, had hooked up with a man called Canje Blaise. It was a holiday romance that had boosted my confidence and given me the spring in my step I needed to know that that side of my life was not yet over. After ten years with D, it felt significant to clamber back on the sexual pony and prove to myself I was still viable.

Canje was a bright man who worked in one of the hotels on the island, took me to dinner and behaved impeccably. I would go diving by day, keen as I was to achieve my PADI advanced diving certificate and at night we went dancing and drinking. He was fun to hang out with, younger than me, and, did I mention, he was hot?

The night before I left the island was spent drinking with an American couple in the hotel bar. They had arrived the day before and were from Ohio. He was a small, round-faced man who was an anaesthetist in a large private hospital, his wife was tall, rather glamorous with auburn ringlets and much clanking silver jewellery, and she taught art at their local high school. We had chatted to them briefly on arrival when they insisted we join them in the bar the following day.

I was late to arrive that evening and they were all pretty merry by the time I clattered in, dragging diving equipment and flippers behind me.

Further drinks were distributed and as the evening drew to a close, they suggested we all go and smoke a joint in their room. Canje was up for it, but I declined as that day's dive had been exhausting and I needed to pack.

The tedium of packing completed, it seemed churlish not to pop along to their room as it was my last night on the island and real life was only a plane ride away. Why not prolong the fun?

Knocking gently on their door, it took a long time for anyone to answer. I could hear fumbling and mumbling and the little round-faced man opened the door bare-chested. He was clearly pretty stoned and it was obvious I had missed the best of the party, so I said my goodbyes and left.

Fifteen minutes later Canje came to my room. 'What was that all about?' I enquired, keen to get the lowdown on what I had missed.

He pulled out a bundle of 20-dollar bills and looked a bit sheepish.

The round-faced man had apparently been keen on a foursome, but when I declined their offer of a joint, he offered Canje 300 dollars to have sex with his wife while he watched. Canje dutifully obliged, although was slightly alarmed when the round-faced man started touching him on the bottom as he was in action and he was forced to tell him that this was definitely NOT part of the deal.

We both laughed uncontrollably at this turn of events and Canje confessed that this was not the first time he had been propositioned in this way.

I could have been taken aback or annoyed, but what was I though, other than another sex tourist? True, no money had changed hands between us, but wasn't I exploiting him too in some way?

In the morning, Canje took me to the airport and we said our farewells. He told me he would write (really?) and I scribbled down my address before hurrying through the departure gates, waving and blowing kisses.

I had been in my new Marble Arch apartment for three months when the doorbell rang. It took me a while to process this tall dark stranger beaming at me on the doorstep. I knew I vaguely recognised him, but this was the wrong setting and he was wearing a woollen suit despite the fact it was mid-June.

It was, of course, Canje Blaise.

He had apparently come to London to deliver something for a friend. I wisely chose not to ask what it was that he was entrusted to deliver. He had my address but nothing more so had just turned up in the hope that I would be welcoming.

What choice did I have? It would be churlish not to show him the same hospitality he had shown me, but how long was he hoping to stay and how on earth would I entertain him?

I decided that the only option was just to include him in my activities and hope he enjoyed them.

We went for drinks with friends around the corner in Connaught Square. A Brazilian couple who worked for the embassy had a swanky flat and a small fox-terrier. They were most taken with Canje and pleaded to be allowed to show him off to their gay friends. 'He is a man of exquisite beauty,' Max whispered to me as I helped him with the drinks.

I mentioned that I wanted to hire a bike, in order to show Canje the sights of London Town and capitalise on the good weather. Max's partner Georgio said, 'No! Do not hire a bicycle. I have one in the basement that he can HAVE. I will never ride it again, too many killers driving white vans.' He wasn't wrong.

At the end of the evening, a little worse the wear for drink, we traipsed down to the basement to see a rather smart but dusty Trek Marlin mountain bike. Canje loved it and we all set about pumping tyres and struggling to position the seat and handlebars as high as they would go to accommodate his height.

'Are you sure I can't pay you for this?' I said, suddenly feeling that this gift was a little much. 'No, no,' said Georgio. 'But please can you come back tomorrow, so I can get a photograph of Canje riding it?' A small price to pay and a request Canje was more than happy to accommodate. Ah, the power of beauty. I was still riding the white mountain bike and marvelling at how long it had lasted.

Cycling around London with someone unfamiliar with cycling, let alone the foibles of traffic systems, thoughtless drivers and the sheer heft of double-decker buses was a little testing to say the least. We practised in the inner circle of Regent's Park, then the cycle lanes down to the Serpentine in Hyde Park, along to the Albert Hall and back up through the trees to observe the ranting at Speakers' Corner. Speakers' Corner is an area at the top of Hyde Park and backing onto Marble Arch. It is an historical landmark, a Sunday soapbox where speakers such as Karl Marx and George Orwell once tried to convert the masses to their respective ideologies. Canje loved the Sunday morning babble of crazy folk armed only with an old beer crate, a loudhailer and a firm belief in whatever doctrines they needed the world to hear about.

There was an old bloke wearing a placard that predicted 'The end is nigh, repent NOW', who we struck up a conversation with. He had thin wispy hair, a pockmarked complexion and a frayed tweed jacket grown stiff with age, dirt and Brylcreem residue. He was called Moses, although I feel it unlikely that name was on his birth certificate. Moses told us that mixed marriage was wrong and that we would be punished for our sins. I politely informed him that we weren't married, weren't planning to be and asked him why he thought such a thing.

'It says in the Bible you cannot mix white blood with black blood,' he spat, with great conviction.

'Which Bible is that?' I asked. 'Surely our blood is the same whatever the colour of our skin?'

He started to get cross and told me black blood was evil and held the secrets to black magic. He was clearly bonkers, but I could see that Canje was becoming vexed (as he liked to say) so I dragged him away. I felt the awful middle-class need to apologise for the madness of this old chap's ramblings and to explain that freedom of speech meant exactly that. This was an area of London that folk could argue the world was flat, the moon was made of cheese, or that aliens were already among us. In retrospect it feels more dangerous, the beginnings of the conspiracists. Racism of this kind is nothing new but it was something I was seeing first-hand, through Canje's eyes.

We became more adventurous on our two-wheeled adventures, cycling around the streets of Notting Hill along the canal footpaths of Little Venice and Camden Town and locking our bikes outside Marine Ices where we had knickerbocker glories and banana splits.

Canje quickly mastered the London roads, but would always make me cycle ahead, despite the fact he was twice as fast as I could manage with my little legs pumping as hard as they could.

Seeing London through someone else's eyes made me see things differently too. The beauty of our parks and trees, the equality of being on the road with chauffeur-driven Bentleys and gold-sprayed Porsches, the exquisitely varied architecture and the history around every corner.

It was when we were returning after a long day of pedal-driven sightseeing that we had our only mishap. A van that jumped the lights at a T-junction saw me miss it by millimetres. I had to slam on my brakes and turn into the curb sharply, shouting obscenities as I did so. Canje, following slightly too closely, hit my back wheel from behind which caused us both to fall into the road and my back tyre to burst. The van naturally disappeared into the distance leaving us to be tended by passersby and other motorists.

We both sustained injuries. Canje had a large gash in his calf and I banged and cut my knee on the kerb where I fell. There was a considerable amount of blood which made things look much worse than they were, everyone was brilliantly kind, offered handkerchiefs and tissues, lifts to hospital and someone even went and purchased cups of sweet tea from a street vendor. Despite the pain, this was the London I wanted Canje to see.

The willingness to help others and the generosity of spirit.

We patched ourselves up, bandaged our knees and legs, thanked all the lovely people who had helped and trundled the bikes back home on foot.

In the great scheme of things, it could have been a lot worse and we had got off lightly. Once we had cleaned up our respective wounds and applied antiseptic and plasters, there was a huge heap of bloodied bandages on the bathroom floor. Canje suggested we save them and take them to show Moses the racist madman at Speakers' Corner that our bloods had mingled and the world hadn't ended. 'I want to show him that black blood isn't made of acid,' he said.

A few days later I was meant to be going to dinner. Despite our matching injury limps and bruised limbs, I took Canje along. It was just the four of us, an old friend and her new partner who was an academic at the London School of Economics. Even I found this man dry and dull and the conversation was halting. We soldiered on through supper with the academic overly pronouncing his words and entering into lengthy explanations for Canje as though he were a child. Being the consummate liberals, they tried desperately to get to know this stranger in their midst. At one point the academic asked Canje, 'What is the current population of Antigua?' Not really a conversational winner by any standards. Canje shook his head and said, 'No idea, bro.' I chipped in helpfully with, 'I think it's about 80,000,' and we all nodded, then fell silent. I could see Canje was struggling not to laugh.

Walking home I asked him what he had thought of the evening. 'It was nice,' he said, 'but they seemed a bit frightened of me.' Not a great success.

We fared a little better with my godson aged nine on a skateboarding trip, both of them traversing along the road by the Serpentine Lake, doing tricks and dodging pedestrians, laughing and falling before finally retiring to safer ground and gabbling enthusiastically about Tony Hawk (American skateboarder) over tea and cake in the café.

We walked my godson home with him sitting astride Canje's shoulders while he told him stories of the village he grew up in, how he learned to kill a chicken and the perils of being stung by a sea snake. Unbeknown to me, the godson had been unravelling Canje's dreadlocks all the way home, leaving him with a big poufy Afro where tidy braids had been and an emergency trip to a Brixton hairdresser.

It was while I was watching the lady laughing and braiding, with fingers moving dexterously through the frizzy mass, that I wondered what our children might look like and if I would ever be able to learn the clever braiding skills. A brief moment of sadness for what might have been and an acknowledgement that whoever one co-creates with is something of a lottery.

The sadness was fleeting much like the brief fertility window that was starting to creak on its rusting hinges.

Canje loved to party, so I took him to Heaven in Charing Cross. Ostensibly a gay nightclub but welcoming to all comers with three floors of dance music and multiple gyrating bodies getting on down to the selective beats. Canje loved it and within a matter of moments had stripped off his shirt and joined the revellers on the podium of dance.

I had to go away for work for three days, but Canje returned to Heaven each evening as though he had found his spiritual home. I asked him if anyone had tried to pick him up for sex and he laughed and said, 'All the time!' before adding, 'I told them I don't go with men, but it only made them try harder!'

It was an interesting experience seeing London through the lens of a man from a small Caribbean island and I delighted in his wide-eyed wonder, but it also made me question my participation in the place I had called home for 25 years.

Friends all seemed to have small children or had moved away to the countryside, which apparently one only does in pairs. Drinking in clubs was starting to make me feel a bit like the character played by the actress Beryl Reid, that of a middle-aged, middle-class barfly.

Not a role I was tremendously keen to mimic.

Canje returned home after two weeks with countless pairs of jeans and trainers to sell to his friends. It had been a brilliant trip, he exclaimed, having seen the Queen (visited Buckingham Palace), met George Michael (watched him leave a club in a limo with blacked-out windows), and cavorted with scantily clad dancers in Carnaby Street (a pop video we stumbled into). He had loved his time in the capital and had anecdotes aplenty to entertain his pals back home. Knowing our paths would never cross again, I naturally made promises to visit Antigua the following winter.

He had wanted to take his gifted mountain bike back to Antigua, but the airline costs were prohibitive, there was no room in my flat, and so we decided to lock it in the Marble Arch underground car park where he could reclaim it at a later date, should he ever come back to London.

Life returned to normal, jobs dribbled in, but the creeping sense of what to do next started to weigh heavily. Work was OK, but did I want a partner?

It wasn't easy to re-enter the dating world so long after I'd left it and being a slightly past-it singleton was another hurdle. It wasn't that I really wanted or needed a partner, but I had to relearn how to be without one.

I happened upon an article written by the comedian Joan Rivers, who talked about the suicide of her husband Edgar Rosenberg and how she briefly contemplated joining him, until she realised that it would mean leaving her beloved dogs. We all need to be needed and this seemed like a good enough reason to stay alive, so I set in motion a dog search and finally arranged with a gay vicar in Haywards Heath to collect a small Maltese terrier puppy. As usual, a rash and hasty decision.

The night before this bundle of fluff was to enter my life, I had

Posing in the South of France, 1979.

NOT topless! Bad *Sunday Times* publicity shot.

Christmas Day swim.

Ill-advised
publicity shot.
Northcott Theatre,
Exeter, 1998.

Riding on the
beach, Langkawi
Malaysia, 2018.

Showing off with embarrassed Dolly.

Showing off in Vivienne
Westwood shoes.

My 'only' wedding, on a TV show.

Stephen B. Whatley:
'Maria McErlane', 1998.
Oil on canvas. 30"x24".
Collection of Ms McErlane.

With Nigella.

ABBA party with Nigella and Hettie.

Carnal Knowledge wrap party, 1992.

Hungover on New Year's Day.

With Dina Martina in NY.

Virgin promotion pic.

At Radio Two.

This Morning with Sarah Silverman.

With Stormzy.

With Tony Bennett.

LOLs with Armistead Maupin.

Someone turned me into a biscuit! I was delicious.

Sharon Gless – *Cagney and Lacey*!

Dolly Selfies . . .

. . . Donny Osmond . . .

. . . James Norton, Priscilla Presley, Carlos Acosta, Johnny Marr.

Agony Aunting on *This Morning*.

Charity shop recreation of Gucci 2019 autumn collection.

Queen's Jubilee on Thames. (Esther Rantzen taking pics.)

2022 Graham's wedding in Bantry, Ireland. Pete Hawkins, Tom Oppenheimer, Simon Rayner Langmead, Jeremy Rayner Langmead.

attended a fashion launch in a swanky restaurant with my writer chum Andy O'Hagan. It was quite a drunken affair and saw us both sashaying down the catwalk in the style of Martha Graham, Pan's People and Eddie the Eagle. There was a waiter who was showing unusual interest and, encouraged by the naughtiest element of O'Hagan, I took the cute waiter home with me for some meaningless sex.

So far, so middle-aged barfly. He was a sweet chap, handsome blond, funny and we drank and danced back at the flat. It was all going as you might expect, until he had to take his clothes off. This action revealed a large angry scar across most of his back and side, down his thigh and a large chunk of his left calf missing. It was clearly a very big deal and he started to cry as I ran my hand over the misshapen flesh on his back and sides.

Whatever I may have had in mind for the evening, this was not part of the plan. We made tea and sat in ill-fitting dressing gowns (him), talking for several hours about the tractor accident on a farm when he was a teen that had resulted in his near death and, as he called it, 'a lifetime of explanation and disfigurement'. As sexy foreplay, this was quite far away from anything I had previously encountered.

The emotions needed were now strictly maternal and I recounted the story of Mark, my boyfriend who had died and how I had found his scars beautiful and positive. I told him about the Japanese art of Kintsugi, which encourages us to see potential for beauty in the reconstruction of broken pieces. Based on the idea that by embracing flaws and imperfections, one can create an even stronger, more interesting work. Every scar and blemish is different and while this 400-year-old technique is mainly applied to pottery, it is now used as a metaphor for healing ourselves; that sometimes in the process of repair, we can actually create something more unique, stronger and resilient. Breakage and restoration is an important part of our history, which the Japanese celebrate rather than disguise.

This seemed to be something of a breakthrough and while

retelling it now sounds hippyish and creepy, we spent a long time looking at and touching all his scars and disfigurements while he talked about how they felt to him and what they represented. We both had a little weep and it was all way more memorable than a quick knee-trembler.

In the morning, hung over and bleary, I had to rush off for a voiceover.

When I returned with coffee and pastries, I found the bed had been strewn with sweet smelling rose petals from the garden, the beautiful boy was freshly showered and we resumed what we had intended twelve hours earlier with clear heads and a deeper connection.

I suddenly remembered I was supposed to pick up the new puppy and scrabbled around looking for the number to cancel. Beautiful boy urged me to reconsider and promised that he would come with me to Haywards Heath and collect the little scrap of skin and fur awaiting his new home.

Singing and laughing around the M25, it was a delight to share this mission with someone. Strangers in time who the fates had thrown together, it remains in the memory as an important act of humanity on both our parts and one for which I am very grateful.

The Haywards Heath vicar was a tad shady, seemed more interested in the boy I had with me, before eventually remembering why I was there. The puppy was clearly the runt of the litter, was brilliant white with pink skin and small enough to fit in the palm of my hand. I naturally fell in love immediately, paid the holy man a wad of cash before the teensy canine vomited all the way home.

Just like that, I owned a dog.

Chapter 17

The Power of Dog:

Death of the White Mountain Bike

'Dogs are not our whole lives but they make our lives whole'
– Roger Caras

Wₕₐₜ was I meant to do with this living, breathing creature with nasty expulsions that I had deliberately invited into my life?

There had been limited preparation for its arrival and all necessary arrangements were makeshift to say the least.

Other than a bag of puppy food and a vomit-covered blanket, this pink-skinned, white-furred, Lilliputian refugee was ill equipped for London living.

He stared at me with needlessly large black eyes and squeaked continuously, only stopping when I picked him up and popped him down my jumper and into the cup of my bra. What had I done?

When I told my friend Nigella that I was getting a dog, she looked sceptical.

'What?' I asked, like a naughty child about to get told off.

'Well, either you won't love it and that will be bad, or you WILL love it and that will be bad,' she said, before adding, 'And then it will die and you will be sad.'

Owing to his diminutive stature, I decided to call this furry tennis ball Goliath. A joke that quickly wore thin and he became 'Puppy' to everyone other than vets, passport-control officers and the BBC risk-assessment panel.

When Daniel left, for obvious reasons I had begun to drink rather heavily.

Not Oliver Reed levels or during the day, rather just clinging to friends' legs as they tried to leave at 2am, imploring, 'Just one more bottle, the night is still young!'

At Alcoholics Anonymous there is no particular requirement to attend other than the desire to stop drinking. A kindly friend Fiona recognised that need and took me along to a meeting. I stayed in the programme for exactly a year and remain a mystified but massive fan of the methodology. Quite how a bunch of drunks gathered in a room have the power to stop one drinking I can't fathom, it's a bit like transubstantiation; it makes no sense unless you have blind faith. Anyway, it worked for me and I highly recommend it to you, should you need it.

At AA they advise you not to get into new relationships for the first year, not to get pets and to begin with a house plant. If you can keep your spider plant alive for 12 months then you may want to move on to something with a pulse. I had dutifully maintained my spiky shrub and had moved up the food chain to a puppy. It was a big responsibility, but I was determined that under my care and with my love, this little creature would thrive, not understanding then that it was a two-way arrangement and I would blossom too.

Within months I became a leading expert in canine husbandry. I was Barbara Woodhouse, Paul O'Grady and Dr Noel Fitzpatrick rolled into one.

Puppy had his own basket that he never slept in, became adept at the retrieval of choking hazards and twigs, learned to sit for treats and how to alert me to his emptying needs. We made friends in the park, swapped tips and stories with other doggy nutters and had playdates with a yappy Chihuahua who mirrored its owner, a petite pointy man who never stopped talking.

It became necessary to take my old friend Stephen to an AA meeting. A last-chance saloon in an unmanageable life (membership of this club can produce evangelism). He was doing brilliantly and one afternoon I asked him to look after the puppy while I went to a work meeting. After an hour he rang me in distress. 'I can't cope,' he cried down the phone. 'I don't know how to make him happy.' This little phrase still touches my heart, a beautiful existential projection onto a sentient being unable to communicate its needs.

It wasn't very complicated, Puppy's happiness was generally reliant on a warm lap and licking access to his own reproductive organs.

Stephen is now 17 years clean and sober, he has his own dog that he knows how to make happy and is a very successful comedy writer at the BBC.

Having taught Puppy to sit in a basket on the back of my bike, we would zoom around London with gay abandon. In bright sunlight, I would see the outline of his shadow ahead, a tiny patient Buddha behind me with ears flapping in the wind.

It was an act of trust on both our parts that he wouldn't jump out and that I wouldn't crash the bike. We understood each other.

I saw the beautiful boy several times but it became obvious he was more interested in playing with the puppy. This was entirely expected, he was fifteen years younger than me and at a totally different stage in his life.

We parted as friends who were lucky enough to share something that felt true.

One week in early spring I swapped Puppy for a small boy when I took my godson skiing in the French mountains and Nigella took charge of the four-legged fiend. Puppy certainly ate well and got a gig with his temporary owner on the cover of the glossy Waitrose magazine, sitting in a picnic basket on a red and white gingham table cloth giving it full Blue Steel realness (yet to receive payment).

The decision to get a dog had proved to be a splendid one, it was all working out very well and Puppy was very amenable to being farmed out when the need arose. Having a small cute puppy is an easy ask if you need to go away, certainly easier than a bull-mastiff or a Tyrolean mountain dog with poos the size of a birthday cake and the exercise needs of Olympic athletes.

Never in a million years did I think that a dog would or could be what I needed.

There were no childhood pets to give me an inkling of interest in animal husbandry, other than a family budgie that went stiff in the cold of the ferocious winter of 1963.

Having a mum who was afraid of dogs regardless of size or timidity meant this entire area of companionship was an alien concept and one that had never been considered or explored. I wasn't aware that my Puppy was a little lacking in the personality department as I had nothing to compare it to. The small areas of character he did exhibit were enough to delight me.

I hadn't anticipated how much love I would have in my heart for this dog, love that had found an outlet and was returned tenfold.

It was only when a friend who had enjoyed multiple pets through his life proclaimed one day, 'I can see no point to that creature other than as a glorified glove puppet!' That I even considered the possibility that this little animal wasn't the brightest in the box only made me love him more.

Perhaps it was just that there was something else other than me which needed help and assistance to stay alive.

Happy as I was with my new status as 'mad dog lady', London had ceased to delight me. It was hard to know where and how to fit in. When you are young, there is never a point that you can imagine anything other. It's a wonderful feeling of omnipotence and an important method of propulsion, but I was now in a sort of age limbo.

I didn't really want to hang out with young unsuitable boys. Besides not being a good look, I needed to share an element of history with someone; be it old Blue Peter programmes or music you used to dance to. Naturally, wild sexual chemistry is important, but it's not enough.

For those who have been in long-term relationships, we know that the heady honeymoon period only lasts a short amount of time. Around two years. It is another of the biological imperatives, enough time to procreate and for a baby to be born.

A relationship wasn't high on the priorities list anyway, but a need for adventure was. I had wanderlust and I couldn't get the line by Eleanor Roosevelt out of my head: 'Today is the oldest you've ever been and the youngest you'll ever be again.'

I had owned my custom-built bike for some years with many happy miles on the imaginary clock. The lock, while heavy and annoying, had been an invaluable investment.

One morning, I cycled to Tottenham Court Road for a voiceover. I secured the bike along with several others in the safety of the bike racks just off the pavement near a computer shop. I was playing the wife of my old *Fast Show* colleague Mark Williams in a radio ad for breakfast cereal and after the recording we went for lunch where I burbled out my dating game failures and asked Mark to marry me. He said no.

When I returned to collect my bike, I was met with a scene of devastation. The computer shop had a smashed window and the bike racks had been flattened. Two policemen were surveying the damage and painstakingly stretching yellow and black sticky tape between two lamp posts.

My lovely bike lay on its side, a mangled wreck. Wheels disfigured beyond recognition, spokes sticking out at crazy angles, the frame resembled something a strongman had bent in half and the handlebars had sheared away completely.

One of the policemen told me that a refuse lorry had mounted the pavement, hit the bike racks and come to rest in the front window of the computer store. 'It's a miracle no one was hurt,' he said. I looked down at my broken bike. It didn't feel much like a miracle. Three other bikes had suffered a similar fate to my own, which in some small way I found comforting.

I was unsure as to what I should do next. Unlock the remains of my transport and take them to hospital? To the scrapyard? Or the cemetery? Of all the possible outcomes to my day, this was definitely not on my list.

The policeman told me I must leave things as they were as photographers and CID were due to inspect the scene. He also told me that the driver of the refuse truck had been arrested. 'Do you think it was drink driving then?' I asked. The policeman was silent but tapped the side of his nose with his forefinger, which I took as a yes.

I was given various crime numbers, the address of Camden Council and a patronising pat on the back by the policeman as I gazed down at my lovely dead bike. 'It could have been worse,' he said, 'you could have been riding it.'

This was certainly true and made me shudder slightly at the thought of the damage to a squishy body given the twisted and broken metal that lay on the ground in front of me.

I was very shocked by this turn of events and also, once again, without a two-wheeled companion. I then remembered the Trek Marlin mountain bike that Canje had used which was locked in the underground car park at Marble Arch. Despite the many months it had been resting there, aside from flat tyres and liberal amounts of grime, it filled my heart with joy to liberate it once more and get it and me on the road.

Having long since abandoned the idea of insuring a bike, owing to the prohibitive costs, with one insurance broker telling me, 'Nah, we stopped doin' bikes, the average time before a decent bike gets robbed in London is 16 months.' My only recourse for this unforeseen incident was Camden Council and their questionable insurance. In short, it took two years before I was awarded the sum of £147.60, an entirely random amount based on the wear and tear of my machine rather than the cost of replacement.

I think it was shortly after the cheque plopped through my letterbox that I decided there really was no point in riding expensive equipment and that I would now only ever buy secondhand or beat-up bikes that no one wanted to steal. I had been unlucky, certainly, not everyone has their bike run over by a dustbin wagon, but the copper was right. It could have been a lot worse.

The journalist Simon Evans said, 'A bicycle is the nearest thing to a living creature an inanimate object can be.' I heartily agree with this sentiment. I had owned the custom-built mountain bike for so long that when it got crushed beyond recognition it felt like a member of my family had suffered a terrible injury and ultimate death.

The relationship one has with their two-wheeled machine is exactly that, complete with the requisite pain of loss.

Chapter 18

Follow Your Dreams:

Marin Mountain Bike

'Only from the heart can we touch the sky' – Rumi

One sunny morning with no work and a pressing need to get out of the city, Puppy was strapped into his car seat and we set off to Brighton for low-tide beach walks. I had been saving some money for a seaside getaway and this was something of a reconnaissance mission. It was a day of snap decisions and Brighton was quickly dismissed as being too flat and boring.

We drove east along the coast.

Eastbourne had beautiful Victorian architecture but had very little energy. Another possibility crossed off the list.

Bexhill was also sweet and pretty, although there were a glut of retirement homes and the estate agent I called laughed as he told me of its nickname: 'God's waiting room'. Not quite ready to shuffle off the mortal coil, we sped along to St Leonards-on-Sea and Hastings where I parked the car and set off with the dog to discover what was on offer.

St Leonards was pretty run down. Shutters of the properties along the seafront flapped open and hung from lone hinges. Windows long since broken had seagulls perched on their sills and the front doors of once grand houses were now filled with a multitude of buzzers, doorbells and entry phone systems for the multiple occupancy within. It reminded me of photographs of post-revolution Cuba.

Past the pier into Hastings, where the quaint medieval old town nestled in the valley between two large hills, west and east, it too shared the same jaded, broken quality. This seemed to be the fate of many of Britain's seaside towns, long abandoned by the public for the guaranteed warmth of a Spanish package holiday.

The entire three miles of promenade was 180 degrees of sea, sky and horizon. However one feels about life, turning your face to a vast expanse of sea is a most calming experience.

Nursing a lager in a pub called the Pump House, which dubiously claimed to date back to 1066, I got chatting to an old man with brown leathery skin and chiselled crevices of sun-made wrinkles. His head was covered by a beaten-up woollen hat and his white beard and moustache flecked with the foam of a long-nursed Guinness. Captain Birdseye sat before me.

It's always useful to find out from a local what they think of where they live and although he had fished in the waters of the channel since he was a boy, he told me that along the south coast, many properties and unused boarding houses had, in the 1960s, been sequestered by London boroughs for problem families and other so-called undesirables from the East End. In return, the local councils had been gifted large chunks of money to deal with any difficult issues that arose and free reign over their spending with no questions asked. He talked of poverty ghettos, third- and fourth-generation unemployment and little or no investment from central government.

I hadn't been expecting a sociology lecture but the phrase 'you can't tell a book by its cover' was proving pretty accurate.

I bought him a pint and he told me his name was Eddie, but everyone called him Chalkie. It was best not to ask why as by now he was talking of Ronnie and Reggie Kray, Mad Frankie Fraser and other East End bad boys, some of whom had houses in the town during the 60s apparently.

This may have been blarney, but Chalkie was suddenly on a roll: 'Often the villains and gangsters would do someone in on a Saturday night, fling 'em in the boot of their MkII Cortina, then drive down to the Hastings harbour arm to wait for the fishing boats to go out and get rid of the corpse.'

At this point I was scribbling down the film treatment in my head and hastily popping on my journalistic hat. 'So you're saying that the Hastings fishermen got rid of bodies for the Krays?' *News of the World* headlines formed fast in my brain: 'Krays' watery Graves!' 'Hook line and SINK 'EM!' 'Swapping fish for a stiff', etc.

'No, no!' Chalkie cried. 'I didn't SAY it were (sic) necessarily the Krays, did I? Don't go saying that!'

In this moment I saw a very real look of fear in his eyes and decided he could possibly be telling the truth, so I'd better shut up.

'Let's just call 'em villains,' he said, and went on, 'Yeah, they would drop the skipper a ton (£100) which was a lot of money in them (sic) days and he'd take the bloke out.'

'How do you know it was a bloke?' I interrupted.

'Oh, it was always a bloke, they didn't do women,' he said, as if there was some code of conduct. I couldn't imagine the skipper peeking inside the sheet or whatever some hapless soul had been wrapped in to satisfy himself that this was indeed a bad man who deserved his watery fate and not a member of the fairer sex.

'So, the fishermen would just dump them in the Channel?' I asked, redundantly.

'Yep,' Chalkie said. 'Out into deep water and chuck 'em over the side. Easy money really.'

I thought it all through and it was certainly plausible. This was many years before DNA testing and underworld crimes often remained unsolved. A villain going missing was just one less villain for Johnny Law to worry about.

'You gotta remember,' Chalkie went on, 'that no one bothered us back then, Hastings kind of worked out its own laws because no one wanted to get involved.' He laughed enigmatically, before adding, 'We're all descended from smugglers here, so it makes sense.'

I told Chalkie I'd better get back and he did a half threatening look, before saying, 'Don't you go spreading that about now!'

I giggled nervously and left, telling him that I would love to hear more. Exhausted by the sea air and a bit drunk, I checked into a guest house near the car and while the kindly landlady fussed over puppy, my heart sank slightly at the sight of nylon sheets on the large double bed in a room that could have been decorated by my mum or My Little Pony's mum.

There was a lot to take on board in this strange little town, but it felt good and I was quite excited to find out more.

I loved having my small dog. There is such comfort in having another heartbeat in the room and he would wake every morning with unshakeable enthusiasm for the day ahead. Should you be blessed with that temperament, you are lucky indeed.

I rang the estate agent and arranged to see some flats. The first was on the last remaining residential square in St Leonards. Warrior Square. An uncharacteristically knowledgeable agent told me, 'The name Warrior is likely to be a corruption of Warehouse as smugglers used to secrete goods in the vicinity.'

'Smugglers get everywhere,' I muttered rather incongruously.

Warrior Square is surrounded on three sides by large, five-storey Victorian houses, it features a rose garden at the top, with steps on either side down to a larger playing field of grass surrounded by a border of plants, shrubs and trees. On the lower section are crazy 1950s-style flower arrangements over eight semi-circular beds and Queen Victoria's statue standing at the centre of the seaward end of the square. The magnificent monument was erected in 1902 and the skirt of her robes thrillingly show a large bullet hole inflicted by the Luftwaffe in World War II.

The entrance to the flat in the slightly run-down Howard House was on the street behind Warrior Square. Mattresses and other unwanted appliances littered the street. Walking through the rabbit warren of a poorly designed entrance hall, the agent finally opened the door of the flat onto a wonderful vista of sky, sea, trees, green foliage and bursting daffodils beyond.

High ceilings, windows you wouldn't want to clean and French doors leading out onto a Regency balustrade porch and steps into a lovely little garden. There was a circular decking arrangement in the middle, further waist-height balustrade fence and gate, then the municipal rose garden and square ahead.

It was a breathtaking view and I fell in love immediately. Two bedrooms with equally high windows and ceiling, a bathroom towards the rear of the flat and a modern galley kitchen were all just as charming and sealed the deal.

'I'll take it,' I cried.

'But I have others to show you,' the estate agent countered.

'No need. This is the one,' I beamed.

£120k and a few weeks later, I was in. Like I said, a day of snap decisions!

The flat was quickly furnished with retro and junk-shop finds and I would visit every weekend to explore this new territory and hopefully make friends.

That I knew not a single soul wasn't a problem, I was happy making home and chatting to locals for the lowdown on what to do and where to see. I attended my first dinner party a few weeks into my residency with the local window cleaner and his wife. A charming couple who practised some form of ancient Korean taekwondo and encouraged me to take it up. I went along to a few classes and social occasions before deciding it was all a front and that they were pretty dedicated swingers. Life could have taken a very different path, but I declined their kind offer and moved along the bus.

Warrior Square definitely had its own personality. I would often find multiple syringes in the gardens beyond my flat and there was a temporary accommodation block that mainly housed Serbian and Croation refugees.

Clearly no one had thought this through and there were often fights after an afternoon of drinking which would tax the local police force and provide entertainment for the Warrior Square residents.

I loved both the geographical and sociological levels of this funny little town, but high unemployment and limited opportunities meant taking on board some of the results of grinding poverty which couldn't be ignored but could be ameliorated by turning one's face to the sea and volunteering at a shelter.

My philosophy for my new life was to say yes to everything and everyone (apart from swinging). I made friends quickly, reluctantly eliminating as I went along. Every town has its tribes and it's just a matter of time before you find the one you are most comfortable within.

There is a saying for Hastings that it's a 'Drinking town with a fishing problem', which certainly rang true. Parties and crazy events were plentiful. An acronym I learned for London folk and blow-ins was FILTH. Failed in London try Hastings. I (rather defensively) didn't really feel this applied to me as I was still working in London while investing in the town, although I understood the resistance from some of the locals.

Summer rolled around and was filled with swimming and outdoor living. The gifted Marlin mountain bike had been nicked outside a homeless shelter when I had popped in to drop off a donation. I was only away for a moment but that was all it took. It hadn't been locked and the temptation or the need for someone was too great. I was getting better at a philosophical approach to loss, seeing myself as a mere guardian of my belongings rather than an owner.

There was a Marin bike supplier on the outskirts of Hastings in a built-up industrial estate. I went to check out the possibilities. All very swish but all quite pricey and I was wary of investing too much money after the fate of my last but one beautifully crafted two-wheeled machine. Antique, pre loved junk shops were plentiful in St Leonards and browsing through other people's lives became a favourite past-time. I happened upon an old, bright orange, 1990s Marin priced at £90. There were 90s smiley face stickers all over the frame and I imagined its former owner shouting 'Aceeeeed' as he or she cycled home from a rave. A little bit of bartering brought the price down to 70 quid and lo and behold I scored myself a bike! Cycling along the bike-friendly seafront was an instant spirit-lifter, puppy in the basket, the sun twinkling on the breaking waves and the wind in my hair made me unspeakably happy. Why hadn't I done this before? My little garden was planted up, the flat painted and along with my new gay neighbours, most weekends were spent on the beach with picnics, wine and small dogs. It was a permanent holiday with fun and laughter in abundance.

Our needs change as we get older, gradually and without us really noticing. A stunning sunrise or the world-on-fire thrill of the golden orb bidding farewell to another day could fill me with joy and was something I would never have contemplated in my twenties. Cliches work in truth and the simple pleasures were exactly that. Life was good, I was still getting jobs, had a seaside bolt-hole, yet I was inexplicably about to throw a massive spanner into the works.

In a final attempt to become a mother, together with a gay friend, we embarked on an attempt at surrogacy. This possibility had been on the backburner for some time and after long and in-depth discussions, we decided to set the wheels in motion.

Perhaps the imminent onset of menopause with all of its fertility finality made me long for what was about to be out of reach. I had been resigned to my child-free status, yet couldn't quite resist a last throw of the dice.

For anyone thinking this is an easy option, much like IVF and adoption, it is an expensive and emotionally costly journey that no amount of counselling can prepare you for.

We met our lovely surrogate Jamie who had been arranged through an agency, underwent tests, took all manner of helpful medications and after several months and many disappointments, two viable embryos were implanted and had bedded in for what everyone hoped was the necessary duration.

We painstakingly worked out all the practical arrangements, saw lawyers and met with others who had been in the same position and had been lucky enough to achieve much longed-for babies.

It was a very exciting time and despite being cautioned against it, I secretly bought many matching newborn outfits and squirrelled them away in the manner of a shopaholic concealing the true extent of their addiction by hiding guilty purchases at the back of rarely opened cupboards and drawers.

We never know what others are experiencing and life goes on in all its silliness while we quietly conceal sadness or hope, pain and longing, and although the thrill of what was to come was for new lives and infinite joy, it also reminded me of the weeks and months after Mark died.

The burden of the secret kept inside weighed heavily and flickered into view constantly, bringing with it a sense of dread and the growing realisation that I wasn't entirely sure I could take another body blow.

Weeks passed agonisingly slowly, all the while I was monitoring the size of the babies from apple pip to olive to strawberry. Quite why the fruit chart was ever chosen is a mystery, but I drew creepy size-accurate pictures in my diary of tiny fruity foetuses with large dark circles for eyes and teensy budding limbs. The progress was good, Jamie was healthy and despite suffering morning sickness, felt happy and glowing.

My secret was a happy one and I looked forward to the time when I could tell the world that I was going to become a mum. 'Mum'. I said the word in my head a million times a day and recalled a line in a book by Martin Amis of the 'pain in the childless woman knowing that no one will ever call her MUM'.

I lost some weight and got fitter than I had ever been in preparation for what would be a massive shock to the system. The arduous task of two small humans needing attention at all times. Someone unaware of my situation told me in a world-weary fashion that 'when you have children you are no longer the picture, you become the frame'. This delighted me. I would surely be the best, sturdiest, most ornate frame that had ever been made and I was ready for the perfect picture to fill my loving rectangular embrace.

By week nine through to week 12 of pregnancy, arms, hands, fingers and feet become fully formed. Fingernails and toenails are beginning to develop and two little external ears are formed. As I wasn't experiencing any of the pregnancy physically, knowing what was going on seemed the next best thing, but I got ahead of myself.

On week 11 Jamie called. Something wasn't right. She was bleeding and had been advised to attend an ultrasound scan. The sudden thud of dread in my solar plexus made me nauseous. I called the babies' daddy and we attempted consoling words and sanguine acceptance. Having a child with someone who you love dearly but are not intimate with is a strange but acceptable experience. Discussing the possible loss of that baby or babies with the same person felt alienating and stilted; almost like we didn't know each other as we had never had to deal with such a thing before. It was upsetting for both of us that our individual panic couldn't be shared.

I remember saying, 'Oh well, at least we tried,' as though I were talking about the impossibilities of erecting a flatpack Ikea wardrobe. We ended the conversation with,

'Are you OK?'

'Yes, I'm OK. Are you OK?'

'Yes, I'm OK.'

And we hung up.

Jamie called. 'They could only find one heart beat.' She started to cry. A lost twin. I tried to offer kind words but they wouldn't come. Strange vowel sounds filled the air before I managed, 'Darling, I'm so sorry, it's not your fault.' I thought of the secret matching outfits, of the double buggy I had been searching for, of the little fully formed heart that had stopped beating. How many beats had there been? The tiny heart tubes start beating 65 times a minute by the end of the fourth week. How many was that? Jamie interrupted my mad internal equations and said, 'They are keeping me in, to monitor the other twin. I will call you back if anything changes.'

The following morning a second ultrasound was silent. The other twin had died. Both babies gone, a week before the end of the first trimester.

If you've ever wondered how one grieves for something that

never was, ask a woman who has tried for many years to conceive a child. Having crossed that particular bridge some time before, it was now a case of grieving for two lives that very nearly were. Though a terrible time for me and the babies' dad, there was relief that the secret hadn't been shared and that other elements of our lives could now return without the need for explanation or discussion.

Without warning, I slipped into a deep, dark hole of gloom. Much has been written by many folk better qualified than me on the nature of depression and I won't bore you with it here. Perhaps mine was linked to the menopause as well as the babies, but the only real symptom I had was one of no longer wishing to take up space on the earth. It wasn't suicidal thoughts as much as just wanting to dematerialise, to fade away and never to have existed. Work and life continued and to the untrained eye all was well. Make-up would be applied, smiles painted on, jokes enjoyed much as before, while in the darkness of home, I would retreat under the duvet and long for terminal illness.

I would take my bike out on long arduous rides. Puppy in the basket, we would cycle the coastal path to Normans Bay and then on to Eastbourne. Sometimes deliberately cycling against the wind in order to feel the physical pain of exertion. I would cycle so hard that my lungs would be screaming for air. In Eastbourne, I would watch young mums with babies in pushchairs and marvel at how casually they treated this miracle of life. Then we would cycle home, Puppy and I. Small innocent dog, unaware of anything wrong, calmly accepting his fate and bobbing his head low in the basket to avoid the punishing wind.

I became obsessed with the bike and how far and fast I could cycle. The bike and the sea took on ridiculous importance and I started to feel for the first time that my bike was a receptacle for pain. I could scream into the wind when the cramp in my thighs became unbearable. Something in my mind was slipping and it was frightening.

I visited the doctor. She asked me how I felt and all I could do was recite the line from Hamlet, 'Oh, that this too too solid flesh would melt / Thaw and resolve itself into a dew!' (quite pretentious).

I didn't return to London for three weeks, cancelled all work, was prescribed the mandatory antidepressants and given a number for the Samaritans, which is how we deal with mental health in this country.

Once home, I talked to the small, not overly bright Maltese terrier about this other black dog that was encroaching. He rushed off to the door and returned with his lead before sitting patiently with it in his teeth. A trick I'd never seen him do before and it made me laugh. In truth, Puppy didn't do any tricks apart from sitting for treats. I pulled on my boots and we went for a walk. I had a responsibility for this animal who never asked to come and live with a nutter, so I needed to feed, water and walk him. Every morning we would cycle for miles, in country parks, meadows, across low-tide sands and ornamental gardens where he would leap and jump, run and twirl, until exhausted he would flop gratefully back into his mobile basket to be pedalled home. My only task was to keep this creature alive, which meant that I mustn't allow this too too solid flesh to melt.

I would often find myself mindlessly blithering away to his uncomprehending gaze as he trotted along beside me, blissfully unaware of anything I was saying.

Little by little as the days passed, thoughts of the future started to creep to the forefront of my mind and notions of dematerialising drifted away.

Six months later, on the day the twins should have been born, the squirrelled-away outfits were donated to a mother and baby unit and Puppy accompanied me as far as he dare, down to the breaking waves on the beach, where I placed two red rose stems for two little lives.

As I did so, I remember thinking how filmic it was, the sun was shining, my hair blowing in the wind, Puppy sitting patiently. It was when I was choosing the music to accompany this scene ('Moon River') that I started to laugh. It would appear my ego was back, which surely meant that I wasn't very far behind?

Surrogacy didn't work out for me, but there are no regrets in having a last throw of the dice.

I am still in touch with Jamie our surrogate who has birthed three babies for lovely folk and I couldn't be happier for them all.

Regret is one of the saddest emotions but the disappointment of not trying at all would have been much worse.

Chapter 19

Agony Aunt:

Day-Glo 90s Marin

Being able to help with other people's problems is WAY easier than addressing one's own issues. It is extremely difficult to be objective about situations you're in the middle of when all available emotions are battling for supremacy.

It is presumptuous though to think that problems can be solved easily. That is not always the point, sometimes it is enough to confide in another, to share a worry and to hear yourself say the bad thing out loud.

To have lived a life with umpteen ups and downs is also a handy tool. Experience counts for a lot, although some of the problems I have heard, read and commented upon have been of much greater heartbreak than anything I have been through.

During my increasingly extended stays by the seaside, I took the puppy to be risk- and suitability-assessed to work as a PET dog. Pets As Therapy has proved to be extremely useful in children's homes, hospitals and hospices. Allowing folk to find outlets for difficult feelings by playing with, stroking or interacting with animals. The science on this is a little sketchy but it involves vulnerability and empathy.

As Puppy was a quiet, timid little creature and not especially touched by the clever stick, he seemed as though he might be a likely candidate. Boisterous, bouncy, inquisitive animals aren't really suitable, especially if patients or inmates are connected to life-saving wires and machines. Puppy passed his many tests with flying colours as he was able to channel his limited levels of concentration towards the person providing petting, kind words or treats.

Once I had spent a day on my own training, which mainly involved dangerous objects, slippery surfaces, fire hazards and end-of-life emergencies, we were good to go.

Many would assume that hospices are grim, sad and grey hellholes filled with people clinging onto life by their eyelashes. This assumption would be wrong. They are social, cheery, bright and lively hubs where life goes on in all its silliness until it doesn't.

The temptation for some might be to find out why people are there, how ill they are and how long they have left. Not only would these enquiries be rude and unwelcome, but you would quickly realise that such information is redundant and irrelevant. There are few long-term projections other than tomorrow.

Puppy and I would wander through the common room, peek around doors and visit whoever felt up to it or was in need of a cup of tea or a fluffy dog and its fluffy owner. We quickly got to know most of the clientele and Puppy would be delighted with all the attention.

A lady we saw a lot would save titbits for the dog and beckon us into her room with a bent forefinger like a pantomime villain.

Louise was a nutty ball of energy and something of a repeat offender. Being extremely poorly on three occasions only to bounce back into remission and return home. She had been a dancer in the 1960s and showed me endless photographs of her with stars of the day where she always looking sultry and gorgeous. Freddie and the Dreamers, The Bachelors, Matt Munro, The Walker Brothers, she knew them all, some better than others as she would tell me with a wink. Louise was always impeccably turned out with full make-up and long slender legs clad in inky black 20 denier tights. She had a plentiful amount of slightly over-processed red hair and would never allow a grey root to poke through, instead asking me to replenish her stock of Nice and Easy Auburn Sunset with alarming frequency. Louise would tell me outrageous showbusiness stories and screech with laughter. In return for the lurid tales I would smuggle in Eccles cakes that she wasn't supposed to have (sugar) and hide them in the back of her cupboard. Louise also had an odd conversational tic where she would say at the end of a sentence, 'Does that make sense?' It would always be used after a collection of words that made perfect sense. For instance, 'I put a wash on that takes 45 minutes, can you remind me in 45 minutes? Does that make sense?' Or, 'If you get me some hair dye from Boots, I'll give you the money when you bring it in. Does that make sense?' I often pointed out the nonsensical use of this phrase but she would just laugh and carry on as normal. It seemed churlish to chide her.

Another little chap we visited was always delighted to see the puppy and would stroke him until the poor mutt was flattened on his back with his feet in the air while Andrew tickled his tummy. Andrew was eight and extremely bright; the ward sister used the word 'precocious' but he was a little darling. Small for his age with jutting cheek bones, I often pondered what a handsome man he would never get the chance to become. Andrew's mum had three other children at home and couldn't get in to visit as often as she would have liked, so he and I had long, involved discussions about Peekachoo and other Pokemon creatures he had extensive knowledge of. He had a large box of cards featuring Ash , Snorlax, Charizard and other madly named animals that he would flick through endlessly, babbling about who he had swapped this one and that one with, what they were worth and that he had filled an entire album at home.

One afternoon when we were discussing Doctor Who, he told me in a matter-of-fact way, 'Mum says that I will probably die soon and that I have to go to Heaven.' I didn't make any comment and he chuntered on, 'Thing is, I don't really want to go to Heaven. I won't know anyone?'

'Well, you didn't know anyone before you went to school and now you know lots of people,' I said, trying to be reassuring.

'Yes, but it's nearly Christmas and I'd rather stay here and be with everyone else and get lots of toys. Do you think I should stay here until Christmas?'

'Why don't you see how you feel,' I said. 'You don't have to decide today, do you?'

Satisfied with this, Andrew went back to his box of cards and said, 'Yeah, I'll see how I feel.'

Some of the residents we visited would confide their fears. It was usually of a practical nature. Worried about who would look after their dog and would I have it? Or wondering if they would manage to finish a cardigan they were knitting and might I find some extra wool. I'm not sure anyone ever told me they were frightened of dying, rather that they were frightened of pain and not being in control.

Just before Christmas, Louise was circumspect. Not her usual nattery self.

She told me she had a daughter and that they were estranged. Louise seemed to have broken contact with all her family for reasons never discussed. She gave birth to her daughter Sage at nineteen who was then brought up by her eldest sister while Louise continued her dancing career. 'I would just like to see her before I go,' she said. 'I know it's stupid but I'd just like to let her know how much I loved her. It doesn't matter that she doesn't love me. Does that make sense?'

'Yes Louise, it does make sense,' I said. 'What can I do to help?'

She gave me a small, battered address book filled with scrawly writing and said, 'Someone in there will know where she is.'

This was quite a tall order and I was daunted by the task, but in her usual cheery fashion she asked, 'Are you sure you don't mind, Maria?'

What could I say? It was Christmas after all.

The search proved fruitless. Most of the numbers in the address book were landlines of people long since moved. Messages were left and other suggestions given but to no avail. Louise was disappointed, so to cheer her up I suggested she ask a member of staff to bring her to the Christmas day swim.

I had managed to acquire a rented beach hut on the lower prom in St Leonards, sharing with my friend Emma. We painted it gold, filled it with driftwood, Coronation mugs and upcycled furniture and created a camp spectacle of the 1950s. It became something of a tradition to hold a Christmas Day swim and along with the huts either side we would serve mulled wine, mince pies and boxes of Cadbury's Roses to swimmers and spectators alike. Owing to the freezing temperature of the English Channel in December, we called it the 'Dip 'n' dash', whereby hordes of enthusiastic nutters would charge into the sea up to their necks, scream with pain then struggle out with disappeared testicles, raw pink skin and hypothermia.

For lots of regulars, the swim meet-up was something of a lifeline as Christmas can be quite lonely. To have had a cup of warm wine, a chat and a laugh with strangers, going home to a turkey dinner for one doesn't then seem quite as bad.

I had cycled to the hut with bags of beakers and boxes of tiny pies and set up camp at the hut. Decorating the doors with bunting and cheap tinsel, the crowds started to gather as the sun broke through the murk and the sky turned azure blue. A perfect December morning, crisp and cold with a golden yellow orb. Large pots were placed on the stove to be filled with red wine, brandy, orange segments and spices.

Just before 11am I spotted Louise with one of the male nurses from the hospice and found her a chair to sit and watch the action by the hut. She was bundled up in a bright pink swing coat with a fur collar, matching pink hat and looking sensational in a heroine-chic-end-of-life way. Bang on eleven o'clock, the horns started blowing and we all ran squealing and hollering across the shingle into the waves. The sea was very rough that year and several unsuspecting souls took a pummelling, but it was all part of the madness and once everyone had been helped back to shore, it was time to dry off and have a warming glass or two, turning our lips from blue, though purple and back to pink.

As the last of the revellers ebbed away to deal with turkeys, Brussels sprouts and family dynamics, Louise came to say goodbye.

'Maria, it's been lovely but before I go, I'd really like to have a ride of your bike. Can I?'

'Whaat? Are you joking?' I laughed.

'I used to love riding a bike, there are no cars here and it's such a beautiful day! I'd just like to have one more go, does that make sense?' She looked very small and suddenly very ill.

'It makes no sense whatsoever, Louise,' I said. 'When did you last ride a bike and haven't you got enough on your plate without inviting further injury?'

'Oh, let the woman have a go on your bike,' said my friend Craig, as he was filling black bags with wine-stained paper cups. 'We'll run along with her, won't we Jason?' he said, to the bemusement of his boyfriend Jason, who wasn't really paying attention.

The old Day-Glo orange bike was pretty balanced, but was Louise balanced? When people say, 'Oh, it'll be easy, just like riding a bike,' I'm not sure they take into consideration that riding a bike is trickier than it looks, especially if you're over 70 and have been depleted by cancer.

Craig knew the male nurse who had kindly brought Louise to the hut and shouted, 'Brad, darling. We'll bring Louise back to the disco in the car! Go and enjoy your Christmas.'

So it was that Louise got her wish. She was helped onto the saddle where she giggled and batted her lashes before tentatively setting off with a gay stabiliser either side. Clutching a shoulder each, they trotted alongside the bike like perfectly behaved, highly trained dressage ponies.

Louise was beaming. I saw the vibrant woman she would have been when young. Twisting men around her little finger. She was singing 'Along the prom, prom, prom, tiddly om pom pom,' and the boys joined in with breathy gasps.

'Just for a tiny moment will you let me go?' she asked. 'I just want it to be only me. Just for a second?'

And so they did. They took their arms away for ten seconds and Louise sailed on. Just her, the sunshine, the sea and the bike.

Once we'd prised her out of the saddle she was glowing. 'Oh, I so enjoyed that! It was glorious. It must be 40 years since I've been on a bike. Thank you!'

'Now she tells us,' said Jason.

'That has made my day and my Christmas!' she laughed.

The boys took her back to the disco, as they called the hospice, and I locked up the hut. The day was warm and lots of people were on the beach.

'Lovely mulled wine!' someone shouted. 'Happy Christmas, Maria!'

'Isn't it just?' I shouted back.

Sometime during the Chrimbo limbo, or 'perineum' as some wag called it, between Boxing Day and New Year's Eve, I had a phone call.

It was Sage, Louise's daughter. She had got wind of my enquiries and curiosity had compelled her to call me. This was going to be tricky. I had no idea of the relationship she had with her mum, or how this call was going to pan out. I went for brevity and honesty, a short explanation of my involvement and that the doctors had predicted a month to six months.

Sage was very quiet and I resisted the temptation to say more words. She was letting the information sink in.

'I'm not sure I can face it,' she said, finally.

'I completely understand that,' I told her, 'but this is something you won't get a second chance at. I know very little about the relationship with your mum, but she IS your mum and soon she won't be here anymore.'

Sage said she didn't want to bring up old emotions and that her life was settled. We ended the call with her agreeing to think about it.

I had done my best but it sat with me for a long time, as did many of the problems that were sent in to Radio 2. We often never found out how things had been resolved with difficult dilemmas, although occasionally we would get follow-up letters detailing outcomes both good and bad.

There was a lady who was trapped in a violent marriage but couldn't leave because she had two children. There will always be reasons not to change the situations you are in and until you can separate the problem and what is in your way you will remain stuck. It can be a slow process to gain strength and the will to address what is needed.

Graham and I had both urged the writer of this letter to get help and to leave an increasingly dangerous relationship. We had provided (off air) details of women's refuges and other areas of assistance.

A good ten months later, she wrote again: 'I managed to leave the family home with the help of some amazing women at Women's Aid and Next Chapter. The children are settled into new schools, thriving, and no longer scared. I went to the police about my ex and this time I found the strength not to drop the charges or take him back. Thank you. My confidence had been worn down but you helped me to believe it WAS possible.'

Another problem that stuck in my mind detailed a mother who had left an extremely divisive will. She had told her four children that her funds, house and estate would be split equally between them. After her death they were informed by the solicitor that the lion's share of all revenue had been bequeathed to her only son. To knowingly and actively cause such upset after your death beggars belief. It is a final act of anger guaranteed to create hurt, division and pain.

We had suggested all the siblings meet and discuss this situation without rancour or bitterness. The best solution was to rise above this hateful act, remain united and to divide the spoils equally.

I loved the follow-up letter that told us they had done exactly that. All four siblings had become closer as a result of this decision and had exorcised all resentments towards their mother and forgiven her. 'She was not a happy woman,' read the final sentence.

It's certainly true that unhappiness makes people behave in unexpected and damaging ways. After 12 years of 'Agony Aunting' (ridiculous phrase but I can think of no other) I conclude that most difficulties can be resolved with communication and total honesty.

So easy and yet so very hard.

Little Andrew made it home for Christmas, presents and all, but didn't get to see in the New Year.

Louise soldiered on until February and I was delighted to hear that she had been reunited with both her daughter and granddaughter who had visited twice before Louise's departure. I still think of her sailing along the seafront on Christmas morning and often smile to myself when I hear folk use the redundant phrase, 'Does that make sense?'

Chapter 20

Understanding Vulnerability:

Day-Glo Marin

Being admitted to hospital when coronavirus was rising at terrible speed was NOT quite what I had planned for my pre-Christmas run-up, but after eight days of pain and a middle-of-the-night call to 111, that was where I found myself.

Self-diagnosis is never a good idea but when other members of my sea swim group went down with a Norovirus-type bug, so did I. Bloated tummy, sickness, nausea, fever and a temperature of 39 degrees.

They got better, I remained ill and chastised myself and my immune system for letting this illness get the better of me.

There is, I believe in all of us, a strong primal instinct to stay alive. Something I experienced once before when throwing myself out of a plane at 10,000 feet over the Egyptian desert, undertaking a tandem skydive.

Every fibre of your being screams 'this is not conducive to life!'

So it was that same primal instinct took over early morning in late December when, on all fours as if giving birth, I breathlessly panted out my symptoms to the kindly soul on the other end of the NHS emergency phoneline. 'It sounds like your appendix, get to the hospital straight away,' was the response.

The prerequisite three hours in A&E saw me slumped across the socially distanced seats waiting for blood test results. You are properly in pain when you couldn't care a jot how the hell you are perceived. That morning in the Conquest hospital, a new system had been implemented. Written physical notes had been dispensed with and now all patient details were to be put online for ease and speed. It had, apparently, 'been a long time coming'.

Despite the march of technology, the new system caused much consternation to virtually everyone in a position to care and the explanations of why and how were gone through again and again to anyone, including me, within earshot. 'It's a whole new system, it started this morning, all physical notes are now online, I KNOW! It's a nightmare.'

Someone called my name and informed me I was to be admitted to the surgical assessment unit where they would immediately organise pain relief.

The small, kindly, Irish porter came to collect me pushing a trolley chair bigger than he was. He waited patiently at reception for my notes.

Having heard the phrase repeatedly over the previous three hours, I helpfully regurgitated it myself, 'There aren't any notes, it's all gone online, the new system started this morning.' He stared at me and nodded, 'Is that right?' Nonetheless, he clearly felt it best to wait. People came and went, he made half-hearted attempts to engage with harassed administrators behind the Plexiglass and to obtain my notes that weren't there because they had gone online that morning.

After ten minutes and no notes, I set off alone for the assessment ward leaving porter and trolley chair trailing in my wake.

Once on the ward, I noticed my name in green ink on the white board at the nurses' station. Somewhat reassured by this, I was nevertheless sent to yet another waiting room, this time with reclining chairs.

Having been physically sick with the pain 30 minutes previously, things were now desperate.

I stomped out to the nurses' station and declared, 'Where's the joined-up thinking here? I need pain relief! I am there on the board. Look! There's my name, please can I be given SOMETHING?'

Eight or nine pairs of tired eyes stared back at me in disbelief. Even I wondered who the hell I thought I was?

Rude and out of character, it nevertheless did the trick. I was hooked up to a drip, given an IV cannula and my veins were quickly infused with a clear soothing liquid that eradicated all feeling. After eight increasingly agonising days, this outcome was nirvana.

Next, I was taken to a bed on the ward with my own little side cabinet and a set of control panels to operate my high-tech bed.

At this stage it seemed the bed allocation was temporary and that it was merely a more comfortable way to administer drugs. Information is hard to come by when everyone is so busy and it's hard to ascertain where the big decisions are being made.

Having reached the ripe old age of 62 I have been lucky enough never to have been in hospital, other than an appearance on *Holby City* where I played Martine, a good-time girl with a predilection for booze and fags.

It remains one of my favourite jobs and involved lying around in bed wearing hospital pyjamas, reading *Hello* and *OK!* magazines while eating Quality Street and gossiping with other actors.

The short bursts of 'acting' were tedious interruptions to my rather lovely social club which only came to an end when my character Martine died suddenly from complications and an infarction of the heart. Being paddled with a defibrillator was the only time I had to really put in any acting effort, as when they shout CLEAR! and the pretend electric shock goes through you, a full body spasm is required whilst lying flat on the trolley and keeping your face from scrunching up in laughter.

Just one take on the defibrillator and my hospital stay was over as Martine's death was called at 3.38pm. Meaning me and the remaining Quality Street were in a cab home before rush hour.

Television is not real though, diagnoses are made, treatments implemented and patients discharged all in a neatly tied-up hour.

A man in full hazmat suit appeared and gave me a Covid test, another for MRSA (Methicillin resistant staphylococcus aureus) and yet a further check for C Diff (Clostridium difficile infection). All this before being seen by a doctor and prior to any diagnosis.

I was in a 'holding pen' until my Covid test could be processed, a negative result meaning transfer to the main ward (were that to prove necessary) with other non-Covid inmates.

The lady in the next-door bed was in a lot of pain, she was rigged up to saline solutions and other medicines to help with what I gathered was some form of gall bladder blockage.

She was my neighbour, but all that separated us was a flimsy nylon curtain hastily pulled across to give the illusion of privacy. For a nosy parker like me all audible info was perfectly accessible.

Her name was Cathy and she was from Ireland. I heard her telling the nurse checking blood pressure levels that she was 88 and had been married for 65 years. 'We have never spent a night apart, he will be very worried.'

All this in a quiet soft Irish lilt that made my eyes water.

It also made my eyes water when some moments later she let out a full-bodied fart that lasted over a minute. This would be Cathy's signature and unique calling card which would ring out throughout the night, competing with the buzzings and beepings of her multiple monitors.

No longer in any pain, I felt pretty chipper and was able to mince about the ward getting cups of tea and generally behaving like Barbara Windsor in *Carry on Matron*.

My main nurse, Stefano, told me he was from Italy and we swapped stories of sea swimming and temperature levels. He was also some sort of martial art ninja despite having kind, smiley eyes and a bedside manner that should be taught in medical school. He could only see my eyes as masks were 24/7 and I could only see his behind his mask and visor. Funny to think of the nurse–patient intimacy with someone I would now fail to recognise in the street.

Stefano informed me that the earlier blood test had revealed my pain bio markers to be very high. This relates to the white T-cells called in to do the heavy lifting when infection is detected.

He also explained the raised chicken pox-like rash covering my chest and tummy was another way the body was showing distress.

All very clever but as I'm not a qualified doctor, my diagnosis/treatment had been heat rash, aloe vera and a Twix.

I was taken up to have a scan and injected with some form of coloured liquid that the operator told me would make me very hot and feel as though I had wet myself. I told him it all sounded delightful and that I was looking forward to both side effects.

Holding onto the hope that I would be home for dinner, my scan results failed to materialise. Stefano and the other nurses left for the evening and the nightshift took over. Everyone on my ward was asleep or drugged or dead and only Cathy's noisy trumps kept my spirits up.

The lady opposite me woke up and I waved a cheery hello. Her name was Pauline and she had failed to recognise her broken leg for ten days, preferring instead to see it as a 'sprain'.

She also admitted that Covid and 'not wanting to make a fuss' had kept her away from A&E. That she arrived when she did meant her leg and her life could be saved.

Her leg resembled a dead fish washed up onshore, bloated and discoloured. It looked, to my untrained eyes, beyond help. She explained that a seizure had caused the fall, epilepsy from the age of 21. She was tearful and afraid but seemed quite keen to chat.

A very beautiful woman, now 68, her story unravelled easily.

Her mother had had an affair with a man from the Caribbean and Pauline was born.

Her siblings were white and she never managed to fit in with either the white or the black community.

A relationship with the drummer in the band Hot Chocolate saw Pauline give birth at 16. A son she is supremely proud of and grateful for.

Then came an affair with the football manager Malcolm Allison, or 'Big Mal' as he was known. A former West Ham player who went on to manage Manchester City and Crystal Palace.

Allison was 44 and married when he met the beautiful, impressionable 20-year-old Pauline. He promised her many times that he would leave his wife and they would be together, but of course, in time-honoured tradition that never happened.

After one disappointment too many, the emotional and reckless now 21-year-old Pauline took a lethal overdose.

She was saved within a whisker of death but suffered a massive stroke that left her disabled and with epilepsy. 'I fucked up my puny life at 21,' she said with a weary acceptance of her own youthful folly.

Being the only mobile patient on my ward, I got Pauline a cup of tea and attempted cheery platitudes.

The ward lights were dimmed around 10pm and I kept trying to imagine Pauline's life as a mixed-race child in 1953 Britain and how that must have shaped her painfully low expectations.

Sleep in hospital is not an easy ask. The machines, nurses, general babble and woodland sounds from other inhabitants are relentless.

Pauline put up a strong performance as the Queen of snoring, as she had to lie on her back; I couldn't help but forgive her but there was a considerable cacophony of competition.

Both Pauline and Cathy had loud and lengthy botty chats with occasional gaseous interjections further up the ward.

It was rather touching to listen to 88-year-old Cathy talking in her sleep and quietly laughing, her subconscious having taken her to a happy place where she wasn't ill, worried or missing the man who had been her husband for 68 years. At one point she started giggling like a teen and muttering, 'Oh Jim. Hee hee hee, come on now!' in a gentle Irish burr, as though Jim was teasing her from a place in her mind long ago.

Getting old is a really bad joke, was my take on it all. Not an original thought, granted, but all I could muster after a troubling day.

The morning (6.30) brought a change of shifts. Bleary-eyed nurses left and were replaced by an equally bleary but fresh to the fight set of selfless angels.

We also welcomed a new arrival to the Covid holding pen.

Jonty. Jonty had been thrown from a horse, had broken her collarbone along with several ribs that caused her to be very vocal about the considerable agony every movement involved. Shocked, frightened and new to the idiosyncratic ways of the ward, it was clear she was best left to acclimatise alone, without Mrs Nosey Parker shoving her beak anywhere near her.

I remained 'nil by mouth' until the scan results revealed my fate and was feeling slightly light-headed with hunger. The solution was a saline drip into my overworked IV line after the morning infusion of antibiotics.

As I actually felt OK and no longer in any pain, I was able to phone in for my slot on the Radio 2 morning show with Graham Norton. I checked with the ward sister and shuffled my drip off to a patient waiting room away from the ward. Much ribald hospital chat with Graham ensued and endless beeping from the drip every time I bent my arm and affected the cannula, gesticulating as I would have had I been in the studio at the BBC. My half-hour radio slot was much like normal apart from my natty J-cloth pyjamas, unbrushed hair and gut-crunching hunger.

Back on the ward in time for rounds and my consultant Andrew had my scan results.

It appeared the appendix had ruptured and caused a wall of infection around both itself and my lower bowel. This seemed like a rather clever way of stopping sepsis. Whilst this wall may have contained all the life-threatening nastiness, it also meant operating would not be possible as it would be too difficult to determine the exact whereabouts of the appendix in amongst the infection of doom that I imagined as a wasps' nest of fuzzy gases, old crisp packets and small flying insects.

My treatment was to be IV antibiotics for the next two days, plus a further scan and colonoscopy once the infected fuzz ball had dispersed. Andrew told me that once the appendix ruptures, it often shrivels up and dies. This sounded like the correct and noble thing to do in the circumstances, but he added that there may be some 'appendiceal malignancy' that we might need to investigate.

I was in hospital, the word malignancy had been mentioned and there was nothing else to do but plan my funeral, choose lovely representative songs and compose an amusingly poignant speech to be filmed whilst wearing full make-up and big hair but only once I had reached the optimal cancer weight and just before I started to look terminal.

Rescue by Drama is how I view this morbid streak.

My Covid test came back negative so I was jumped from the holding pen onto a ward with my own window. This was the preferential treatment I had been waiting for! I was also no longer 'nil by mouth', so ordered chicken peas and roast potatoes for dinner.

Of course hospital food is never nice, but after 38 hours of hunger it felt like fine dining at the Ivy and I only just managed to stop myself from licking the plate.

My new neighbour on this ward was an elderly lady with nicely done hair and two rather alarming black eyes. My smiles went unreturned though and she seemed to be lost in another place. Her name was April. She talked a lot to herself as if someone was beside her bed and I heard her mutter 'that brown one is SO lazy, she will never bring a bedpan'. She was talking about one of the nurses, Faber. As troubling as this was, the old lady was sick and the nurses could not have been kinder or more patient. My guess was that April voted Brexit.

Before bed, I popped back to see how Pauline was in the Covid holding pen. She raised her eyebrows and shook her head. 'How will I sleep with Jonty shouting and screaming?' she said. Poor Jonty was really in trouble and nothing or no one was able to help. She had gone into full defensive battle mode and the pain was making her nuts.

As sorry as I was for both Jonty and Pauline, I was quite glad to have moved wards and have a Brexity old racist as my bedfellow.

At 6am the following morning I managed to sneak off into

the shower before anyone was awake. Lovely Stefano found me shampoo, towels and clean pyjamas and the buzz from such a simple pleasure kept me buoyed up until lunchtime.

As I returned to my bed, April asked me rather curtly if I would change her pad before adding triumphantly, 'I have wet the bed too!' I probably could have changed her pad but couldn't trust myself as to what I would do with the soiled one. *Pulp Fiction*-like visions of stuffing it in her mouth and suffocation briefly appeared in my head. Whilst I like to think of myself as a compassionate being, the heady cocktail of drugs may have momentarily unhinged my thinking.

Instead I smiled and said that I too was a patient and I would try and find a nurse who was free and able to change both pad and bedding for her. This was not the correct answer and April scowled at me, muttering something under her breath. All I heard was 'blonde bitch'. Perhaps April has dementia, I thought, but 'No,' the nurse told me with a smile, 'she is just a little curmudgeonly.'

A mental note was made to kill myself before reaching this 'curmudgeonly' stage of life. (Please remind me.)

All the while I was on the ward, patients wore masks 24/7, the staff wore masks, visors, goggles, and rubber gloves changed at every use. Covid also meant a no-visitors policy. I appreciate that this was a very difficult situation for everyone and kept my communications to friends and family as silent text messages only.

It surprised me somewhat when a new lady without a single tooth to her name arrived on my ward and immediately FaceTimed her family on a speakerphone, her iPad set at ear-bleeding decibel levels. I listened as baby Kylie sang her grandma an endlessly tuneless ditty and her son guffawed about how many pints he had downed the night before. 'Wait a minute, I'm gonna show the other ladies on the ward my lovely granddaughter,' bellowed Gummy Granny.

I smiled thinly at the blurry image and scurried off to get myself tea and to marvel at the total lack of awareness for others.

When I returned, Gummy was still gabbling on to further members of her brood and Curmudgeonly April had a glamorous visitor sitting beside her bed.

Her daughter. 'I've driven six hours to get here,' she told her mum, who wasn't really comprehending.

The daughter had a lovely swishy haircut, blonde highlights and a real fur gilet over tight jeans and high boots. She coughed a lot and complained about being starving. 'I'm so hungry I could eat one of these patients!' she said.

'You wouldn't like us, we're all riddled with infection,' I drawled from behind the curtain.

Daughter went on, 'I have asked that bloody nurse THREE times to come and wipe your face, Mum!'

Trying to keep my counsel and not yell, 'Wipe your own mum's face!' it seemed wise to leave the ward and lower my blood pressure.

I bumped into the ward sister and questioned the wisdom of visitors on an open ward that was a tinder box for infection?

She took me to a quiet room and told me that poor April was 'end of life' and that, for compassionate reasons, her family had been allowed to visit and say their goodbyes.

This seemed fair and humane, but after all the safety measures staff and patients were following to the letter, perhaps a private room would be more Covid-secure?

The ward sister agreed and gently let me know that all efforts were being made to find such a room.

My fury at this situation was almost certainly a combination of tension, fear, anxiety and sadness for poor, curmudgeonly, black-eyed April.

Ward sister Sarah was lovely. She had clearly seen this transference of anxiety a million times before. We had a cup of tea, talked nonsense and I trundled back to the ward.

Gummy was still gassing on her iPad, but someone must have politely asked her to turn the volume down owing to the sad farewells being said in the bed opposite.

April's daughter was also in animated mid-flow, telling her baffled mum about her new trick with jigsaw puzzles. 'What I do is, I cut the picture out of the box, put all the jigsaw pieces in a Tupperware container – well, I say Tupperware, it's all Lakeland now, isn't it? – and then I throw away the box, pop the picture into the container and seal it!'

I know there's nothing profound to be said in end-of-life farewells, but jigsaw puzzle maintenance seemed so unspeakably banal that I wasn't confident I could contain the hysterical laughter about to burst through my lips.

April's son arrived. Where the daughter was glamorous and chatty, the son seemed incapable of holding eye contact and had the look of a trainspotter, rather like Roy Cropper from *Coronation Street*, all foldaway pac-a-mac and elasticated slip-ons

The daughter reminded us again of her six-hour drive, gave her mum a perfunctory pat on the arm and left, relieved her shift was over.

The son attempted a conversation with his mum, but April couldn't hear him. 'I'm not gonna shout, am I?!' he said, before spending two hours, head down, scrolling through his phone while April dozed. The nurses brought further fresh sheets and scrolling son saw this as an opportunity to leave.

'Be back next week, I hope!' he shouted from halfway down the ward to a mum who couldn't hear him.

It was a sorry and poignant scene to witness and I wished I hadn't.

Sure enough, April was moved to a private room. Not before haughtily telling the porters packing up her possessions, 'Ohh, I'm not going anywhere!' April seemed blissfully unaware that soon, she would be gone in every sense.

Her children returned to their lives unencumbered while the NHS made sure she had a peaceful and pain-free death.

Having been raised as a Catholic, some small part of my old self insisted I say a silent prayer for her imminent departure.

My consultant Andrew whizzed in and informed me that my bloods had shown greatly reduced pain markers and that there was a strong possibility I could be released the following day. This was my cue to pack my meagre possessions and to divvy out my foodstuffs/chocolate to the other patients.

Still in a great deal of discomfort Jonty didn't really know what to do with herself and was still on high alert, eyes darting like a cornered animal. She seemed to be refusing all offers of drugs on account of the fact that, 'I didn't come to hospital to be pumped full of drugs!' This left me wondering quite why she did come to hospital?

There was a pattern emerging of the late-middle-aged women who, having grown so used to being in charge of a thousand different things in their own natural habitat, found it almost impossible to relinquish any of that control when they were compromised by illness or pain. Despite the obvious lack of medical qualifications, they all seemed to know what was best and most effective for their assorted maladies. My own sense of control was assuaged by asking endless, irritating questions. Knowledge is power, and all that.

Jonty, the new arrival in April's freshly and hastily changed bed, and who had fallen from her horse, was cajoled into sitting up in bed and spoken to in gentle tones, but such was her distress nothing could be done to alleviate any of the horror. The nurses wheeled in an 'on demand' morphine machine and the ward sister came to answer questions and instruct her in its simple press a button use: 'Yes, it administers a very small amount.' 'No, you won't be able to overdose.' 'No, you won't become addicted.' 'Yes, you can stop any time you feel weird.' 'No, you won't die in your sleep.'

Jonty allowed them to connect it to her IV line but was adamant she WOULD NOT be using morphine.

En route to cleaning my teeth before bed, I smiled at Jonty in what I hoped was an empathetic way, but she was too lost in her own agonies to respond. Final evening blood pressure checks and drug administrations by the nurses meant further movement for Jonty and tiny yelps of tortured pain.

Another sleepless night loomed.

Sometime around 3am and after the screams, shouts and moanings had finally, mercifully, subsided, the next-door blood pressure monitor went off in an ear-splittingly urgent fashion. Something of an old hand at this, mine had repeatedly bleeped insanely the day before, I knew that it was when the plug had not been put back in and that the battery was low. Leaping up mid-dream and all of a bother, I raced around the flimsy nylon curtain to turn it off.

Jonty looked scared by this wild-haired apparition, breasts spilling from pyjamas and mask askew. The monitor silenced, I rearranged my mask and bent down towards her ear to hiss in a no-nonsense fashion, 'Take the fucking morphine!'

She whimpered in agreement as I attempted to keep some semblance of reason in my tone. 'You are exhausted, your body needs rest to heal, it will help your muscles relax and you need to stop fighting this now.'

Both half asleep, we scrabbled for the morphine button, she pressed it once and I returned to bed.

The dawn brought sunshine and a becalmed bedfellow. I brought her some tea and we chatted though our masks. Her face no longer strained and tense, she looked like a different woman. With the aid of her magic drug pump button, Stefano and another nurse, she was able to leave bed, sit in her chair and even managed a snail-like hobble to the loo (no one likes a bed pan). She told me about her accident, that her horse had been spooked by a local dog and that after being thrown, she lay on the damp grass nearly passing out with the pain until the ambulance arrived.

By now Jonty was loving the morphine, it had given her back some agency over her battered and broken body. Unfortunately, it was wheeled away soon after in the '12 hours on, 12 hours off' ruling that made her look slightly scared and sad.

Discharge papers arrived for me soon after breakfast and my last intravenous infusion before two weeks of antibiotics taken orally (how retro). Four days had felt like four weeks and my gratitude turned into embarrassed blubbing as I said goodbye to Cathy, Pauline, Jonty, Stefano, Faber and all the wonderful staff.

We talk about the NHS as some form of faceless behemoth, but it is made up of a zillion different faces from all avenues of life with care and compassion in their hearts and a belief tattooed on their souls that help and medical assistance should be free for all.

I gave the Conquest hospital five stars on Tripadvisor so am hoping for an immediate upgrade and limitless supply of Quality Street should I ever need to return.

Being in hospital for the first time in my entire life was an experience I am not keen to repeat.

It was a perfect reminder of one's fallibility and that without the wonderful work of Alexander Fleming and his antibiotic marvels, I would have doubtless shuffled off the mortal coil. Where once, as a young woman my immune system may have been capable and steely, it now needs a small amount of assistance.

Reality finally hit home that I am now on the last stretch, in the third age, over the hill and descending. Nothing to be done about it but move forward and maintain the joie de vivre, curiosity, interest and amazement at this ever-changing, beautiful world.

Looking back on this mad, bad and crazy life causes me to smile. Sad that I never got to find a cure for cancer, implement world peace or negotiate an end to poverty; surely the hope of every right-thinking child and/or triumphant beauty queen. Yes, I know there is still time for these noble achievements. Even so, I am left with the firm belief that I have filled my life to the brim.

I have been to ALL the parties, drunk all the wine, taken all the drugs and had sex with all the men. I have worked hard and tried not to be unkind, I have friends I love dearly and have laughed long and hard almost every day of my existence.

Dying is clearly rubbish, but none of us get out of here alive. It would be my hope to go after being given some notice. A week or two to get things in order and to write a long and boring speech to torture attendees at my final shebeen. I would like fun and laughter, celebration and a small moment of quiet reflection for loud and unseemly sobbing.

If given the chance, I would like control over the end of my life. Tucked away in the back of a cupboard are two bottles of morphine, left to me by my old friend John Diamond 20 years ago. Despite the fact it is almost certainly out of date and useless, it has given me comfort in times of distress to know that it's there. I have loved life too much to ever want to ingest this tincture, but there may come a time when given the option, I would rather have agency over my exit than fade away in pain and distress.

Witnessing as I did the final days of some of my fellow hospital inmates it would most definitely not be my first choice to suffer the indignities and loneliness of enforced incarceration with albeit saintly, overworked, NHS personnel.

Suffice to say there will be zero regrets. It's been a blast and it's not over yet!

Chapter 21

Flirting:

Rolls Royce Gifted Marin

To be brutally honest and all things considered, what I miss most about getting older is the flirting. It's an overwhelming acknowledgement of what has drifted away.

Flirting has always been an overriding passion for me.

Not the drunken, eight pints, getting off with someone kind, rather the harmless yet delicious pleasure, charm and cheekiness that a damn good flirt provides.

Good flirting must never flip over into bawdiness or smut but remain a tarantella of clever moves, parrying and playful candour.

Flirting can be employed when dealing with everyone, regardless of gender. It is a clear indicator of understanding and attraction, but it absolutely doesn't have to result in sexy time.

One of the best flirts I have ever encountered was the late Paula Yates. Observing her on set during one of the 'in bed with Paula' segments on Channel 4's *Big Breakfast* was to watch a woman who clearly enjoyed the rough and tumble but also realised the attraction of intelligence cleverly deployed. We got chatting after the show, such a tiny little Thumbelina of a woman, and I commended her fabulous flirting techniques. She looked at me very intensely. 'Use it or lose it,' she trilled. 'There is a finite flirtation window,' and off she went to wrap her legs around another pop star.

During a very brief period of online dating, the ability of my suitors to flirt became key as to whether there was any hope for further encounters. If the response to good-natured teasing was a stony-faced glare, my heart would sink and I would revert to the manual of 'Let him talk about himself'.

Talking AT someone is fine for a bit and essential to impart crucial information, but hearing someone's life in Curriculum Vitae is no one's idea of a good time.

'Tell me your grades,' one chap asked.

'You are a terrible flirt!' I replied. 'Literally. Terrible.'

The first online date I went on started quite well. We met in the Kings Road for drinks and he was tall, impeccably groomed and rather funny and camp with his flirtations. It was going well until my gaydar started screaming to be turned off. He was lovely though, a photographer of 50 who lived with his mum and had never been married. (Beep, beep, beep!)

Let's not jump to hasty conclusions here, we were having a nice time, albeit devoid of any chemistry, but a few hours into the evening and after a couple of drinks too many, I proffered the notion that maybe he was, ahem, gay?

Perhaps I shouldn't have been so bold, but why not call something out if you are potentially barking up a wrong tree?

He didn't seem unduly worried by my enquiry, told me that, no, he wasn't gay, although I wasn't the first to mention it.

We finished our supper, went through the pointless process of exchanging numbers and he very gallantly put me in a taxi home.

I found myself chatting to the cabbie about my introduction to the online world of possibilities and how charming my date had been.

'That bloke who put you in a cab?' he asked.

'Yes,' I said.

'But he's gay, isn't he?' came the response. QED.

Many months later I got a peculiar text that took me ages to fathom who it was and what it meant.

It simply read, 'You were right, I just wasn't ready to admit it.'

'Hallelujah!' I texted back. 'Go and enjoy your best life.'

When you encounter someone who gets you and are able to

verbally spar with, it really is one of life's greatest pleasures. Flirting can be the absolute best foreplay, employing the brain long before any physical contact. To extend that period of exquisite excitement is to have a never-ending supply of surprise presents to open.

A member of a very successful boy band once told me, 'It's SO easy to have sex with anyone I want, that what I want most of all, is the chase. Once you have the prize, that's it, bored now.'

Not that I can match his bedpost for notches, but I absolutely get it. We all know how it ends and that, in many ways, is the least fun part. Alright it IS fun, but it doesn't last that long, whereas flirting gives you prolonged gratification.

Aside from the absence of anaesthetic, the appalling pongs and lack of women's rights, I would have loved to have lived in the 18th century when hand fans were a popular fashion accessory and which women used to convey messages to potential suitors. Such a fabulous way of flirting to flutter your fan in a myriad of ways, hide your eyes, signal to someone you love them, warn of possible danger and even to snap shut your fan in fury and stomp off, tripping over your crinolines.

There was said to be certain codes that aristocratic women could learn called 'fanology' with every fan movement having a meaning. A hand fan was used for so much more than just keeping cool or wafting away a nasty stench.

This from Joseph Addison in the *Spectator* (1711) in a satirical article advertising his school for ladies: 'The purpose of which was to instruct ladies in the proper use of the hand fan so that they "May be entire mistresses of the weapon which they bear".'

The 'weapon'. How sexy is that?

Hiding behind a fan had its pitfalls though.

Imagine the horror of a potential paramour hoping for more, if behind the allure of a delicately embroidered hand fan, sits a tired old crone?

Of course, none of us need become the grey-haired crones of yore and we can all go on to be fabulous in middle and late age, albeit with a packet of hair dye, a bit of exercise and a goodly dose of chutzpah. However, the biological imperative is way stronger than all the L'Oreal, ferocious workouts, or surgeons' knives in Beverly Hills; and Paula Yates was right about the 'finite window'.

Once one is no longer able to conceive or produce children, the flirting success rate drops like a stone. It magically disappears overnight when the ovaries stop chucking out alluring little eggs with whatever witchy pheromones come with them.

Menopause seems to be a literal indication of being past your sell-by date. It pains me to say this and I urge you to disagree, but once the reproductive system starts drying on the vine, the gig is up with the come-hither eyes.

This doesn't mean that life is over, or that all hope is lost. Merely that the flirting game becomes much tougher and you'll need to be wily. It's as if someone has thrown over us a cloak of invisibility. A cruel and nasty trick that Mother Nature has played. What a killjoy.

I am not giving up that easily. No Siree.

We can now use our skills in other ways.

Wearing the cloak of invisibility means much mischief can be achieved as no one sees us anymore!

Where once there was a need for approval, to fit in, this disappears along with fertility. Abracadabra, it's gone. Being afraid to speak up? Yep, that's gone too. There is a newfound confidence about getting older, which has nothing to do with the way you look, what you have achieved or how desirable you are.

It is something waaaay more important. It's the right to be you without any of that nonsense getting in the way or making any difference whatsoever. No one warned me about any of this, and it does take a bit of getting used to.

Flirting can be about the deployment of language, wit, humour and verbal dexterity. I'm the first to admit it could be seen as creepy when attempting to flirt in this way with a younger man, but older men lose their abilities in this department and quickly revert to innuendo and baseness.

I can only assume that the older man may not be quite as successful as his younger self in terms of sexual fulfilment. The urges are still there but he has lost the thrill of the chase and wants to get straight to the bedroom.

Buyer beware.

During my time with Graham Norton at the BBC, I would often come up from the coast and stay with my friend the broadcaster Paddy O'Connell who has a house around the corner from Broadcasting House (he presents a Radio 4 show with the same name). As a gay man of a similar age we would discuss the viability of flirting. For him, he felt the difference between straight and gay was that gay men are more concerned with a potential hook up, having sex and saying goodbye. I pointed out that for a lot of straight men on dating sites, the anticipated outcome was often the same, but the waters were muddied by women wanting both sex AND life partners. A combination that often led to disappointment.

Paddy and I often went to parties and events together, he always made me laugh and was great company. But for his sexual preference we could have been the perfect couple. In the olden days, this was considered a perfectly acceptable arrangement. Form a respectable marriage while maintaining a secret life. I am certainly not advocating this throwback existence and am delighted that we can all be who we want to be, but it does make me question companionship in later life and what it really means. Are we overlooking living arrangements that could access all areas?

After one such extended chat into the early hours of the morning, I stumbled out to work and to collect the Marin safely chained to Paddy's railings. It was gone. Despite there being a Boris Bike rack only yards away, some little tea leaf had seen fit to nick my bike leaving only the cut-through chain to show that it had ever existed. The familiar rage and fury started to build along with a weary sadness that yet again someone had taken something that belonged to me. It's true to say some thefts affected me more than others. I really liked this bike and it was lovely to ride. I was still upset when we went on air and told Graham about my latest loss and that there was little point even reporting it to the police. I surprised myself by hearing a catch in my voice as I spoke. While accepting the inevitability, it still caused me heartache.

A couple of days later, I was contacted by the boss of Marin Bikes UK who told me he had heard me speaking about yet another theft and would I like to choose a bike from the latest range to replace my 90s Day-Glo oddity. Such a kind offer, but I had to explain that I wouldn't be able to thank him on air owing to BBC advertising guidelines, etc. He understood and wasn't bothered. 'Look in the catalogue and choose something that suits your needs,' he said.

That was it. No price cap, no strings attached, a lovely, brand-new, top-of-the-range Marin bike, as a gift!

I was embarrassed about this gift and felt a little unworthy and spoiled so I asked a cycling friend to choose something for me. I didn't want to appear greedy, but Marin bikes aren't cheap and I was boggled by the array. My friend Emma chose a beautiful sleek road bike with alloy frame and specialised wheels, but as instructed, didn't tell me how much it cost.

It was only when I took this magnificent machine to my local bike shop for adjustments that I found out it cost two thousand pounds. It was lovely to ride but I was in a constant state of panic about leaving it anywhere. Several heavy locks were employed, but I never felt relaxed about where it was parked or how long I would be. It was almost as if it wasn't mine and I knew how terrible I would feel if something happened to this graciously gifted piece of kit.

I had also, by chance, picked up a secondhand Marin for a good price (£120) not long after I took possession of the whiz bang wallop spendy one and would often use the cheapo version as it didn't cause me stress. It felt as though I were stockpiling Marins in anticipation of the super spendy machine being robbed.

All this is madness, I know, but after six months of owning the posh bike I felt like giving it back. A ridiculously ungrateful option but we didn't really work well together. Can that be said of some wheels, a frame and pedals? I talked to the man in my local bike shop and decided that he would sell the bike for me, take a cut and the money would be given to charity.

Once this was complete, I felt happy again. It had never felt right to be given something so expensive merely because I had a national radio platform to moan about theft. It was an extremely kind gesture of Mr Marin CEO, but all the bikes I have loved and lost have meant more to me because I have been the one to bring them back to life, to rescue them from garages or to liberate them from junk shops. It surely wouldn't take a psychiatrist long to unravel the above, but it's probably something to do with a little girl who wanted her own bike and to do things her own way.

Chapter 22

Advice to Self:

Junk Shop Marin and Claud Butler Racer

Hitting milestones is tough. As an agony aunt with Graham Norton on BBC Radio and now Virgin Radio, a lot of letters we receive are concerned with the gloom of getting old. As Bette Davis once said, 'Ageing is not for Cissies' (it may have been a ruder word). With a 60th birthday on the horizon I decided to jot down how to cope and the main advice to myself was to 'Be The Best You Can Be'.

There is nothing easier in the autumn of our years than to sink into comfort, complacency, get set in our habits and feel that in some way the party is over. This of course is entirely your choice, but as we're living longer and staying healthier, I'm here to warn you not to metaphorically hop off the bus before your stop.

We all know that whatever the outer covering looks like, the inner you remains the flirty 22-year-old with the same grand plans and aspirations.

You don't get to be 60 without a lot of baggage in your rucksack. Events unimaginable to you at 20 will have filled your life. Some of it will have been brilliant and some of it will have been painful. This is what has made you who you are. Not the events themselves necessarily, but how you have dealt with whatever tribulations came your way. The longer you've been around, the more experiences both good and bad will have danced through your door and tested your resolve. The wheel goes up and the wheel goes down.

What I've noticed is that the bad, sad, tragic and unpleasant events in our lives have a tendency to get a lot of airtime the older we get. Ruefulness can set in and change the narrative:

'I would have been running Microsoft if Geoff hadn't divorced me.' 'If I hadn't had the children to worry about I could be winning Oscars in Hollywood.' 'If I'd HAD children, I would be more fulfilled and wouldn't feel so lonely.'

You get the picture. Regret is very ageing. Bitterness and disappointment are the gifts that keep on giving, but they are also dull to listen to and will hold you in your history. It's not over yet so do it now!

Everything that has happened has made you who you are, you have survived the awful, enjoyed the fabulous and kept getting up in the mornings for the 'Meh' bits in between.

Some academic or other said that the notion of time speeding up as we get older is because there are fewer 'new' things happening, the brain can process the same old stuff without too much effort, whereas when we were younger there were way more firsts to download. Avoid the groundhog days and continue looking for fresh activities to stimulate the brain. It couldn't be more important to get away from the known by challenging ourselves, it will keep that grey matter bubbling and the synapses firing.

Is it time to slip off the elasticated flares and Nurse Jackie shoes? Time to assess what you show to the world? Not in any way to body- or fashion-shame, merely to confirm that you are happy with this picture and that you are looking after the piece of equipment that has got you this far in one piece.

Accept that it will not be the same image that stared back when you were 22. Children, gravity, hormones and the passing of time will have seen to that. This is not about vanity anymore though, it's about maintenance and repair.

Keeping the engine ticking over, oiling the wheels and getting the paintwork touched up. Be careful about weight too, do NOT try and get back into the jeans you wore at 30. Losing too much weight can make one look haggard, an element of plumped-up flesh will do us more favours. We're on a hiding to nothing to think that youth can be reclaimed, it really can't. Surgery doesn't make you look young. Surgery just makes you look like you've had surgery. Smiling is a way better option and considerably cheaper.

At 60, it's stretching it to go around calling yourself middle-aged. Generic middle age was a comfortable club, but what term does one use now? Old age? The third age? Pensioner? All unpleasant and pejorative. My advice would be not to mention it at all. Who cares and why do they need to know? Do you really want another pigeonhole to sit in where you can be safely patronised? I don't think so.

I have noticed a lot of contemporaries begin sentences with 'I remember when . . .', or 'In my day . . .' These conversation openers are VERY ageing and also invariably not terribly interesting. Try and stay in the present, in the moment or even the future. Keep up with contemporary issues, hang out with the young, ask questions and stay current. The only people who may be interested about what happened 'in your day' will be others who were there and even they couldn't really give a hoot or won't remember. Staying in the moment is where it's at. Learn a language, go and see modern art, travel, read the Booker Prize shortlist, maintain interest.

Staying healthy is the best thing you can do for yourself. No one needs you to train for the London Marathon, but a walk every day and some form of load-bearing exercise will make you feel so much better than a Viennetta on the sofa watching *A Place in the Sun*. Riding my bike gives me as much pleasure now as it ever did, but I am reminded of an aged gentleman I saw cycling extremely slowly up a hill in Bantry, Ireland. I smiled at him as he wobbled past and he shouted, 'Sure this old bike is slowing down!' I understood completely.

Moaning. Stop it. There's a theory that somehow you have earned your right to be miserable by being older. I'm not sure where this came from but it's wrong. Moaning is exhausting both for those who are world champions at it and the poor blighters who are forced to listen to it. It also affects the negative part of your brain that makes you want to do it more. Moaning and complaining is destructive and tedious. Of course things go wrong in life and it may be that you find everything more stressful than it used to be, but an endless litany of complaints really will NOT make you feel better. Instead it will bring everyone else down and turn you into a gigantic bore.

There is nothing more appealing than happiness and enthusiasm. This may be a tough one to put into practice, but fake it till you make it and you'll really notice the difference.

Be realistic. Annoying as it is to know that I will never be Young Musician of the Year, it's still possible to hold on to personal goals and achievements as yet unmastered. There will always be new challenges ahead and although it may be easier to talk yourself out of attempting them, think of the joy and delight in finding out that you CAN accomplish the 'Couch to 5k' challenge, learn the lambada or date someone ten years younger. Whatever floats your boat, you can be sure that there is a version of it that is available and the only thing stopping you is you.

I can't be too prescriptive here and if you really want to magic-marker your day's viewing into the *Radio Times* and await the rat-a-tat of the hooded man with a scythe, then who am I to argue, but we only get one shot at this and it's all there for the taking. As a man of almost ninety told me the other day as we were both lurching into the crashing waves of the English Channel for a nine-degree sea swim, 'You know what, Maria? We're a long time dead. Might as well live now'!

Yes, I now have an electric bike, along with an old-fashioned Claud Butler manual machine, and both give me great joy.

I have let it be known to friends and family that once I am no longer able to get out on the open road, they can let down my tyres and send me off to the velodrome in the sky.

Epilogue

My dad taught me a poem when I was six by the 11th-century Persian polymath, mathematician, astronomer, philosopher and poet, Omar Khayyam. I'm not sure how a working-class boy from Greenock knew about him, but I loved this poem then as much as I love it now:

Now isn't it strange that Princes and Kings

And clowns that caper in sawdust rings

And ordinary folk, like you or me,

Are builders of eternity,

To each is given a book of rules

An hourglass and a set of tools

And each must build 'ere his time has flown

A stumbling block or a stepping stone.

I came across my own version, written when I was at school aged 12. A very poor imitation lacking in subtlety, but a clear indication of my strong ambitions to be a woman at wheel!

Isn't it strange that sad little girls, grow up to be women who clutch at their pearls.

That life is decided in our early years, the portions of laughter, your quota of tears.

With saddle and pedals, a frame and some wheels, all roads can be travelled, all maladies healed.

No need for status, grand titles or wealth, this simple contraption will give you good health.

It can spirit away bad thoughts and all worry, whatever your strengths, there's no need to hurry.

The hills may be tough and could take a while, keep going, you'll get there and it will make you smile!

Acknowledgements

I would like to thank David Burrill, Ross Jamieson and all at Great Northern Books for their hard work in publishing *Bumps in the Road*. The girls who hopefully get all the PR! Jackie Gill, Heather Holden-Brown. Culinary thanks to Jason Fellows, Craig Masson, Ed Ray and Mark Lease for delicious sustenance. Marin bikes for their support. All my Hastings friends and family for continued encouragement and support.